Concrete and Culture

Essays by Robby Porter

Bar Nothing Books
Montpelier, Vermont

CONCRETE AND CULTURE
Published in the United States of America

BAR NOTHING BOOKS
100 State St.
Suite 351, Capitol Plaza, Box 3
Montpelier, VT 05602
802-223-7086
info@barnothingbooks.com
SAN 256-615X

Preface

To the random stranger reader:

I meant this to be a short writing project for my children, Ceres and Ford, to read someday, but like so many good intentions, especially those involving one's children, it got complicated and much longer and more important to me than I expected.

The marvelous advances in technology have given us YouTube, email, improvised explosive devices, fake news, and many other good and bad things, including, for a person like me without the credentials or aptitude to be interesting to mainstream publishing, the ability to distribute my thoughts cheaply and easily. A bound book of your own creation is reward enough for the effort, especially now that the effort and cost of publishing has been so greatly diminished.

I wrote this for my kids. When I was stuck or despairing (often), I asked myself what it was I wanted to explain to them. This was my lodestone and it proved a true compass for moving me forward.

When I was younger, my father, who has always been a more natural writer than I, would say, whenever I could coax writing advice out of him, that I should think about who I was writing for. In the case of this book, that was an easy question to answer but not such an easy instruction to obey.

Often the boasting toad inside me couldn't help hoping that I might have a larger audience. As my simple project grew in length and complexity, I strayed from the path of addressing my kids and, conceited, mounted my soapbox, unsure of who my audience was. Before long, stuck and humbled, I would return to writing for my kids.

By rewriting, I've tried to remedy these flaws and the bumps they create for the reader, whoever that may be. But as anyone who has done a sloppy job installing drywall and then tried to spackle over the mistakes knows, at some point fixing it only makes it worse. With building, the correct solution is to tear out back to the mistake and start over. This should be easier with writing because it would seem to be simply a matter of hitting the delete key. I've tried, but the physical simplicity of writing compared to installing drywall is outweighed by the mental difficulty. When you rip out drywall, you can replace it with a new, flat piece. Sometimes, when you rip out the old words, the new ones lack the spirit of their predecessors and are flat, which, while it is a virtue in drywall, is a death sentence for writing. I've rewritten these essays multiple times and rounded off a lot of rough corners but, occasionally, patching over is the best I've been able to do.

Therefore, allow me to give you a suggestion on

how to read this book. Skip around. Read what interests you and ignore the rest. Whenever you encounter an awkward curve in the text, remember I should have paid more attention to my father's advice.

The ideas and experiences I write about span my life. I have separated them into four groups. The first group contains essays that came from experiences in my childhood. The second group of essays mostly originates in the period of my life between 18 years old and when I was 30 and got married. The third group covers my life from that point until the present (2020). The fourth group contains essays that felt related to each other. Because this is a book of stories and ideas, the groupings are not strictly chronological. In some essays—the first one, for instance—ideas and experiences from my childhood carry into my adult life.

My family, like all families, uses a variety of nicknames, from the common "Mom" and "Daddy" to more unusual terms of endearment (after seeing a John Wayne movie, my brother called me Pilgrim for years). To simplify things, when I use someone's name, I use their given name rather than the names they call each other.

Acknowledgements

My most helpful critic, Erica Heilman, pointed out to me that my father, Bill, is a frequent character in these pages but my mother, Ruth, only makes a couple of appearances. This was not by design. I didn't seek a theme. Whenever an idea for an essay came to me, I jotted it down. Eventually the ideas dwindled, although they haven't completely deserted me. I don't know where they came from in the first place.

I can hazard some guesses as to why my father shows up more often than my mother. It was my mother who did most of the child raising while my father worked. As a result, the experiences I had with him may have seemed more prominent to me, while the lessons from my mother may have been more subconscious. Or perhaps there is a natural tendency for a male child to look to his father for instruction.

Maybe it has to do with my parents' individual character and methods of teaching. I would say that the art of teaching comes more naturally to my mother than to my father. Just as a skillful carpenter leaves no hammer marks, perhaps a good teacher leaves no trace.

Whatever the cause for my father's prominence in these stories, the actual writing was influenced almost entirely by women.

When I was making furniture, I used to drive to the Adirondacks every fall for a great furniture show at the Adirondack Museum in the town of Blue Mountain Lake. As the years wore on, I got sick of making furniture. On one drive, in the late 1990s, as I turned onto Route 74 and headed into the mountains, it occurred to me that I should try to write a page a day. Then by the time the next year's show rolled around, I would have 365 pages of something written, which I thought would be satisfying in a way that building furniture wasn't.

Several years in a row, as I passed over the spot where I first had that idea, I had to face the reality of another year gone by and no writing to show other than a lot of half-started essays and stories. I expressed this frustration to my wife, Beth Ann, who suggested that I needed to pick one writing project and stick with it until I was finished. For some reason, which must be a flaw in evolution, it is difficult to take advice from your wife.

I think another year went by before I admitted to myself that she was right. I have made it a policy ever since to finish one writing project—at least a complete draft—before starting another, and without this rule I probably never would have finished anything.

As I mention in chapter 39, "What I've Learned about Writing," it was my mother who gave me invaluable advice and direction on writing and, by extension, on life when I was in high school. She also read two different drafts of the book, gave me helpful opinions, and corrected the record in several places where I misremembered events.

At different times and in various essays, Lori Martin, Cathi Buni, and Deb Fleischman gave me useful advice. My cousin Jane Harding-Gurney, despite her poor eyesight, read the entire manuscript, and her encouragement helped me push on and finish it.

Erica Heilman, certainly my earliest and most enthusiastic critic, read the first draft of this book and made many comments, most of which I used when I rewrote.

My sister Molly also read almost every essay, some of them, I'm sure, more out of duty than interest. She has a painter's sense for spotting where I stray from telling what is true.

And, finally, Anita Warren took my punctuation-challenged prose, put the commas where they are supposed to be, and made gentle but persuasive comments about where things needed changing.

I am grateful to all of them. No doubt there are ideas in this book with which they individually and, perhaps, all together disagree. I'll take sole responsibility for those.

For Ceres and Ford

Introduction

Dear Kids,

During the winter of 2007–08, the year we homeschooled you, it occurred to me that it is a parent's duty to pass along to his children everything he knows that's worth knowing. By the time I had this realization, we were already following lesson plans for history, math, and English. I wasn't sure quite how to implement it anyway, but the idea stuck and became, at least in my mind, an obligation.

There are things I want to tell you, but you roll your eyes at my regular menu of lectures: "It may not be your fault but it is still your problem," and so on. I have a kind of gallows humor because I know before I open my mouth that I can't convey in that moment and with those overused words what I want you to understand. So I speak with a grimace, the kind of expression you might see on the face of a dog when it tries to beg a treat it knows you will not give.

Underneath these attempts is an experience of mine. I've always been a builder and a problem solver, a contemplator trying to understand how things work. I'm proud of the things I've built, things that are beautiful or functional. Thinking and problem-solving support these creations, as much as wooden beams and nails.

In college, when my girlfriend Aliza hunted down a copy of *The Way Things Work* in a used bookstore and gave it to me as a present, I saw it as a practical addition to my library and immediately looked inside to learn how hydraulic pumps worked. The summer before, my neighbor Roy Haggett (more about him later) had meshed his fingers together as a demonstration of the functioning of a hydraulic pump. I professed to understand, but I didn't and wanted to find out. What I also didn't understand was that *The Way Things Work* was a comment on my character.

I'm a Yankee mechanic, convinced there is a solution if I can just figure it out and build it. There's a certain cold optimism to this outlook on life. Things can work out, but you better have done your sums correctly and not have made any sloppy mistakes.

Had I been raised as William Faulkner was, in the Mississippi Hill Country—a place where the fertile, bountiful landscape is the result of ancient winds and a powerful river draining half a continent—I might have focused less mechanistically on how things work and more, like Faulkner, on the subtle, immeasurable, and sometimes irreconcilable actions of my fellow human beings.

In the stony, mountainous New England

landscape of my life, every knoll and valley presents a unique opportunity to contrive a living, and every winter tries to bury that struggle under a glacier. This terrain, by turns inviting and unforgiving, encourages a person to look for a device, a particular construction that will make living a little easier.

The puzzles I've struggled with are common and fairly general—relationships, money, purpose, all of the questions you are growing into. I've dealt with them as a Yankee mechanic, contemplating how I thought the pieces fit together and functioned.

We identify people by their work, but a person is more than the part of them that is their work, although it took me years to realize this. Here are many parts, disparate parts, from the whole experience of life, the same way a whole person is the work part and many other disparate parts.

Maybe, like me, you will choose to live close to your parents and gradually pass from admiration to disdain and back to . . . what is it, really? Resignation with appreciation? Do we have a word in English, or is there some compound German word that manages to capture the combination of love and sadness, frustration and fulfillment that is a child and parent? Even living close by, my own parents are mostly a mystery. From long experience of working with him, I know how my father will act in lots of situations and, to a lesser extent, I can make an educated guess as to his reasoning. But the experiences that shaped the reasoning—that box is just a tangle of misremembered stories and forgotten punch lines.

Yet, someday you will wonder, "Who was that man, what did he think, and why?" Stories are perhaps the most enduring human creations. These are the stories behind the reasoning of what I think. After 53 trips around the sun, this is what I got.

You'll notice, when you get around to reading this book, that when I introduce your mom, Beth Ann, I introduce her as "my wife" to keep things clear for any other readers who may happen on this book. It feels a bit awkward to write those words instead of simply saying Mom. Let it be a lesson on the importance of tone and intention at the beginning of a writing project. I wrote lots of these essays thinking they would be read only by you, and now I've rewritten them in an attempt to make them serviceable to a general audience as well which feels, in places, like an imperfect compromise.

In a way, this problem symbolizes the struggle of being a parent. You put your children first but this doesn't mean that you completely cease to exist (although it occasionally feels that way). Instead, you compromise, taking care of your kids and trying to maintain some of your own ambitions. And that's what I've done here.

Warning

When I told my brother, Louis, that I was going to write down everything I knew worth knowing, he replied that if I worked hard, it shouldn't take more than an afternoon. Whatever the cause for the length of my efforts—a decade now—I make no claim that the following writing is complete, final, or thorough. I especially do not claim to be expert or even knowledgeable about many of the topics. In defense of this cavalier attitude, I say, "That's life." We're dropped into a womb by chance and birthed into this world unprepared. Our existence is the sum of how we use incomplete knowledge and passing notions to meet life's unexpected challenges.

xx

Table of Contents

ONE

1- Concrete and Culture

When I was 16, I made my first real money by cutting a load of pulpwood. I cut mostly balsam fir and a few white spruce trees. These days, the low-quality wood that is destined to become paper is likely to be felled by a mechanical harvester and trucked away tree length, but 35 years ago a lot of pulpwood was still felled with a chainsaw, measured and cut into four-foot lengths, and stacked in neat piles to await the arrival of a log truck. You needed to accumulate 14 to 16 cords—a pile roughly 80 feet long, 6 feet high, and 4 feet wide—before you were ready to call the trucker.

I cut my load of wood in the area where my sister Molly's studio and house now stand. We called this thicket "the swamp" because it bordered a beaver pond. It was my father's objective to clear the whole area and return it to pasture. My cutting of the pulpwood was going to be the first phase. We never got past the first phase, and by the time Molly built her place there, most of it had regrown trees.

One day I would fell and limb trees, the next day I would skid them with my oxen out to the road, where I cut them to length and piled them. I was hardly disciplined, but eventually the day came when I calculated and recalculated and re-recalculated, measuring over the sloping ends of the pile and the curves of the gully I'd stacked it in, and decided I must have enough for a load. I called a trucker recommended by a neighbor.

A few days later, in the early morning fog, a tractor-trailer truck pulled up to my pile, followed by a loader truck with a cherry picker mounted on its back. As they positioned themselves to begin loading, the old adage "Possession is nine-tenths of the law" swam into sharp focus in my adolescent mind. These enormous trucks were going to depart with all of my hard-earned wood, and if I never got paid there wasn't a lot I could do about it.

While they were loading, I imagined various unrealistic teenage fantasies about how I would reclaim what was rightfully mine. An hour of paranoid daydreaming did nothing to reassure me, but the wood was loaded and disappeared with the morning's fog. I fretted for a couple of weeks and then got a check in the mail—$535, as I remember.

I hadn't thought about those truckers in years, until a few summers ago. We were building a solar electric installation and needed several yards of concrete. I called a concrete company, one I'd never used before and to whom I was nothing more than a voice on the end of a phone line. Nevertheless, at the appointed time a massive truck showed up and deposited 16,000 pounds of concrete in our holes.

Nothing unusual about this. It happens every day on construction sites all around the country. I gave the driver a check and the truck went on its way. If I had decided to stiff the concrete company, there is no way in hell they could have gotten either their money or their concrete back. They could have sued me, complained about a bounced check or no check, tried to ruin my credit, taken me to small claims court; it hardly would have been worth it for $1,000 of concrete.

Thirty years ago, as the log trucks loaded my pulpwood, I realized how vulnerable I was to the dishonesty of other humans. This time, older and on the other side of the transaction, I had a different realization.

We live in a trust and honesty culture.

In this day, when litigious scumbags troll the airwaves and internet for their next cases and when big corporations seem to hate their customers and look for any opportunity to trick them into spending money, it may seem counterintuitive to say that we are a trust-based culture. And it is true that predatory corporations are doing their best to ruin this culture. But underneath, as a culture, individual to individual, we believe that your word is your bond, and when some guy calls up, gives his first name and an address, and says he wants concrete, the concrete company sends out a truck and assumes he will pay.

Most of what you see in everyday life obscures this fact. The financial industry—the pinnacle of commercial transactions and the sector of the economy that attracts the brightest, most ambitious minds—collapsed (again) in 2008 under the weight of its own lies. One trip through the security line at an airport would convince anyone that we are a fear- and deception-based culture.

But the vast majority of transactions take place within the bounds of the law, not because people are afraid of punishment for breaking the law but because most of the time and for most people—in other words, as a culture—we have ingested the assumption that we should be honest with strangers. Take away the culture of honesty, as has happened in the financial industry, and the law, far from being an enforcer, becomes just an inconvenience that must be avoided or purchased.

If you run your hand over a piece of sanded wood, you'll feel one small rough spot even if the rest of it is perfectly smooth. Similarly, it is easy to see examples of dishonesty and harder to see how much trust there is. But once you start looking, and I never noticed until I ordered that load of concrete, you start seeing the strong, smooth sheet of honesty everywhere.

This is a cultural choice. Trust and honesty between individuals, even strangers—especially strangers—is a slender and perhaps peculiar, yet enduring, first principle of our culture.

I know it isn't this way in every business or in every place in this country, and in some ways Vermont is a bit of a throwback to an earlier time, but this really just makes my point. A trust and honesty culture is our heritage.

Our heritage also includes slavery and genocide of the first Americans. Ta-Nehisi Coates, whose writing I admire even when I disagree with some of his conclusions, argues that black Americans have lived in a culture of white supremacy, bondage, and theft of their lives and bodies. A person with dark skin can look at our history and conclude that it is a culture of deceit and theft directed at anyone without white skin.

I don't disagree, but I don't think this invalidates my observation. The trust and honesty culture has always excluded people and treated those people it excluded from the culture—dark-skinned, women, Asian, Native American, the list goes on and on—as having no or fewer rights. What's changed over time is that the culture has gradually become more and more inclusive until now, by ideology, it includes every American, even if there is still a big gap between the ideal and reality.

Even making allowance for how poorly we live up to the ideal and how the ideal itself has had to evolve, the trust and honesty culture seems to me to be somewhat unique in history. Usually trust has been extended between men along familial, tribal, or sometimes religious or political lines. Somehow, despite the white, male, wig-wearing, slave-owning, female-excluding genesis of our country, we've expanded the idea of trust between strangers to mean *all* strangers. It is a remarkable leap ideologically. Practically, we've got a long way to go.

If my voice had been female or if I had "sounded" black, would the concrete company still have sent the truck? I don't know. I've had the privilege of living my life as a white male. This limits my perspective, but it doesn't stop me from seeing that a trust and honesty culture is a good thing within my experience and believing that the more completely and thoroughly that experience is shared by everyone, the better.

2- Granny's Rug and Muh's Casserole

The music of my childhood (and by "childhood" I mean the period after I was seven and we moved from Clarendon Springs, near Rutland, Vermont, to Adamant, Vermont, because I don't have any particular memories of music before that), the music I remember, was the album, mostly traditional country music, *Will the Circle Be Unbroken*; another record that my father often played of black Mississippi prisoners singing as they worked; and a Doc Watson record.

A number of those songs have stuck with me. Some were fun to listen to, like the song "Tennessee Stud." A lot of the songs had vocal harmonies, which, to my young ear, sounded dissonant, and I thought those were places where the singers made a mistake and hit the wrong note. This last observation reveals two character traits, arrogance and tone deafness, which, unfortunately, I realize have been with me starting even in my childhood. And some of the songs, Doc Watson's version of "Tom Dooley" chief among them, confused and perplexed me.

I couldn't understand how Tom Dooley killed poor Laurie Foster if he also hadn't harmed a hair on her head. And given that, I couldn't understand why he wasn't protesting his innocence more and seemed so resigned to his hanging. But what really got me was the verse *"You can take down my old violin / And play it all you please / For at this time tomorrow, boys / It'll be of no use to me."*

The macabre image of Tom Dooley encouraging someone—he says, "boys," I pictured his sons—to take his prized possession was even more uncomfortable to my brain than the vocal harmonies, and it disturbed me in a way my young mind couldn't resolve.

We're all going to die one way or another, and many of our possessions will outlast us. What's the right attitude and treatment for the possessions of deceased relatives?

We have several rugs made by my grandmother and given to us by her while she was still alive. When I look at the rugs, it is easy for me to remember Granny's hands and how she pulled the braids together extra tight so the rugs would last. Her hands were knotted by arthritis, like an old root, by the time she died at 97, but I think it was blindness not arthritis that caused her to give up on rug making a few years before her death.

The rugs have lasted, though. I think every relative has a rug and maybe several. Ours have survived wet boots and dogs, firewood and moths, and the same passage of time that wears us out. The rug in front of the woodstove has given way in one spot and no matter how many times I tuck it under, a small tail of wool braid always manages to find its way onto the hearth, like a pointing finger reminding me that I should have taken better care of this heirloom.

From my other grandmother, Muh, I don't have many keepsakes: a couple of pieces of furniture, a small, ornate clock, and a round, red casserole dish. Not too long after she died and her possessions were distributed among her descendants, I stowed the red casserole dish under the sink counter, sure that it would get broken if we used it. There it stayed for a few years until we were going to a potluck dinner party and I saw that my wife had retrieved it from its hiding place and filled it with food.

Perhaps I said something, I suspect I did, about how we really shouldn't use it because it might get broken, and Beth Ann wisely ignored me. What I do remember is that the dish, which is red on the outside and white inside, with a couple of scrolled handles, made it home and I washed it. The handles leave little indentations on the inside which are impossible to get entirely clean, and there are several flutes at the rim that you need to run a sponge around several times. When I turned it over, on the bottom I saw a small, yellowed piece of masking tape with "Mary Grahl" written neatly in pen. All of a sudden I knew that my grandmother had taken this pretty dish to her own potluck parties, carefully putting her name on it to make sure it came back to her.

Unfortunately, Beth Ann never met Muh, but despite the miles and years I felt a connection between these two women, both reaching for the same pretty but difficult-to-clean casserole dish to take to a party. The red lid eventually got broken but the casserole dish still survives, a veteran now of innumerable parties. Someday it will break and someday the rugs will wear out, but I won't feel guilt when that happens. And until then, every time I wash the dish I think of Muh, and every time I tuck under the frayed end of the rug I think of Granny. This is the way it should be—the right way to let go

of someone, a little at a time, thinking of them as you do.

So when I'm dead and gone, take down my old tools and use them all you please. They'll get broken and lost, but don't feel bad. And until they do, I'll live on a little in someone's memory.

3- The Dignity of Not Hanging Trees

Jim Bornemeier was a friend of my parents. He worked at the newspaper with my father, Bill, and, like a lot of my dad's friends, he occasionally came over to our house and hung out. Hanging out meant drinking beer and doing whatever my dad was doing, and one fall it meant going up in the woods to cut firewood.

Bornemeier, as my father always called him, had a flare for language, and he and my mother liked to talk about books. I noticed that when he spoke, he looked for the right word, not in the way of a taciturn Vermonter looking for the most economical version of a sentence, but in the way, I suppose, of a poet, a person who wants just the right word and is always reaching into a corner of the grab bag of language, hoping for an unused word. This quality and his general demeanor gave Bornemeier a certain dignity. He always seemed poised and thoughtful.

On my parents' woodlot, at the top of the main hemlock stand, the hemlocks start to thin out and the hardwoods take over. Right on this periphery, my dad cut a dead beech, which fell downhill and got all tangled in a hemlock. The beech was light because it was dead and the bushy hemlock held it tightly. My father's solution was to pick another beech tree and fell it into the first one, hoping to dislodge it.

When you're logging, every tree is different, every skid is different, and there are continually opportunities for things to go wrong. You are constantly judging the skid road, the mudholes, the direction gravity wants a tree to fall against the direction you want it to fall. Things usually go along quite well until you misjudge a tree and hang it in another tree.

These errors all start with a misjudgment or downright self-delusion. You think to yourself, "It'll slide between those two trees" or "It'll roll off that tree" or "It'll break through those dead branches," and it doesn't. Then you're left trying to fix a mistake.

Whatever your attempted solution, it is bound to be more dangerous and much more time consuming than simply getting it right in the beginning. And getting it right in the beginning is usually a matter of taking a few more seconds of preparation. Cut the other trees first, see if it is possible to take your tree in a different direction, some little choice that takes a hundredth of the time you eventually put into unhanging the tree, but you don't make that choice because you err on the side of thinking things will work out. Optimism is not your friend when you are cutting trees.

My dad's hopes were ill-founded, and although

the second tree succeeded in lowering the first tree, it didn't bring it all the way down. Now the second beech tree was leaning on the first beech, which was itself still caught in the hemlock.

He examined the cut on the first beech and determined that while it was still propped on its stump, it was broken completely through, and he concluded that we could bring the whole mess down if we could just dislodge it from its stump.

If we had had a winch in those days, we would have simply winched it off the stump. Instead, he put a wedge in the cut and started tapping on it with a sledgehammer. This was not best forestry practice since, if it was successful, it would mean that as the first beech fell, the second one would come down on his head. Naturally, he planned to run at the first sign of movement, and after several false alarms it looked as though the beech was ready to pop off the stump. On one of these false alarms, my dad ran a little distance and Bornemeier, with manly courage and the instinctual camaraderie of men doing stupid, dangerous things, reached out his hand for the sledgehammer.

He and my dad then took turns. One of them would walk in and take a swing at the wedge and then turn and run. Each hit moved the tree a fraction of an inch closer to the edge of the stump. Finally, Bornemeier took his swing and the tree slid off the stump. Just as Bornemeier started to run, he tripped. The trees started to fall with an enormous cracking and rearranging of branches, and Bornemeier started speed crawling through the leaves and forest litter. Crawling was the right choice. Taking the time to get up could have been fatal. A second or two of crawling, palms open, fingers grasping whatever traction he could get from the leaves and the soft ground of the woods, and Bornemeier threw himself in a headlong plunge and lay on the ground, looking back at the trees, which had settled somewhat lower but had not come all the way down.

It was the first time I had ever seen a man, a dignified man, stripped of his pride and reduced to a dog in sheer desperation to keep himself alive. The lesson is that it is safer and more dignified to avoid hanging trees in the first place.

4- Frost and Rust

Rust and frost are two natural forces I was exposed to in my childhood and that shaped my outlook on life. One is the result of climate, and the other, at least in the manifestation that plagued me, is the result of humans struggling against the climate.

Newton's first law states, roughly, that objects at rest remain at rest. While this may be strictly true for the physicist, it is not true for a New England farmer. A stone wall rests on the ground but the stones somehow manage to topple off and spread around both sides of the wall. The dry stone foundation moves around underneath an old barn. Nothing in this climate seems to stay where you put it.

I understood from a fairly young age that frost was the force moving these stones around. Had I known when I was in my early teenage years and starting to build things that there was something called Newton's first law of motion, it might have changed my perspective. Or if I had grown up in a warmer climate, where there was no foundation-cracking frost in the ground, I might have had a different and perhaps less defensive and cautious attitude toward life.

As it was, I liked building things and wanted anything I built to stay built forever, but I saw that every building in this climate was under seasonal attack from the frost. Rather than understanding frost in the context of Newton's first law—in other words, understanding that the stones and buildings would have, by law, stayed where I put them, but for the renegade Jack Frost—I understood frost in the context of my life. Anything you build, there's some damn thing that will try to tear it down. That's the law I observed in nature, personal and somewhat adversarial, more like the Old Testament of the Bible than the impartial reality of physics.

Every rusted fender, broken tailpipe, and failing car frame just added to this conviction. We got the cars of my childhood cheap, used, and mostly worn-out. Repairing the inevitable breakdowns meant confronting rust. Disassembling any one part often involved breaking a rusted mounting bracket or cutting off bolts too corroded to be spun loose. Nothing came apart easily.

I knew, of course, that this rust was the result of the salt spread on the roads to melt the snow and ice in the winter. Had I traveled to New Mexico, as I did later in my life, and witnessed the underside of a 40-year-old pickup truck with perfect-looking emergency brake cables, I might have seen rust less as a perennial condition of life and more as a collective choice—rusted cars in return for passable roads. Instead, my provincial upbringing caused me to believe that the things I cared about and needed to maintain were under continual assault.

I expanded this into a general outlook on life, a skeptical eye convinced not only that there is weakness and vulnerability in everything, but also that there are forces, adversaries, quietly, invisibly at work against everything you need. The law I derived was to view the world as a dynamic place where everything is in motion all the time and usually in opposition to your efforts. This is not an optimistic way to understand the world, but it does seem to be a common attitude among those people like myself—grim Yankees who have lived in such a way as to have the rigors of this climate interact with our own personal designs and ambitions.

It seems now—older, a little traveled, and more knowledgeable about the laws of physics—that I am perhaps a bit softer, but mostly I'm still formed by the climate I grew up in and still live with. I'd rather not take the afternoon off or wear bright, cheerful colors because I know winter is coming, again.

5- God

Every child, at least every child of skeptical parents, as soon as they are introduced to the concept of God, naturally wonders about God's existence.

Throughout history, the priests and clerics of all religions, damn them, have done their best to take the wisdom of the true spiritualists and contort it to empower and enrich themselves. It is not fair to categorically condemn all ecclesiastics for the selfish, power-mad actions of many of their colleagues, but the crime is so heinous and so widespread it is probably the one case where the saying "Kill them all and let God sort them out" is not entirely unreasonable.

Religions are built primarily around the clergy, not God, so it is difficult for anyone, but especially for a child, to separate God and the existence—or not—of God from religion. Since my parents are pretty much agnostic, we didn't get any pressure from them, although I think once, at the request of my father's mother, Muh, we did get sent for a dose of Sunday school.

Nevertheless, religious ideas are all around us and kids pick them up by osmosis, even when they aren't directly indoctrinated. By the time I was 12 I had a good friend, Sean, who was Catholic. He impressed on me the necessity of prayer for myself and especially if I wanted to save my family from eternal punishment.

Superstitions of all kinds multiply in the same part of your mind, egging each other on and creating a riot of worry and misunderstanding. Around the time I started fearing hell, I also developed a fear of vampires. My friend Sean informed me that if I kept a cross near my bed, not only might it help with salvation but I could use it to ward off a nocturnal vampire attack, so for several years I had a little cross on the shelf where I kept my book. My parents encouraged reading before sleep rather than prayer, but I followed Sean's suggestion and after reading I prayed every night for my family.

I can't remember now exactly what I prayed but I do remember that the thought of asking God for something stuck in my craw because it seemed rather presumptuous to interact with God primarily by asking for things, even protection. So, in my prayer God was implied but not directly called upon, something like, "I pray that my family will be safe." And then I enumerated all of my family members, including dogs and important farm animals, like my oxen and the horses. I wasn't sure about the souls of dogs or other animals but I figured it couldn't hurt. In refusing to ask, I think I probably missed the whole point of humility and prayer.

Praying seemed to me like a small but potentially powerful insurance policy. When I had to read Pascal in college, I saw that he made pretty much the same argument—namely, that you don't have a lot to lose by believing in God and you do have a lot to gain. I didn't think much of the logic of Pascal's Wager when I read it, although the impassioned convictions of someone like Pascal can be quite persuasive and I was surprised at how emotionally moved I felt by Pascal's entreaty, but by that time I had long since given up on this logic. And that really gets to the heart of my problem with religion, especially Christianity, Judaism, and Islam.

Any religion that claims exclusive rights to the one and only God pretty much forces you into a choice between that religion's God and justice. Your choice is to worship a God who punishes those, often through no choice of their own, who don't worship him—a God of injustice—or to choose justice.

Years before, I had put a version of this question to my Catholic friend. Were Asians doomed to perpetual torment even if they hadn't had a chance to be exposed to Christianity? He thought so; he wasn't certain, but he was sure they weren't eligible for all the good stuff that awaited righteous

Christians in the afterlife.

I don't know if a sense of the Almighty is hardwired into humans at birth, but a sense of justice seems to be. I found this idea of a God who would punish people through no fault of their own to be unbearably unjust. It didn't stop me for a while from taking out an insurance policy by praying. But I couldn't stomach the idea of obedience to a God (and at this time I don't think I had much of a concept of god other than the Christian God) who would unjustly punish the unbelievers. After a year or two, I decided that if God was going to punish a bunch of otherwise innocent Asians, then I would have a lot of good company in hell, and I gave up on praying.

When I got older and read the Gospels, which, after all, are not the word of God or Jesus but rather Jesus's story and sayings as recollected by other men (and a woman or two, although their versions didn't make it into the Bible), I saw that most of the injustice in Christianity and all of the pageantry and fearmongering was twisted into the religion later by priests.

I brought up this topic to address the existence of God. It is easy to dismiss all of organized religion—history is chockablock full of monstrous deception (and also superhuman generosity) in the name of one religion or another—but dismissing organized religion just sidesteps the

22

question of the existence of God.

When I was in my praying and cross-trusting phase, I did, in a simple, shameful way, test the existence of God. I bring it up now in the spirit of honesty, but I am ashamed both by the nature of my test and also the waste because, as I realized shortly after, you only get one of these opportunities per lifetime and you should be careful how you implement the test.

I was sitting on the toilet, staring out the bathroom window, alternately puzzling the existence of God and watching the chickens who scratched there in the summer, when it occurred to me that I pretty much always produced sinkers, not floaters. "All right, if there is a God, let this one float," I said to myself. In a minute, when I turned around to look, sure enough there was the proof, bobbing away.

Since that is the best argument I can make for the existence of God, I won't try anymore

On the other hand, I am not a vehement believer in the nonexistence of God. Not only is it impossible to prove a negative, but there is an awful lot we don't know about the universe; even the space between individual atoms is vastly larger than the atoms themselves. The physicists, the same people who used to use an invisible "ether" to explain physical phenomena they didn't understand, now tell us that 98 percent of the universe is invisible dark matter and energy. So I think there are big pieces we don't understand, big enough, maybe, to hide or hold a prime mover of some sort.

It is a puzzle to me that after learning to manipulate the physical and chemical and biological world, we have not been able to create life in even the most primitive form. I'm sure the biochemists are doing their best and perhaps one day, instead of cloning a sheep, they will be able to create from dust a single-celled organism, but so far they haven't. Why? How can this be so much more difficult than a thermonuclear reaction? It does seem, at least now, as though there is something special about life, something science hasn't been able to explain.

Religion works for lots of people and I think that is why it continues. A human being is a type of creature that needs a structure. If you have self-awareness, then you understand you exist in a larger world and you want an explanation for that world. The Garden of Eden story in the book of Genesis is one of the most elegant descriptions of the awful realization of self-consciousness and the inevitable need for structure.

Evolution favors pragmatism and we are products of evolution. The fact that we created religions and kept them around for so long is proof of their usefulness. In a way, this is a version of Pascal's Wager. Believing in God and an ordering principle, whether or not it is true and whether or not the insurance policy will pay on your final claim, is almost beside the point because the structure is very beneficial until, of course, it isn't and you find yourself determined to kill your neighbors because they believe in a slightly different fantasy than you do.

I have no idea whether there is an afterlife, but I do want to offer some observations. Despite all of our technological, medical, and scientific progress, we really don't know what life, much less consciousness, is. This means that we can't know exactly what its cessation entails. Is it "lights out," like unplugging a computer? Is it a purely chemical and biological process, like compost, of being reabsorbed into the cosmos? Is it a spiritual journey, starting with a bright light at the end of a tunnel?

No one knows. It seems likely to me that whatever happens after death, it is a natural process, meaning that it will resemble the natural processes we are familiar with. The natural world we are part of and live in has, apparently, no intrinsic justice or kindness, no reward or retribution; these are human values. Nature has just the blank math of physics.

So if there is a soul and it exists within the realm of the natural world and continues somehow after the death of the body, what reason do we have to expect that its experience after death will be any less chaotic or fairer than the one it experienced while in a living body? If this is the case, your experience in the afterlife might be, as some of the ancients thought, somewhat dependent on the manner and circumstances in which you die.

Perhaps the soul, or whatever aspect of a person that might continue after the body's death, goes to another realm, one beyond or different from or parallel to the natural world we are able to observe. I don't see this as impossible, given what we know we don't know about the universe. The old people from whom we are all descended had a much closer relationship with death than we do. Not only were they often around other people when they died, but death came suddenly and in a greater variety of ways than it does now. For the most part, from what we can tell, they viewed death as a passage to another world. I don't think we can completely discount their experiences. Maybe they were right. Then again, they thought lightning was delivered by an angry man in the sky.

My first principle is not knowing. Being a zealot means escaping the awful burden of doubt. For zealots, there is an answer; they know what it is and are certain God is on their side. Even more moderate religious believers think there is an answer or a reason, and when they have doubt, it is just difficulty understanding God's will.

I don't have this comforting illusion. I don't know.

6- Music and Mistakes

As a child, I took piano lessons from Naomi Flanders (granddaughter of Ralph Flanders, the honorable U.S. senator from Vermont who introduced the motion to censure the liar Joe McCarthy). At the time, she was barely older than a child herself. I hated piano lessons and I doubt she enjoyed instructing me any more than I liked the lessons. Years later she recognized me, as she told my mother, because she recognized my thumbs, and this tells you all you need to know about my native talent as a pianist. Nonetheless, even as a child, desire can exist where ability and potential do not. By the time I was a teenager, I sincerely wanted to play the piano.

What I wanted to play was boogie-woogie piano, although I only heard that sort of piano music on a jazz show on the local radio station so I assumed it was a form of jazz. My mother found a wonderful jazz piano teacher, Andy Shapiro, who lived in a cabin in the Northeast Kingdom. He was a transplanted Brooklynite, with a round body and the ability to turn any tune into rocking jazz.

I tried and even practiced with some regularity, at least at first. And Andy tried. He tried to teach me the correct posture and proper hand position so I would have good form in case I ever became good. I played Bach and scales (which I found less tedious than Bach). And, of course, since I had told him I wanted to play jazz, he had jazz songs for me to play. My timing was bad and I didn't have much of an ear and, anyway, jazz is for a more sophisticated musical palate than mine.

I put in enough effort so that occasionally I dreamt about playing the piano. In my dreams, I was playing rolling boogie-woogie bass line with my left hand and spiraling riffs from my right. In my dreams, I could see my fingers on the keys, and one night I woke up and went downstairs to see if I could reproduce the music in my dream. I couldn't.

I gave up on playing the piano.

When I went to St. John's College, the program included a year of music and music theory. After college I went back to live with my parents.

John Ruskey, who had been my sister Molly's boyfriend at college before they dropped out to hitchhike across Mexico, was also living with my parents and going to the University of Vermont. In John's extensive library of abilities was making music. Until UVM, I don't think he had ever had a music lesson, but he could play the guitar, fiddle, accordion, and piano.

Although he was usually a guitar player, sometimes at night John would sit down and improvise on the piano, mostly sad melodies over a light boogie-woogie bass hand. I wanted to be able to improvise like John, to be able to sit down at the piano and make music from nothing more than the full moon and whatever mood was in my head. But when I sat down to play, I was afraid—afraid of playing the wrong note. I sat alone at the piano time after time, timidly tapping a key or two, nervously looking around to see if anyone had heard me disgrace myself with a wrong note. No one cared, and even if they did, what could be more ephemeral than a note that disappears at the speed of sound?

The illogic of it was unbearable. How could I not be able to improvise? Even if the notes were no sort of melody and the wrongest sort of misguided attempt at music, I still should be able to play them, play something, anything.

Hammering the keys with my fists and calling it improvisation would have been a cop-out. The trick was to try and fail—to want to play notes that sounded right and try to get it right and yet to get it wrong and play notes that sounded awful.

I decided I had to overcome this irrational fear, so I waited until no one else was in the house. I wasn't completely ignorant. I knew how to put together chords. From the little bit of music theory that stuck with me, I could figure out a major, minor, or blues scale in any key. There was no harm in trying. But my fingers froze over the keys. I didn't want the shame of making a mistake, even with no one else around to hear it. And why would it even be a mistake?

I'd sat in the same spot all those years ago for my piano lessons with Naomi. It made me angry. Why hadn't I just stuck with it when I was young?

I played a blues scale in C, easy because it was a scale so there were set notes I knew ahead of time, but what next and why? The thinker in me needed a reason. Play an E? a D? or notes in the scale but out of order? I gave up and stood up and then sat down again, disgusted with myself for giving up. Why should this be so hard? There was no cost for getting it wrong.

I forced myself to play some notes. It took what felt like a huge act of will to overcome a nonexistent obstacle. I played some more. It did not matter if they were the right notes or the wrong notes, but it did matter that I *wanted* them to be the right notes, notes that sounded good to me. Most important was to want the right notes and have them be wrong, to try and fail and have that be all right. Playing the wrong note while you're sitting in a room by yourself is the least costly failure imaginable and yet, somehow, I found it almost impossible.

But the horror of playing the wrong notes gave me a window into my psyche. I was terrified of making a mistake.

Over the next few weeks I played some more, not knowing what or why but forcing my fingers to hit keys, emphasize some, lightly touch others. A couple of notes would sound good together and be followed by the clunk of a note that didn't seem to fit in. I'd look over my shoulder. No one was there. It didn't matter. I pushed on whenever no one was around. If I played long enough, I would stumble on a little riff that pleased my ears and I'd repeat it, looking for new notes to add.

John was listening to lots of blues back then and I heard John Lee Hooker singing about how the blues saved him. The blues didn't save me but music did, in a way. Making mistakes, failure, imperfection—these have been pillars of my life ever since. Before this, I had seen that the search for perfection could drive you crazy and that a person only learned through making mistakes, but music made it real for me. Music is the perfect vehicle because mistakes are inevitable and erased as soon as you've made them. Every second of time is new. Put a mistake into it and it's gone; put in a good note and that's gone too. Put in enough mistakes and you start getting a sense for what sounds better.

I pushed on with the piano. I'd find a few notes I liked, build on them, add in a little bottom hand, but I could never really make a complete song. John taught me to play the guitar, and after that I taught myself to play the saxophone. I think of this as a golden period. At night John would play music, often in the pine-paneled room he built for himself on the end of my parents' house. I'd sit in there and play along with John, and sometimes my brother, Louis, would play too.

In my memory, it is dark and John is playing a song he wrote and singing and I'm adding in little bits and pieces with the guitar or saxophone. That's as good as it ever got for me with music. I'm not a musician. I can't hear the pitches of notes very well, my timing is terrible, and the structure of a song is still a mystery to me. Music was a little boat I got on and pushed out into a lake where I didn't really belong, but when I returned to the shore I was more eager than afraid of making mistakes.

7- Money

A father should be able to impart to his children some basic advice on making money. I didn't have much use for money as a child because I got most of what I needed for my building projects out of the woods. But no one is immune from the lure of money, and as a child I had number of futile "get rich quick" schemes. The two that come to mind are mouse pelts and wild turkeys.

Probably after reading too much Farley Mowat or Ernest Thompson Seton, I decided to make money by trapping mice and curing their pelts. I suppose today parents would be worried about their child getting diseases from the mice, but mine took a typically laissez-faire attitude toward this project. My father supplied me with a handful of mousetraps and I went to work placing my sets around the grain box in the barn. In a couple of days I had 10 or 12 mouse pelts salted and tacked to a piece of cardboard. I had planned to create a value-added product, like mouse fur gloves, but beyond trapping the mice, skinning, and salting the miniature hides, I can't remember what happened to that project.

I was a little older when I tried to raise wild turkeys. I got some baby wild turkey chicks from a neighbor. I'm not sure what my plan was because, before he sold me the birds, he told me that it was illegal to raise and sell wild turkeys. This was back in the days before the Fish and Wildlife Department had successfully reintroduced wild turkeys into northern Vermont and even their existence seemed to me to be a fantastic Early American novelty.

This neighbor also had an incubator and said he could incubate the wild turkey eggs for me when my birds got big enough to lay. I don't remember if I was planning to sell the wild turkeys as food or pets, but I did a little calculation on how many eggs I thought each turkey would produce and convinced myself that it wouldn't be too long before I had dozens, if not hundreds, of birds and lots of money.

What sticks in my mind is the turkey shed I started to construct. After scouring the property, I settled on a spot below the garden. It took me a while to choose this spot because I wanted a place with the potential to expand my operation and I also wanted to build a solid structure that would outlast me. I had to convince my mother that I could keep the turkey shed low enough so that it wouldn't block her view from the kitchen sink where she washed dishes.

With the spot chosen, I set to work collecting the largest flat stones I could find and transporting them one at a time by wheelbarrow to support the corners of the building. It was spring and it rained hard all that day, but I insisted, despite my parents' objections, on working on the foundation. I ended the day completely soaked and my clothes so caked in mud that I had to hang them outside, but I had four nice slate piers a foot or more tall and ready for the turkey shed. My dad shook his head in admiration at my persistence and concern over my bullheadedness.

There was a lesson in there, one applicable to making money, although it has taken me many years to recognize it. Persistence and determination are important, but they are put to better use if you choose your battles carefully. God knows why I settled on mouse pelts or decided to build the foundation on that particular rainy day. I never worked on the turkey shed again. I raised the turkeys in an old chicken coop behind our house. They frequently escaped and fell victim to raccoons. The one that survived the longest took to living in the woods but came back occasionally for food or to roost on the peak of the house roof.

My early entrepreneurism ended with a whimper. My parents considered money an unworthy objective for life and I didn't really give money much thought until I became a parent myself. Before that a pretty minimal amount of work was sufficient for me to get by. I was more interested in having money for road trips or free time than for buying possessions.

For me, money has always been a means to an

end. I want money so I can use it to do something, whether it is paying bills or taking a trip. I see money as a tool, but it is not this way for everybody. Some people like money just for its own sake. I can understand this. Although I like to use a good tool, I have some tools I probably will never use. I like having them just to have them. Some people are this way about money; just having it is the point.

So my understanding of money is mostly theoretical and my practical interest started late, motivated by need. Be forewarned that what works in theory often doesn't work in reality, and as for the practical, when it comes to money you've probably noticed by now I'm not particularly successful in this area.

There are basically three ways you can make money. You can exploit yourself, you can exploit nature, or you can exploit other people. In truth, any form of moneymaking involves, to a greater or lesser degree, some of all three.

Exploiting yourself seems to be the most honorable way to make money. You can do this a variety of ways, the simplest and most common of which is to sell your labor to someone who needs your work.

An artist may paint a picture motivated purely by creative impulse, but when that artist sells the picture and money enters the equation, it becomes a form of self-exploitation. I use the word "exploitation" because it has a negative connotation, "unfair treatment." But the secondary meaning, "use of something to produce a benefit," is also the meaning I am seeking. The two somewhat contradictory meanings perfectly sum up what you do when you make money.

There is a sense—deserved, I think—that self-exploitative people have a slightly superior moral position to the rest of us. People are envious, but very few are disdainful of an artist who hits it big and makes a lot of money from their art. When an industrialist makes a lot of money, people are also envious, but on some level everyone knows that the money was made not by creating something exclusively from their own effort but by taking a bigger share of the wealth created by the labor of many people.

Exploiting nature—a farmer or a miner, for instance—can, in a very limited sense, involve exploiting only your own work as well as nature, and this too seems to be an elevated moral position, but it quickly involves exploiting other people so as to more effectively exploit nature.

And exploiting other people, in both senses of the word, is certainly what it means to have people work for you. Most people, myself included on most days, can't get out of their own way and need structure and discipline imposed on them not only so they provide adequately for themselves but also because it makes them happier. That's a fact, sad or not, of human nature.

An employer who ultimately takes more value from a worker than he pays them (otherwise, why employ them?) is providing a benefit to the worker and to society as a whole by maintaining an organizing structure. You have to grant that the employer does this because he believes he will have the greatest material gain. But when the proportions are properly allotted, exploiting nature, each other, and ourselves can be a mutually beneficial arrangement among people. Civilization is another word for this mutually beneficial exploitation.

Most people have no other choice and work for wages. If you want to make more money than you can get from wages or exploiting yourself, you have to employ some form of leverage.

In its simplest form, leverage means borrowing money. If you use borrowed money to produce a greater return than the cost of borrowing, then you are making money with leverage. Obviously, this can make you a lot of money or bite you in the ass. But there are other forms of leverage as well. Any time you get more out of your work than the work itself pays, you are using leverage. Employees are forms of leverage for the employer.

For instance, if you're a lawyer and work for a firm that charges by the hour but pays you a salary, no leverage. If you become partner and take home a piece of the firm's profits every year, then you have a little leverage because you are making money on the other lawyers working at your firm. If you use your skills as a litigator to win personal injury cases where your cut is a third of the whole settlement, then you're using a lot of leverage. You don't get to build a pyramid in ancient Egypt or pile up a huge fortune without some type of leverage.

A musician playing for tips in a coffeehouse has no leverage, but when they cut a CD that sells millions of copies, they've got leverage, although the recording company has more.

Now, take me. When I was making rustic furniture, I had to make a piece of furniture to get a piece of money. Sometimes I charged a lot and the pay was good; sometimes it wasn't. Since each piece of furniture was unique, there was no way to make more money than the amount of furniture I was able to make and sell. Had I made furniture that could have been mass-produced, and even if I had established some sort of brand and hired other people to make "my" furniture under my name, that would have been leverage. Another option would have been to make some sort of name for myself as a furniture artist and sell the furniture as art where the functional or even aesthetic value of the furniture became an insignificant part of its price. I wasn't opposed to any of these forms of leverage, I just didn't know how to get started.

Leverage seems simple when I write it down, but I did not consider these facts when I started making furniture. I wish I had. If I had been able to make more money making furniture, I might still be doing it and maybe employing other people. I didn't think through the business and financial aspects of making a living as a craftsperson; instead, I focused on wood and design. As a result, I am very proud of the things I built and I'm not building them anymore.

Life is a compromise between what you want and what you have to do to get it. The parameters of the compromise have to be constantly reassessed as circumstances change. Money can ruin something or make it possible, including your own self-worth.

I'm not saying that money is a good way to measure yourself, but you can't entirely escape it. Even if you choose to pursue something other than money and value your accomplishments by a different standard, other people will still measure you by the money you make, and no one's self-worth is entirely separated from what other people think. Money is the measure in our society.

Religious hierarchy seems to be the measure in other parts of the world, and between money and religion I'd take money as the less evil measure. The religious zealots are always patrolling to make sure everyone stays within the boundaries, and they tend to draw the lines tighter and tighter as they gain more control over people.

Money as a measure allows for greater freedom and meshes nicely with our culture of individuality. In subcultures, people are measured by their achievements—musical, literary, car races, what have you—but these are not universal cultural measures. One of the nice things about money as a universal measure of worth is that, if you want to, you can more or less opt out of this game, and although you have to deal with the general societal scorn we heap on the poor, no one hangs you for being heretical.

8- Stuck Cars, Chrissy, and Chess

Most people try to use the power of a car to get it unstuck. This obvious solution—bear down harder on the accelerator—is usually unsuccessful. Assuming you are stuck in snow or ice (this is not so true for mud), momentum is your friend and power your enemy.

The problem, when your tires are spinning, is that your power exceeds your traction. More power doesn't solve the problem since you already have too much. The deficiency of traction you can remedy with shoveling, sand, ashes, or tire chains, but often you can get unstuck simply by using momentum. This is what people do when they try to rock their car back and forth. It is often a successful strategy, but usually they still overdo the power.

Here's the trick: Say you're stuck or, better yet, you feel yourself about to get stuck. Do not tread down on the accelerator in a futile attempt to avoid the inevitable. Admittedly, this is a judgment call. If you think you have the traction to power yourself out of the situation, then apply just enough accelerator to match your traction and try to drive out. But spinning your wheels when you don't have the traction will just polish the snow and make it harder to get free

I am talking about a garden-variety stuck situation—the kind that is frustrating, often time consuming, and in the hands of an inexperienced driver usually made worse, not better. If you slide into a ditch and are wrapped behind a tree with two wheels off the ground, you need a wrecker, not momentum (in fact, you are a victim of too much momentum), but if you are stuck in someone's driveway, try this:

Using the lightest touch so as not to spin the wheels, roll the car either forward or back, whichever way it will go, even if it is only half an inch. Then reverse direction using the same light touch. Usually you can gain a little, maybe an eighth of an inch, maybe a full inch. In this way, rock the car back and forth, each time gaining a little bit but being very, very careful never to spin a tire. Most people, when they feel that they have gained a little on the situation, get greedy or fearful or both. Sensing that freedom is within reach and afraid they will lose the opportunity, they lunge for it by giving extra gas. The result is they get stuck a few inches in front of where they were.

By going back and forth and never spinning a wheel, you can pack yourself a tire track through the snow. Before you are able to get free, occasionally you will be driving back and forth several feet or even several yards. It is a test of your will not to get greedy for the freedom until you have created a sufficient runway. It is also a test of courage because once you are a little way from the spot where your tires originally got stuck, it is scary to back up and return to that spot, but that is what you must do.

When I get stuck like this, I rejoice a little because it is a chance—a small, low-risk opportunity—to test your judgment and psychology. What you want, being unstuck, is right over there, but you have to go away from it, maybe several times, before you can get it.

Sometimes, however, there is no room to go back and forth or make any mistake at all. One winter day, Louis and I drove to a spot near Woodbury Mountain to go hiking. It was snowy and the road hadn't been plowed but we didn't think much of it because we were driving a four-wheel-drive Land Rover. The terrain was rugged and the mountainside came almost to the road, with a little brook and a steep ravine in between.

I backed rather hastily into the small parking area and felt the sickening drop of a back tire sliding over the edge of the flat and onto the steep slope of the bank. The Land Rover listed a little and we got out to inspect. Not only was the back tire down the bank, the front tire was also over; it hadn't slipped quite as far because it was still supported by the snow that had concealed the edge where the parking area stopped and the steep bank began.

It was, as they say, a tight spot. We could both see that as soon as we tried to go forward the wheels would spin and slide farther down the bank. The bank was steep. Any sliding and the situation would get worse, and the wheels wouldn't have to slide too far before the Land Rover would tip over.

I knew what to do, however, because I had learned years before, playing chess with my sister Chrissy. Back in the pre-computer, pre-internet days, we whiled away the winter hours with archaic activities like reading and playing chess.

At chess I could usually beat Chrissy, who is four years younger than me, but occasionally a dead calm would settle over her and she would focus on the game with a quiet deliberation. Neither of us had much strategy or knowledge of chess moves, and so the games were won or lost based on who made mistakes and lost pieces through carelessness. When Chrissy focused, she didn't lose. I couldn't beat her even if I tried to bring my focus up to her level. Sooner or later, eager for a quick kill or thinking I already had the game in the bag, I would make a mistake. She didn't miss anything. The only way to compete against her was to give no ground, even a pawn, and to make every provision for defense.

This was the same strategy I applied to the Land Rover. We didn't have a shovel, but using a windshield ice scraper and a jack handle we chipped down to bare frozen gravel in front of all the tires. This was a tedious undertaking though an obvious one. We also chipped behind the tires in case the Rover slid back a little. And in front of the tires we chipped paths all the way out to the road, widening as they went out in case the Rover went a little off course.

These last two steps might have seemed unnecessary, and it was certainly tempting to skip them because chipping ice with a jack handle and a window scraper is unpleasant work, but this was where the chess lesson came in. If you're in a tight spot and you have the time, make every provision for rescuing yourself, however slight, before you give it a shot. The extra effort may seem pointless, tedious, and wasteful, and usually it is, but it helps in an important secondary way by bolstering the discipline necessary to focus on every aspect of the situation at hand and causing you to not overlook something that might turn out to be critical.

We were only going to get one chance. The Rover was either coming out or going farther down the bank. Next, we found an unfrozen spot under a snowbank and mined some gravel, which we spread in front and in back of the tires. It took about half an hour to make these preparations, and when I put the Rover in low range and idled forward, it crept slowly up the bank.

I often wonder, and cannot answer, why I don't put this same sort of preparation into all of life's struggles. In fact, it is a discipline I only seem to find when there is no room for a mistake. Still, in these tight spots, it is a very useful skill to have.

9- The Boys

Mac and Butch

When I was 13, my sister Molly's cow, Cocoa, had her first calf. Because we cared, maybe we thought fate would deal us a heifer calf. We bought Cocoa from a neighbor, Rick Barstow, who thought her lineage to be mostly Jersey with some Devon. She produced an incredible amount of milk, overfilling a 16-quart pail twice a day at the beginning of her lactation. Sometimes, when the grandfather of one of my friends would come to pick up his grandson at our house, if Cocoa was near the fence as he turned around to leave he would stop his truck and stare at her in admiration. "By Gaw, look at the bag on that heifer," he would say. Then he would mutter something about how he wished he'd had a whole herd of cows like that when he was farming.

Because Cocoa's first calf was a bull, his birth was a tragic event. The future for bull calves is extremely short and dim. The lucky ones get raised for 18 months and slaughtered for beef; the unlucky end up as veal or, as my friend's grandfather recommended, knocked on the head and thrown in the woods for the coyotes.

We already raised chickens, sheep, and pigs for meat, but somehow the doom of this furry little calf seemed unbearable. Molly named him Mac. At a month old, the vet dehorned and castrated him as per the standard preparation for a bull calf on his way to becoming hamburger.

Then one day Rick stopped by and suggested training Mac to be an ox. An ox is simply the castrated male of any breed of cattle that has been trained to work. The idea took hold immediately, and so I started on a project that would shape a lot of my adolescence. It took a couple of months, but by August we found another Jersey bull calf on a nearby farm, dehorned him so he would match Mac, and named him Butch.

Dehorning was a terrible mistake since an ox uses his horns to restrain the yoke when a load, like a wagon or cart, pushes forward, but once done it can't be undone.

There was a time not so long ago when people worked with animals every day. It is easy to forget, or never know, that animals have personalities. Pets have personalities, fun, entertaining, sometimes frustrating characters we interact with on a daily basis. When a house cat walks away, seemingly oblivious to your entreaties, it is a charming example of a beautiful, emotionally self-contained creature. And a dog's abundant affection is a happy dose of unconditional love. Pet personalities for the most part are pleasant experiences that broaden us to some extent and coax us to see the world from a different perspective than our own.

But patting your pet is as different from working an animal as exchanging pleasantries about the weather with your neighbor is from dealing with the people at your job. They are related experiences but you don't really submerge yourself entirely in an animal's point of view until you have to cooperate in order to accomplish something together.

So I spent a lot of my childhood contemplating the mind of an ox, not just because they were pets and I loved to sit next to them listening to their methodical cud chewing, but also because we were in a life-and-death struggle. Mac and Butch needed to be productive in order to justify their existence.

Before the notion of training Mac to be an ox came into my world, I had considered myself a horse person. Molly loved cows because of Cocoa, and one of my chief entertainments was teasing Molly. I teased her about everything and specifically about the relative inferiority of cows compared to horses. Training Mac to be an ox began as a family project but quickly became my responsibility and caused me to switch my allegiance from horses to cows. Sadly, this didn't put an end to my teasing.

I started by putting a halter on each little steer and leading him around. Then I tied the halters together. My knowledge of ox training came from the book *Farmer Boy* by Laura Ingalls Wilder and also the Foxfire books. While this was a somewhat insufficient knowledge base, the larger problem was my lack of consistency and discipline. I'd walk the boys around for half an hour three days in a row and then not for two weeks.

Mac, who was two months older than Butch, was also much larger. I measured and remeasured their girth with a tape that translated the girth measurement into an approximate weight. I worried about their difference in size all the time, taking a break occasionally to worry about nuclear war with the Russians or the return of the next Ice Age prophesied by Walter Cronkite one night on the evening news.

I focused most of my effort and worry on creating ox yokes and bows. An ox yoke is a crude harness but it is beautiful in its simplicity. The wood gets polished by rubbing against the oxen's necks, and the shape of the curved bows can almost speak their function, which is to keep the yoke securely on the ox's neck. Compared to a padded horse collar, an ox yoke doesn't look comfortable even when it fits properly, but oxen are stoic and are one step above using your own body for draft power, so no one seems to have worried too much about improving the yoke. When they were sufficiently prosperous, farmers switched to horses for most tasks.

Unlike a horse harness, which requires a variety of materials and a fair amount of sophisticated craftsmanship, you can create an ox yoke with an axe, a drawknife, and an auger—all tools on the first order of necessity for a homesteader.

I had more tools but fewer skills and even less knowledge than the typical homesteader of a few centuries earlier. Using his chainsaw like a giant power rasp and spraying me with the fragrant red pine sawdust, Rick helped me carve the curved neck pieces of the boys' first yoke.

The oxbows were the real trial. I started with a maple sapling, which I tried to bend in a roasting pan while my mother poured boiling water from a kettle over it. Not only did the sapling break on the outside of the bend, but instead of bending in a consistent U shape, it bent into a V. After a lot of cursing and breaking several saplings completely in half, we got two that, although somewhat V-shaped and badly splintered on the outside of the bend, did have a little wood that managed to survive. I shaved the splinters off the outside edge, and these were my first oxbows. They worked fine for training, even though they were too sharp and jagged for actually pulling anything.

In the Foxfire books, they used hickory, preferably shagbark hickory, for oxbows. We didn't have any shagbark hickory and although my *Trees of North America* book showed some hickory growing in the Lake Champlain Basin, that might as well have been South Carolina for me. So I started experimenting. Whenever I walked through the woods, I grabbed any nearby sapling and bent it into a U. All broke until one day I grabbed a little ash sapling growing close to the forest floor and it obligingly bent into a U without cracking.

It is hard to imagine just how much ignorance was a problem. But it was also a teacher. I spent days in the woods breaking saplings or bringing them back home only to have them break after I had shaped them into oxbows. But I learned every square inch of the woods around our house and every type of tree in those woods.

Occasionally, I would employ the oxen to pull the logs for a new yoke and bows from the woods, but making a new yoke and bows was such a dreaded task that I usually put it off until I convinced myself the boys' misbehavior was the result of being hurt by their yoke and bows. And believing this, I didn't feel right making them pull a log out of the woods until I had outfitted them with a new yoke. In all, I think I made 13 ox yokes over the course of their lives, mostly in the first three or four years.

Making oxbows is how I started to love woodworking—ash, with its fresh smell and easy grain; hop hornbeam, also known as ironwood, the densest tree in the Vermont woods, that turns slightly pink when it is boiled. An ideal bow stave is straight, with no knots, and shaped round, except for the outside edge where the bark is trimmed flat but left adhering to the wood.

You need to steam or boil the wood until it is flexible and then bend it around a form. I used a conveniently sized fence post, but the bows had a tendency to slide forward and bend in a V with lots of splinters instead of a nice, even U shape.

To solve this problem, I made some forms that could be clamped to a heavy table. In front of the U-shaped form was a block to prevent the bow from sliding forward and force it to stay in a U shape. Had I, for instance, seen a video of someone using a form like this, no doubt I would have used this method from the beginning. But I didn't. Instead, I came to this solution reluctantly after repeated failures. It is very difficult to invest your time and effort or money even in a simple, obvious solution unless you've seen someone else do it first.

The first time I managed to bend a piece of wood into an oxbow without breaking it was one of the greatest achievements of my adolescence.

Patience, Discipline, and Repetition

While I was struggling to figure out how to make ox yokes and bows that could comfortably harness Mac and Butch, I was also struggling to train them. Years later, an old ox teamster told me that training oxen boiled down to patience, discipline, and repetition. This is a good, concise definition for learning or teaching anything. At 13 I had none of these qualities. But I did have a temper. When I was in walking in the woods, if a branch happened to slap my face, I made it a point to break the branch off the tree or, if it was a sapling, rip it out of the ground. At the time this seemed a logical response and I have to admit, at least at that age, it was satisfying.

When they were young—for the first summer through the winter and during the next summer—training meant walking the boys around, teaching them the commands "Gee" (right turn) and "Haw" (left turn), "Whoa," and "Get up" (which meant get going), or taking them into the woods to pull small logs.

My training regimen consisted of deciding, for no particular reason, that it was a good day to train them. I would head down one of the cattle paths winding through the woods. These secret, serpentine paths led from one good grazing section to another or to a favorite shady resting spot secluded from the insects, where the boys would lie flapping their ears to keep the flies off and chewing their cuds with their deep bovine serenity. When I found them, I broke a little branch switch and started them on the way back to the barn.

Any sort of misbehavior, from running away to refusing to walk, could and usually did happen. What was predictable was they would be bad, I would get angry, and that would make things worse, and I would either not train them again for a while because I dreaded it or I would decide I had to train them more often and would stick with it for three days before I got frustrated.

One day, in their second summer, I was working on their commands and walking them around the yard. I was having them practice backing up, which no big, ungainly animal likes to do but which is entirely necessary for hitching a team of draft animals to a load. When I told them to "Whoa," they immediately dropped their heads and began feasting on the yard grass.

I lightly tapped them on the nose with my whip, but they continued wrapping their tongues around the grass, so I brought my foot up under Mac's mouth and they both raised their heads, grass hanging out both sides of their mouths.

Now with their attention and standing in front of them, I told them to back up and they shuffled back a baby step or two.

"Come on, boys. Back up," I said. Mac took another small step back and then dipped his head and started to pull his hind end away from Butch so instead of standing parallel they were in a widening V shape. Butch's neck twisted and he started to move his back end away from Mac.

"No. Whoa. Bad boys!" I shouted and laid a swift whip stroke along Mac's flank. Undeterred, Mac kept twisting away from Butch in a move I could never quite unravel in my mind. They spread their back ends so far apart, twisting the yoke on their necks so that it ended up hanging upside down beneath their throats and they were standing on the wrong sides of each other, with Mac on the right and Butch on the left.

The only solution was to completely unyoke them and move them around to the proper sides and re-yoke them. Normally, before I re-yoked them, I gave them each a few viscous strikes with the whip.

This time, however, cold pure rage enveloped me and took me over the edge of an idea I had contemplated but not wanted to admit. I silently unyoked them and returned them to the pasture.

That was it; I would retrain them.

It was an admission of failure and it seemed to imply that all the effort I had put into training the boys had been wasted. I resolved to start at the beginning. So the next day I got them out and walked them around in halters. I saw this as turning over a new leaf and assumed I might have a year and a half of work ahead of me to get back to where I had just given up on thinking that I was.

I walked them in halters singly and then I tied their halters together and worked them as a pair. First, we did easy things—Get up and Whoa. Then Gee and Haw and, finally, backing up. I worked them every day. The same cold rage that often provoked me to lash them with the whip I now channeled into discipline for two weeks without missing a day, but by the fourth or fifth day I knew I was onto something. Not only did I not miss a day, I didn't let myself advance to a new lesson until I was certain we had the current lesson completely under control. The boys got better, much better. By the end of two weeks, they were almost obedient. They were walking around in their yoke, not pulling anything, because I had set a goal of sticking with training for at least two weeks before we went back to trying to do any sort of work.

Start over. Try again. I had chosen this path out of pure desperation. I didn't know what else to do. I had seen "send the boys to become hamburger" as my other option because they clearly weren't working out as oxen. They were pets and I loved them as much as anyone loves their family dog, except they needed to be able to work; otherwise, they were just thousands of pounds of hay-burning mobile steak whose value as a food source was going to start to diminish.

The beauty of Rick's idea to train Mac to be an ox was that it seemed like a win-draw. If it worked out, Mac's life was spared; if it didn't, he became hamburger and he and my family were no worse off than we would have been. Of course, we doubled down on that bet by buying Butch. The part I hadn't foreseen was my attachment. Once I cared for the oxen, it was no longer possible to say, "Oh, well, we tried. They'll become meat, like all other bull calves."

I think this somewhat desperate position added a lot to my anger when I worked the boys. Didn't they know I was trying to save their lives?

As my two-week retraining program rolled along, it was as though someone had opened a door and showed me a parallel universe where I had the power to make the boys do what I told them to do. "Patience, discipline, and repetition," as the old teamster would tell me in a few years. I didn't see it in these terms at that time. What I felt was that I had to give up on the progress I thought I had and start over. And I had to methodically work through the training steps, not rushing into a new challenge until the previous skill was entirely cemented in the boys' behavior.

I was as rigorously disciplined as I had been sloppy and emotional. How this switch came I can't describe. I know that I got to a point of absolute desperation and that forced me to start over, but how or why I knew not to rush things, I don't know. The boys' progress was so dramatic that my method became self-reinforcing.

The boys pulling

Retraining didn't solve all of the boys' or my behavior problems, but it made working them a completely different experience. They had an awful lot of bad habits and tricks by the time I retrained them and some of these would occasionally pop up when they got frustrated in a difficult situation. Even the dreaded yoke-upside-down trick would happen again. Nor had I gotten beyond my outbursts of rage and impatience. And both of these would combine again for another harsh lesson in the way the world works. But we had two weeks that changed everything and which I would go back to when necessary by remembering to slow down and take many easy predictable steps.

Over the next several years, the boys and I had some wild and dangerous times working in the woods together. One time I cut a giant dead maple tree on top of a ridge that was too steep and inaccessible for a tractor. I cut a path up the slope and the oxen would pull one short section at a time down to the logging road where we could get it with the tractor.

On one of these hitches, as they were piling down the hill, the log snagged against a big root and both oxbows snapped. The ox yoke flew over their backs and landed behind them. It was as though someone had performed a magic trick. They were wearing the yoke and pulling a log. All of a sudden, the yoke was gone and disappeared.

When oxen are yoked, they know they are working. When they are unyoked, then they are free. They understand this perfectly. This time they looked around a little perplexed and then, recognizing that somehow they had crossed seamlessly from working to nonworking without the usual intermediary step of going to the barn to get unyoked, they started ambling along as they might in their pasture, pausing to sniff a tasty-looking twig. I collected some of the broken bow parts, threw the yoke over my shoulder, and herded them toward the barn. Then I took the chainsaw and walked out into the woods looking for an ash tree to make new bows.

Another time they ran away while pulling the heavy oxcart I had built for them. This cart had huge old wooden wheels about four feet tall and each weighing close to 100 pounds. I was walking beside Mac's left shoulder when they started to run ahead of me. I ran to catch up and I was gaining when I looked up and saw that we were headed for an opening in the fence.

The gate was gone and the opening between the posts was wide enough for the oxen and cart if they were perfectly lined up. When I built this gate, I'd used old telephone poles the boys and I dragged out of the woods for gateposts. I made a wooden hinge from a piece of ash wood and secured the gate to this hinge with 30-penny nails. At some point, the gate had been ripped off but the ash hinge remained, with a line of spikes protruding two or three inches along its whole length.

At the last second, I realized I wasn't going to get ahead of Mac and also that the wheel coming up behind me wasn't going to clear the post with the spiked hinge and that I was going to be sandwiched between the two. Somehow, I went up and over the post and hinge without even catching myself on a nail. When the wheel crashed into the post and brought the boys to an abrupt stop, I was still in the air. I landed more or less in correct teamster position just off Mac's left shoulder. I shouted, "Whoa," as I landed and Mac, eyes still bulging from the force of being stopped so suddenly, turned his head to me as if to say, "Chill down, we're stopped."

When the boys were three years old, we were skidding pulpwood up a hill through about a foot of loose snow. Just walking through the snow was frustrating, but after I told them to get up, the boys started off and worked themselves into a jog. I was struggling to keep up and yelling at Mac to slow down because he was overpowering Butch and causing both of them to veer off the road.

Once we made the crest of the hill, it was smooth pulling down to the log pile, but if they came to a stop partway up the hill, starting the load on the hill was always tough. Mac ran on, oblivious to my shouts, and just as I thought I might get close enough to slow him down, I tripped and went headfirst into the snow.

I got up, furious, but by that time Mac had pushed Butch completely off the road and they were standing with their yoke braced against a small tree. I backed them up and Mac stepped over the chain. I forced my way between the two of them, their flanks wet and steaming from the snow and exertion. I tried to push Mac back over the chain but he just leaned comfortably against me.

When I got them straightened out and told them to get up, Butch came forward but Mac just stood with his feet planted obstinately, forcing Butch to curve around in front of him before being brought to a halt. When I got Butch backed into position and gave them the command to get up, I gave Mac a sharp whip in the rump and he stepped forward, but Butch stayed still, perhaps expecting Mac to play the same trick he had done before.

The next time, they came forward with the load and made five or six steps toward the top of the hill before Mac stopped again, twisting his head and pulling his back end away from Butch so that they ended up facing the load with the yoke upside down on their necks, the ultimate act of misbehavior.

In the contortion of turning the yoke upside down, they ended facing downhill, with me behind them. In a fit of rage, I kicked Mac right in the soft fur between his legs just above the crushed, furry ball sack that had never grown since the day he was castrated. While my foot was still mid-swing, my mind was justifying this cruel act. "It won't hurt him that much, he's been castrated." I had hit the boys cruelly with my whip when they misbehaved, but it was always under the excuse of punishment. For this kick there was no excuse other than wanting to hurt Mac because I was angry. His leg twitched up toward his stomach, he put it down and raised it again, obviously feeling the nausea anyone feels when they've been struck in the testicles.

I gave him a pat on the flank but was too ashamed to scratch his neck and apologize, as was my usual pattern when I hurt them in a fit of rage. I just waited until I was fairly certain he felt well enough to walk. Then I unyoked them, re-yoked them the right way, and we headed for the barn. I gave them a little hay and went up to the house. It was the first time I had to confront the awful reality that there are some things you can't apologize for and the best you can do is to never make that mistake again.

The boys bring hay to the horses

Mac and Butch lived to be 12 and 13, a ripe old age for oxen. I was gone a lot after I graduated from high school and they didn't get worked very much.

One at a time they got so they couldn't stand up and we had to put them down. Bruce Fitch, whose father had sold us Butch years before, came over with his backhoe and dug graves.

10- War Stories

When I was a boy, the world was full of World War II veterans. They were neighbors, the older fathers of other kids my age or a little older, the guys we bought old farm equipment from; they were everywhere. Any conversation with them that lasted more than five minutes usually involved a war story.

Back then, not only pre–cell phone but even before the advent of primitive, handheld digital games, listening to grown-ups tell stories was part of childhood. Sometimes the stories were interesting; often there were implied references that I didn't understand; always there was the sense of sharing something significant.

The men are all dead now but the stories linger on for me. I can only guess at the veterans' motivations for telling and retelling them. It seems as though they should have been recorded somewhere. Here are three I think of often:

Carl Houghton lived in the house at the bottom of the hill where our long driveway intersected the dirt road. I spent a fair amount of time working with him. He was a physically small man, quite a bit smaller even than me, and the thought of him doing battle with a gun and bayonet always seemed unfair. As I got older, I began to think of him as a good Christian in the truest sense of the phrase. He was humble, rather devout, generous, meek in some ways. I think he had a temper and may have had a drinking problem after the war, but by the time I knew him he seemed rather grandfatherly.

He was in the Pacific theater. I don't remember which islands, although he probably told me dozens of times. We were working in the field above his house near the apple trees when he told me how scared he and his fellow grunts—mostly boys, really—were when they knew they were about to encounter the Japanese soldiers for the first time.

There was something about the admission that was confessional and personal in a way that was out of character. He just said that they were scared, more scared than ever before in their lives. They'd heard that the Japanese—"Japs," as he called them, using a slur that contained more venom in the way he pronounced it than in the actual word—could march all day with nothing to eat but a fish head, that they fought to death without surrendering. And then the fighting started, close combat, I think, and Carl learned that he and the other American soldiers were just as tough as the Japanese.

George Doner lived a couple of miles away from us. I think George was less prone to reflection than Carl. Outwardly, he was rather jovial. I did a fair amount of work with him, although I didn't know him well enough to know if his humor obscured a darker side. I think he was mostly pragmatic and lived his life looking forward.

One year, he cut firewood on our land at the top of the hill near the property line. He told me that the old-time rule was that you could cut trees as far across the property line as you could throw an axe, although he didn't follow this rule himself but instead cut all his firewood in one spot, making a hole in the forest canopy that has since regrown with saplings.

George enlisted when he was 16 and saw action in a trench during the Battle of the Bulge. The soldiers' feet swelled up from days of being in cold, wet boots. George's buddy's feet hurt and so he started to take his boots off. George told him not to because he reasoned that he wouldn't be able to get them back on and sooner or later he'd need to get out of the hole and run, but the guy couldn't stand it anymore and took his boots off. He died and George didn't.

Elbridge Toby grew up in the house I was raised in. One of his Toby ancestors had the original grant for that piece of land. In 1973, when we moved in, we were only the fourth family to live there. Elbridge's family, who knows how many generations, held on to the place from the late 1790s until the 1950s. His parents or grandparents sold it to a family that lived there for 20 years, and they sold it to some people, "hippies," who lived there sporadically for a couple of years before we bought it.

Elbridge had a colostomy bag. I'm not sure when or how we children obtained this information. He lived in the village, about a mile from our house. Perhaps some of the kids in the village, many of whom were related to him in one way or another, told us. This fact, confusing, morbidly fascinating, added to Elbridge's slightly mysterious demeanor.

I don't know if he was in the navy or simply an infantryman being transported, but he was on a boat in the Pacific. A torpedo hit the ship while he was belowdecks. As the ship started to take on water, the watertight hatches began automatically closing to seal off the damaged portions of the vessel. In the dark of the flooding hull, Elbridge slid sideways through one of these openings as the door closed.

I remember him telling us this story while standing on the little knoll in front of our house. I don't remember the exact words, something like, "And I knew there was men behind me." What I remember exactly is how he tilted his head a little and didn't say any more, looking from my parents, whom he had been talking to, down toward us kids as though to make sure we got the meaning, which we didn't entirely and had to have our parents explain afterward.

As a child, understanding that some men got sealed in a flooding hull to save the boat and that Elbridge slipped sideways from one side of this line to the other was fascinating, like the colostomy bag, and ephemeral—a mysterious, somewhat horrifying fact to be bounced around one minute and ignored the next. As an adult, I remember the way Elbridge tilted his head, a gesture that has stuck with me more than the words and now conveys a sense of horror, sadness, maybe guilt, whatever irreconcilable emotions a person has to live with for the rest of their life after an experience like that.

11- Hammer Gods

I take pride in being able to do things myself. This is a character flaw or a fate that has been with me from the beginning, and now I've worked alone for most of my life. Consequently, I've spent a lot of time holding a plank with one hand and trying to pound a nail with the other. Sometimes I start the nail beforehand; sometimes, if the wood is soft, I can push the nail in enough with my hand to get it to stick. Either way, you end up trying to get an extra-hard swat on the nail because the other hand is getting tired holding the plank.

One December, when I was a teenager and building a barn for my oxen and the horses, I was trying to place the 2x10s that hold the rafters. It was snowing and the planks were heavy and frozen. I drove a nail into the upright and rested one end of a 2x10 on this nail. I'd already started a nail in the other end of the plank and I raised it to my mark and held it there with my left hand while I tried to deliver a crushing blow to the nail with the hammer in my right hand. I missed the nail but hit the 2x10 so hard that I dislodged it from the prop nail at the other end. The plank fell off and banged against my shins.

I'd already pounded a lot of nails by this point in my life. I didn't miss very often. The injustice of missing at this exact point when I really needed to sink the nail sent me into a furious rage, lamenting the cruel stupidity of a world I had to live in. After straightening my nail, which had been bent when the plank fell, I flung the plank back onto the prop nail, drew back, and delivered another vengeful swing. And missed again, only this time I managed to brace the plank with my shoulder and keep it from falling off the prop nail.

Nearly blind with rage but more cautious, I took another, gentler swing at the nail. It wasn't a hard enough hit to drive the 20-penny nail all the way through the frozen 2x10, but the next hit was. I sent the nail all the way home with a few more hits and then followed up with three or four vicious educational hits to teach it a lesson.

I felt bitter at my unjust mistreatment by the hammer gods but I also couldn't ignore the math. Considering that I pretty much never missed a nail under normal circumstances, two misses in a row was too unlikely to be a random stroke of bad luck. I observed my nail striking and saw that I was much more likely to miss when I really needed to hit the nail.

When you go over the 80 to 85 percent effort that you can do comfortably and repetitively all day long, you dramatically increase the likelihood of missing. Naturally, the times when you need to exert the extra effort come along at infrequent but critical moments. Trying to do it under pressure or trying to hit it super hard is almost entirely different from regular, everyday effort.

So, either practice giving it everything you've got or remember when you're in a crunch situation to use a normal swing instead of trying to clobber it.

That said, with nails, I still try to clobber them and I still miss. I like to feel the wings of fate brush by and remind me that I am a mere mortal, unable, when the pressure is on, to hit the nail really hard and unable resist the temptation. And then, every once in a while, I manage to really nail it—foolish, eternally hopeful human.

12- How to Split Wood

I've split a lot of firewood in my life. As I got old enough to efficiently handle a splitting maul, probably 12 or 14, I developed a typically adolescent strategy for dealing with difficult pieces of wood.

When you've split a fair amount of wood, you get so you can read the wood. It is the sort of sixth sense you develop whenever you're doing something for a while. You get so that with a glance you have an intuition that a certain piece of wood will split more easily if you flip it over or if you give it a quarter turn. Sometimes you are wrong, which is the beauty of intuition. It is the compilation of everything you know about a subject and it hasn't been processed by a rational filter; it is just the pure knowing based on experience, and it is incredibly good but not omniscient. So sometimes the piece of wood that you know will be tough turns out to split right open.

And sometimes it doesn't. Every so often you run into a particularly bad tree. Usually this is a tree where the wood has grown in a bit of a spiral. Yellow birch has a particular tendency to do this. When I was a teenager and hit one of these pieces, the strategy I employed was, "It's going to be tough, so get the worst over first." I'd nail it right in the middle and pound it relentlessly until it split—or until I bent double over the block, dripping perspiration and rage. At that age, I could deliver well over a dozen full-force blows before I succumbed to the need for a rest. For a person who is skilled with a splitting maul, that's a lot of energy to focus on a piece of wood, and most blocks of wood are not able to stand it. Some are, however, and they faced my impatient teenage determination with an infuriating and impassive silence. When I'd gulped enough air, I would resume whirling my maul and attacking the wood.

Usually I'd win, but not always. After the piece was split in half, the next splits were almost always easier. Attacking the wood from the sides I considered a moral failure. The middle, where the tougher heart wood lived, would have to be split eventually so I might as well get it over with. Pretending this wasn't the case, taking a flake or two off the sides of the block (the tough ones, as you can imagine, were also usually large—a couple of feet in diameter, in some cases), was just lying to yourself about what had to be done. So I faced the music and put everything I had into breaking the blocks in half.

As I got older and perhaps weaker, morally as well as physically, I succumbed to nibbling around the edges. I knew this amounted to putting off the inevitable but I had softened enough to indulge myself. I began to notice that some of the hard pieces—or pieces my intuition told me were going to be hard—I could quickly work down to size by just splitting the next easiest piece off until there was nothing left. Maybe I was just misreading these pieces as being hard. I had faith in my intuition, but it wasn't perfect. The only way to tell, of course, was to attempt to split a block in the middle and determine just how tough it was and then give up and attack it from the sides.

Obviously, after having begun an assault on the middle of the block, giving up and focusing on the edges was an additional moral failure, but in the interest of experimentation I tried it. The results were conclusive and I have applied them to every struggle since then. In short, you can split bigger and harder pieces of wood if you work away the easy pieces first. The difficult splits are still difficult but often much less so after you have stripped away all of the easy stuff.

13- Designing Things

When I was young, I wanted to be an architect. Then Granny told me that architects were the first people to lose their jobs in the Great Depression. Giving up on architecture didn't stop me from compulsively designing and building things.

I don't know where the designing impulse comes from. Not everyone has it. I used to take my furniture to craft shows, and about every third person that stopped into my booth would say, "I just don't know where you get your ideas." I've never had a shortage of ideas. Lack of motivation, conviction, preparation, education, organization, dedication, remuneration, yes, but lack of inspiration, never.

People take whatever natural talent they have and use it to try to correct the inevitable problems in their childhood. So a person with a quick wit and a natural sense of humor will get good at diffusing tense family situations with a joke. In my childhood, most of the drama focused around the farm: the sheep were out of the fence, the roof was leaking, it was March and we were running out of firewood. I got good at figuring out a solution and then implementing it by building.

My eyesight is relatively poor and so I have always been prone to observing shapes and forms rather than details. This carries over into my intellect, where I am much quicker with concepts than specifics. And in designing things it means that I have always focused on proportions and structure. Another designer would have a different inclination, maybe focused on textures and colors, based on their experiences and personality.

Here are some observations on the design process extracted from a lifetime of designing and building things, often with wood:

Ideas come from ideas, and the first idea comes from a muse. When I see an interesting piece of wood and immediately think of how I will build it into a bed, I don't know where this first idea comes from. In most cases, the first idea gets discarded or modified a dozen times. The design process is a long series of problem-solving. I imagine the bed I am going to build, either in my head or on scratch paper. Then I see a problem, so I modify the design, trying not to lose what I feel is important. Then more problems, more changes, new ideas, new problems. It is a juggling act trying to keep the original inspiration alive and solve all the problems that come up. Sell off too much of what you like about the idea and what's the point in doing the project at all? Fail to foresee and solve enough problems before you build it and the inspiration, even if it is brilliant, won't work the way you wanted it to.

When I was a kid I was always designing and building things: a manure trolley that ran on a cable I dragged out of an old granite quarry; a chicken plucker made from electrical wire and an old spool; dozens of iterations of hay and grain feeders designed to prevent the animals from wasting their food; wooden hinges made from saplings; and wooden spoons made from dish-shaped pieces of wood split out by the hydraulic log splitter, just to name a few.

An idea would hit me and I would work away on it, sketching, thinking, wandering between the workshop and the pile of broken farm machines in back of the house. Often I would come up with a new idea that was very different and better than the original. I probably started and abandoned three times as many projects as I finished, much to my parents' consternation since I usually left the half-finished creations lying around for a while before I picked up the pieces.

What I noticed about this process was that I couldn't tell where a solution would come from. My knowledge base and materials list were limited, so I often was trying to solve a problem for which there was an already existing solution—a little piece of hardware, for instance, that would solve my problem, but I didn't know whether it existed or have an easy way to get it and so I would try to fabricate the piece I needed from parts scavenged off old farm equipment. I could see that these limitations, frustrating as they were, forced me to be creative and that the solution to one design problem often came while I was working on another problem. Somewhere outside of my conscious brain, my mind was putting together pieces and seeing possible solutions to one problem while I was working on another.

This same unconscious problem-solving is also at work while you are asleep. I often find after falling asleep, building something in my head, that when I wake, a solution is floating around in my unconscious, waiting to be captured before I get up.

The goal—my goal, at least—is to design something that performs its function, doesn't break, and looks nice. Foreseeing and avoiding problems is a big part of a successful design, and when I work an idea over in my head, I am continually posing the question, What if? and trying to have a solution that takes into account every reasonable possibility.

Inevitably, however, on any halfway complicated project, I make a mistake and design myself into a corner. Midway through the project I realize, "Oh my God, I forgot about that; it's going to be a problem and I'm already committed to the design and the project is half built." Here is the thing: This is the point—the stomach-dropping, "I'm going to have to throw it all away" point—at which I come up with the best design solutions. Modifications that are better than the original design occur when your back is against the wall. Why, I don't know. It would have been easier, calmer, cheaper, faster to have thought of the solution in the first place, but I didn't. Try as compulsively as I might to see every problem and potential problem beforehand, I don't. And yet, often this desperate position gives rise to a design improvement. I don't know why the creative process works this way, only that I have seen it happen in myself over and over again.

The compilation of solved problems in a finished design is a reflection of your character and taste. Since hundreds, if not thousands, of small decisions go into anything you build, each creation reflects who you are. Another person given the same function to fulfill and the same materials would come up with a different solution. This stamp is indelible and unique.

Sometimes designs come easily, sometimes it is a struggle, but it is always a question of keeping at it until you get it right. When I'm designing something, I build it dozens of times in my head and on paper until I feel it is right. And yet, even then "rightness" is often just an illusion.

In fifth or sixth grade, as an art project to promote the importance of clean water, I painted a picture of two deer drinking from a brook. I tried for hours but had to keep admitting to myself that the deer heads didn't look right. Finally, after drawing every sort of deer head imaginable, comparing them with pictures of deer and my own mental image of deer, I felt that I had gotten the right proportions.

I had painted the picture on a piece of drywall that got stored away, and several years later I came across it. The deer were veritable Pinocchios, with ridiculously long, pointed noses. I'd stuck through with my deer painting until I felt that I had it right, the same way I stuck through a design problem until I was satisfied with the solution, but the deer were absurd. So I don't have any illusion that persistence will yield a perfect design. The compulsion to keep refining the design is just that— a compulsion to satisfy some inner urge to perfect the design. But who knows where it connects to reality?

By the time I was an adolescent, I knew this compulsion was what allowed me to make good things, things that worked, or to come up with design solutions for problems we just lived with. For instance, the manure trolley I designed was a solution to the manure thrown out the back door of the barn, where it piled up on an inconvenient bank and was inaccessible by the tractor for spreading on the field. And I also knew it was a compulsion, a perpetual inability to be satisfied.

I understood, or at least came to believe, that I would drive myself crazy if I didn't learn to limit the compulsion, and I knew that by limiting the compulsion I was also limiting my ability to come up with good designs. After having given it some thought, I settled on a compromise. When designing or building something, I resolved to accept as "good enough" designs that were still not completely satisfying, but in order to maintain my ability to build good things, I would put off this concession as long as possible.

This was a sort of theoretical decision. Before I could get good at implementing this idea, my compulsion over design problems morphed into more existential questions, where I was not particularly good at limiting my need for a perfect solution.

14- Roy Haggett

Roy Haggett was the man who built the building I converted into our house. It is the type of cheap, metal-framed commercial building that is often used to shelter agricultural equipment. He constructed it to use as a welding shop. I don't know why he built it so big, 40 by 100 feet, since he never had use for all of the space. But my history with Roy Haggett goes back to long before I started living in his welding shop.

Most people in modern society move around a lot, following a career and interests. There are some huge advantages to the peripatetic approach to life, but when you stay in the place where you grew up, your life becomes a long thread woven together with the other people who live near you. For me, even considering that I live about a mile from where I grew up, that thread is remarkably twisted around the life of Roy Haggett. We're not on parallel tracks and I'm not following in his footsteps, but his actions and creations and also his advice influence almost every hour of my life.

I don't know when the first Haggett settled in this area—long enough ago that the road bears their name—and at one time most of the property along the road was owned by Haggetts.

Once, when I was a boy and we were cutting hay

in Roy's field, which is now our field, Roy's brother, Sonny, stopped by and told me a story about when he was a boy and rode with his father down to the store in Adamant. They bought a box of hot dogs for dinner, but his father stopped the truck on the way home and got out to talk to a neighbor. It was summer and Sonny was bored and hungry, sitting alone in the hot truck. They didn't have a lot of money and the hot dogs were a bit of a treat. Eventually he couldn't stand it any longer, but instead of eating one of the raw hot dogs, he took a bite off the end of each one and then closed the box so his father wouldn't know.

I suppose he was middle-aged when he told me this story, although I was child and so I remember him as being an old man. I'm not sure what the point was, except that he should have just eaten one whole hot dog and probably no one would have known, but the story was still so vivid to him (he caught hell when his father found out) that I often think of it when I drive by that house where Roy and Sonny and their brothers grew up. That's the way it is when you live for a long time in one place. Other people's stories become the fabric of your life as much as your own story.

I was about 10 when I first met Roy. Our hay baler at the time was an old New Holland with a motor mounted on the baler. The head of the motor was aluminum, and somehow my father had managed to crack it. He took it to several local mechanics and eventually someone directed him to Roy. I went with him and we stood in front of Roy's shop, right about where our front door is now. My father handed the head to Roy and said, "I've asked a couple of guys if they could fix it, but it's aluminum and everyone is afraid to weld on it." Roy looked back and said, "I ain't afraid of nothin'." He was a superb welder and fixed the head, which was a tricky job because a head has to stay perfectly flat but aluminum is prone to distorting under the welding heat.

My sister Chrissy called him "Rory Haggis the fix-it man," and this perfectly summarizes both what he did for us and the role I think he wanted to serve in his community when he built his welding shop. Unfortunately for Roy, the farmers and loggers who would have had a regular use for his services were a diminishing breed. Consequently, he spent a lot of his time working away on structural steel and other large fabrication jobs. Locally he was known as the man you went to if you needed something metal or mechanical fixed.

Roy worked hard all day, welding, grinding, repairing greasy machines, and at the end of the day he took a well-deserved and needed shower. One time, we went over to Roy's house after hours. When we got there, with a car key that had broken off and a blank key that the hardware store hadn't been able to cut because their machine was broken, Roy must have already had his shower because he was wearing a large, green bathrobe. I'd never seen Roy out of his grease-monkey clothes and it was somewhat disconcerting, like seeing a teacher on the street outside of school.

We went into Roy's basement and I fidgeted while Roy and my dad talked. In my fidgeting, I managed to tip over the ironing board and break the plastic on the iron, and after that I stood silently and listened. They talked for what seemed like forever and then Roy handed my dad back the key, which, while he and Bill talked, he had filed with a hand file to match the broken one. That was the kind of guy Roy was—resourceful and inventive but, most important, able to jump over mental barriers. Just because we always get a key cut with a special machine doesn't mean that it has to be done that way.

Roy had the disdain for engineers that is common among people who actually build and repair things rather than design them in a clean office separated from the dirty reality of work. I've "inherited" this only somewhat justified prejudice from Roy, but I don't have as much of the chip it put on his shoulder. Roy's chip came, I suppose, from not having the education he deserved and having to follow the instructions of people who were intellectually his inferiors. He never felt entirely appreciated for the person he was. My father shook his head one time over Roy's discontent. "He should get it," Bill said. "He's lived his whole life on his own terms. He's already beaten the bastards."

As a young man, Roy was in the Air Force, which is where he became such a great welder and I think it is probably where he picked up a passion for airplanes. By the time he was in his 50s, he owned a small plane and was working on repairing planes in his shop, our future house.

I went flying with him once in October when the leaves were all orange and so we looked down on a carpet of fall foliage and green fields. We flew up over the Granite Hills in Groton and then landed on a little grass strip somewhere in New Hampshire. Before this flight, I hadn't realized the intense feeling of freedom you get from flying a small plane.

The Great Plains that used to beckon adventurous Americans with their unfenced vastness are all cut with fences. And for centuries, the East has been divided by roads and property lines. If you want to go from one place to another, you must stay on a route laid out by someone else. Not so in the skies. It is a three-dimensional world up there and you can go pretty much where you want. When you see a little grass strip, you can land, and when you take off again, you can go in whatever direction suits your fancy. I could see how flying was a perfect combination for Roy. On the one hand, there was the machine, and he was brilliant with machines, and on the other, the near complete freedom.

Our first winter
in "The Shop"

When we bought his shop, I started moving my woodshop into one end of the building, while Roy was moving his welding shop out the other end. One day I was working on one of the main structural posts high up toward the roof and I noticed a metal electrical outlet box that Roy had spot-welded to the post. For some reason, in that second I thought of all the work Roy had done to build the building—all the cold winter days he had worked inside there, all of the little improvements and modifications he had made over the years, the almost innumerable places he had welded something on or run wiring or fixed the roof, the sort of things a handyman does, the handwork. The next time I saw Roy, I said something to him about it, something about how he was leaving an awful lot of his life's work behind and I hoped he didn't mind.

"Let me tell you," he said, "if you've got something material you can't walk away from, then you've got a big, fucking problem."

I've tried to remember that in the years since, as I've poured my sweat and blood into this building. For people who are builders, like me and also Roy, it is important to remember that life is more than what you make. Your life itself, in the moment you are living it, is your most important creation.

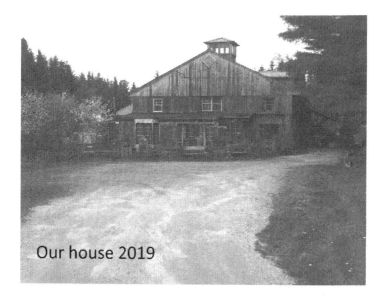

Our house 2019

Roy understood this, and when the time was right for him to leave everything behind—the generations of Haggetts who have lived on this road, his house and land and shop—he did it without a backward glance.

Unfortunately for Roy, he was trying to diagnose the problem with an airplane and he flew it into a high tension wire and killed himself a few years after moving to Arizona. I miss him, but I still feel his spirit in this building.

15- Drinking, Drugs, and Addiction

Drinking beer is more or less a national, cultural responsibility in this country. When I feel bad about not doing my part, I remind myself that our family has consumed more than enough alcohol to more than make up for my abstinence. We come from a long line of alcoholics. My father's father died of it. My mother's mother's parents were both alcoholics. My uncles, Jimmy and Max, from different sides of the family, were alcoholics, although they both managed to dry out.

As a non-drug and -alcohol user, I can't tell you anything from personal experience of drug use and addiction. I'll have to stick to observations from the sidelines.

I was 14, almost 15, when my father's brother, Jimmy, came to stay with us during his downward alcoholic plunge. (In a curious twist of fate, Jimmy arrived at our house on the day I achieved one of the greatest triumphs of my childhood: bending an oxbow without any breaking or splintering.) I always felt a certain kinship with Jimmy since we shared a birthday, were both oldest sons, and were almost exactly the same size physically.

His alcoholism was an obvious cautionary story for me. As an adult looking back, I can imagine how terribly difficult it must have been for my father to see his brother in the grips of the same drug that killed their father, not to mention how horrible it must have been for Jimmy's two sons.

At the time, I focused pretty much entirely on what it meant for me. One day, I walked past Jimmy in the upstairs hall. He was standing and I said, "Hi," as we passed, and our eyes met, or I should say I looked into his eyes, which looked back with no flicker or recognition or acknowledgment, just the vacant, blank stare of a dead drunk. It unnerved me so much that I swore I would never drink. Since I was old enough to recognize the problem was addiction, not the specific drug, I just swore off all drugs. (Jimmy had, of course, done the same thing as a young man and didn't drink until he went to college, although I didn't know this at the time.)

I didn't drink because I was afraid—afraid I would become an alcoholic like Jimmy. When I made that decision, it didn't seem like much of a choice. On the one hand, drink poison and possibly end up wrecking your life and damaging the people you love. On the other hand, don't drink it. It's really not a tough choice from a rational perspective, and teenagers can be maddeningly pure in their reasoning. The risks are relatively high, at least in our family; the benefits, from the perspective of a 14-year-old, are negligible.

That said, my motivation was fear more than reason. I didn't make an illogical choice out of fear, as people often do, but I was motivated by fear nonetheless. Fear as a motivator is not necessarily a bad thing. It's natural to try to protect yourself from things you think are dangerous. But my fear was the fear of myself—fear that I wouldn't be able to control myself, fear that alcohol would make me into a person I didn't want to be.

It was a well-justified fear. I'd seen what alcohol did to Jimmy, but if you are afraid of yourself, what do you trust? How can you trust yourself if you are afraid of yourself? I didn't appreciate the complexity of these questions at the time.

In college, occasionally I had to defend my non-drinking choice. The two most effective lines of attack against it were, "How do you know if you've never tried it?" and "What are you afraid of?"

I never gave too much weight to the first objection. There are tons of things I will never do. In fact, every time you make a choice to do something, you explicitly choose not to do something else. Once you've made a choice and move forward in time, you can't go back and try the other option, ever. You can, in the future, make a different choice, the opposite choice, but it will still be at a different point in time.

I have never killed another human being, although in the course of human history, male human beings killing each other is a more culturally significant act than drinking. Did the people asking how could I know if I had never tried it feel an obligation to try mortal combat so they could know what that was like? Depending on the level of inebriation, this point caused confusion or suspicion but rarely persuasion.

As to the "What are you afraid of?" accusation, the answer for me, obviously, was "I'm afraid of becoming an alcoholic," but people who are drinking are usually quick to dismiss that possibility. These same people are often too prudent (afraid) to try heroin and don't see it in the same light as alcohol. They're right in a sense since heroin is a much more addictive drug than alcohol, but it undermines their argument that you need to trust yourself and not be afraid of what the drug might do to you. We all choose different risks that we are comfortable with; I just happened to draw the line across something generally considered safe.

I stuck to my choice all of these years and have no regrets. Being afraid of something that is culturally normal and even culturally revered put me in an outsider's position. But as a young man, this just added satisfyingly to my bitterness and anger.

Motivation by fear and self-doubt has an internal downside, however, in the lack of trust. I don't think this was caused by not drinking. I was the sort of person to doubt myself when it came to alcohol and probably the type of person to doubt myself in everything.

I puzzled over this a lot as a teenager. If you can't predict or trust your actions in the future, if you're afraid of what you might do, then what's to prevent you from doing bad things? The Nazis, whom we look on as the modern incarnation of evil (how convenient to have a group we can designate beyond doubt as evil and different), were very rational. In fact, the calculated and systematic nature of their regime and crimes makes them seem all the more abhorrent. Horrific as their beliefs and actions were, at the time those actions made some sort of rational sense to an awful lot of people— people who were part of a culture that was as advanced and sophisticated as any in the world. So there's no comfort or protection in rational thought; you can reason your way to atrocity.

If you want to do what is right—and who doesn't, after all—where's the guide? Religion is hardly trustworthy. Not only is there the problem of different religions (or even more absurdly, different sects of the same religion) claiming exclusive knowledge of God and killing people to prove their correctness, but also religions are based on a leap of faith. If I wasn't going to trust myself, why the hell would I have the faith to trust some priest?

You can shackle yourself to someone else's morality in the form of religion or you can strike out on your own, but neither course offers any protection from being wrong. Trust in yourself, but not really, if you don't trust yourself to drink. So, what's left to trust?

Nothing. Imperfection. Accepting the real possibility that you don't know how you will act in the future. You will make mistakes. That's the best I could come up with. In an odd way, it brings you back to faith. You have to trust that somehow it will work out. It may not work out. But you don't have control over that.

So you can die or you can do your best and see how it works out, knowing full well there is no guarantee of being right or doing the right thing. What is that but faith? Faith in yourself? Faith in the universe? Faith in life? Maybe faith is really just the lack of better options. I'm not sure. Maybe what you think is right and dedicate your life to will be, at some point in the future, universally reviled, and even you may have a change of heart and look on your past actions with opprobrium. And yet, that's the deal. Life, emotions, morality—these are cheap, probably worthless in our cosmos. They have a very important and real but constantly changing value for individuals but no permanent axis.

I shouldn't end this painful chapter without making a comment on addiction. Addicts seem to believe the very thing that is killing them is actually saving them. They say, "Don't take it away from me, it's all I've got," or, "Without it, I'd never be able to cope." But this, apparently, is the trick of addictive substances. When people use them to solve a problem, the addiction eventually becomes not only a problem in itself but consumes the person's whole life while they cling to the notion that it is somehow helping them.

It is easy to convince yourself that what you are doing is making things better when in fact you are making them worse. Addictive substances seem to take over this weakness in a person's mind, a weakness we are always vulnerable to, whether or not we drink alcohol.

The other day, I went over to our hydroelectric plant because one of the turbines kept shutting down from low turbine rpm. This was the fault of the sensor, which was incorrectly reading the speed of the turbine shaft rotation. Because the sensor reads better when it is closer, I kept moving it closer and making modifications until it was almost touching. This didn't fix the problem.

As I was leaving to go find someone who could solve this problem, I ran into my friend Dave, who said, "You keep moving it closer and it doesn't get better. Have you tried moving it farther away?" I smiled politely. No, I hadn't, because that was a stupid idea. The sensor has a limited range, and since it was reporting low rpm that meant it was not seeing some of the bolt heads; it doesn't actually look at the shaft but instead counts bolt heads located on the shaft.

I came back several hours later armed with several more complicated diagnostic ideas, none of which worked. So, in desperation I did the opposite of what I thought would make things better and moved the sensor farther away. Of course it worked. By moving the sensor too close, I had made it impossible for it to distinguish between individual bolt heads, so instead of seeing 12 going by, it was lumping several together and calculating a too-slow rpm.

TWO

16- The Purpose of Life

I met Jim Heller in eighth grade PE class. The class
was doing an introduction to wrestling and Jim
Heller ended up as my partner. I'd never taken
much note of Heller before but we were about the
same size so the teacher paired us.

We wrestled a couple times and Heller told me
that I'd won the first match but he'd "dominated the
second match." Neither of us had been pinned
decisively or had any idea how to score a wrestling
match, so it was an act of diplomacy to offer that we
had each won one. But it was a linguistic victory for
him to claim domination in the second match. He'd
made us equals by giving us each a victory, then
claimed a bit more for himself by saying that he
dominated, which sure sounded a lot better than
plain old winning.

In eighth grade I still considered myself a smart
kid and I read a lot. I knew what dominated meant
but I wouldn't ever have used it in a conversation
with another kid. It was a good move on his part and
it impressed me, so I started looking for him to sit
with at lunchtime.

It turned out that Heller was as much of a misfit
as I was and, consequently, he usually took a small

table at lunch and sat by himself. I started sitting with him occasionally and we struck up a lunchtime friendship that lasted for a couple of years, until we drifted apart. It was there, during ninth grade at a little two-person lunch table by the window, that Heller floored me one day. "Rob, did you ever wonder what the purpose of life is?" he asked.

No, I hadn't. His question struck me as so obvious and important that I felt embarrassed not to have thought of it myself. And I didn't have an answer.

The existential struggle that Jim Heller started continues for me to this day, but it was most intense during the two years between high school and when I started college.

When most other kids my age were either prudently contemplating which career would give them the most security and remuneration or happily scheming about which party would give them the greatest possibility of getting laid, I was in that sad, self-absorbed minority stumped by the questions, "Why am I here?" and "How can I be happy in this apparently meaningless life?" Or, as Einstein put it more eloquently than I have, "the nothingness of the hopes and strivings which chase most men restlessly through life came to my consciousness with considerable vitality." Einstein found in the contemplation of physics a "liberation" from this question.

It is not a question that demands much intellect or logic. In fact, unless you are religious and allow the leaders of your religion to set the meaning for you, the answer is pretty obvious. Chances are extremely high that you will live a small, anonymous life, but even if you become Alexander the Great, you will die (at 24, in his case) and your accomplishments will wither rather quickly.

Even if during your life you manage some monumental achievements, the accolades from your fellow humans and your own personal satisfaction are very likely to be useless to you after you die. It follows, therefore, that you must choose the meaning and purpose yourself and find contentment with your choices during your life. But logic is perhaps the least certain road to happiness.

And if you find that you cannot be happy because the meaninglessness of life takes all the pleasure out of it, then you are headed down a road similar to the one I found myself on. Even though there were things I wanted to do, I couldn't seem to believe in them, and without some reason to believe, it all seemed pointless and boring. Try as I did to convince myself that doing something which interested me was all there was, the logic of it did not bring me peace, contentment, or purpose.

Until I left home after high school, I was not plagued by the question of the purpose of my life. I had building projects, school, lots of chores. The seasons and years rolled along with haying and firewood cutting and hunting and sledding and pond hockey and maple sugaring and fishing. I knew that I didn't know what I wanted to be when I grew up and this troubled me, but in a distant, intellectual way.

That all changed when I took my walk, which was a huge failure for me and was the beginning of trying to come to terms with what I wanted to do.

My walk doesn't make sense without knowing about Alex, who was one of my father's friends from the newspaper.

Alex was my childhood hero. Lots of children have heroes who are kind, fun, and playful, and Alex was all of these things. That's all a person needs to be for a child to see them as heroic and want to emulate them.

But Alex also seemed heroic. He'd hitchhiked across Africa and Afghanistan. He was a photographer and a mountaineer. He'd rescued climbers from the icy sides of the White Mountains. He was an athlete. Bill once described him to me as being like Achilles, and the accuracy of that characterization has stuck with me ever since.

My first memory of Alex is from our house near Rutland, Vermont. Alex was racing his motorcycle up and down the road, trying to loosen the exhaust so he could replace it. I sat out in the side yard, and every few minutes he would zoom by and my mother would come out of the house wringing her hands about how fast he was going.

When we moved to Adamant, Alex drove the old pickup with our chickens and a dresser containing my father's boxer shorts, one drawer of which came open and distributed his undergarments along the road. In Adamant, Alex was an intermittent presence in our lives. He would show up unannounced, say that he couldn't stay for dinner, and then stay for several months. Then he would be gone and we wouldn't see him for six months.

While he was with us, he helped with all of the farm work. Alex had worked on a tree service. Bill told me once that Alex was the best man he'd ever seen with a chainsaw and this started in me an ambition to be as good with a saw as Alex, although the truth of the matter is that the athletically gifted have a finesse and ease with their bodies that the rest of us simply can't achieve, even if we get more skilled. Alex was like that with a saw; he had the skill that comes from starting with a more responsive piece of human machinery.

Finally, on January 1, 1976, Alex set out on his greatest adventure. He stepped out of our door in Adamant, Vermont, and walked to San Francisco.

So, let me say I measured myself against giants, and I fell short.

In the fall, after I graduated from high school, I

set out on my own walk. I meant to walk from Washington, DC, where we had friends, south to Alabama, where my grandmother, Muh, lived, and then on across the country, like Alex. Alex's walk was the greatest, most epic thing anyone I knew had ever done, and I wanted to emulate it.

I lasted for three days and 62 miles—winding around on little roads from Culpeper, Virginia, to Charlottesville. I was bored, afraid, shy, lonely, crushed by homesickness, and utterly confused by my motivations. What I'd taken on as a great new project, like building a barn or getting a tractor unstuck from a mudhole, I assumed I could accomplish just the way I had succeeded at those other projects: by figuring it out and working on it.

I didn't know why I was walking, but I knew I wasn't enjoying it. The thought of continuing all the way across the country seemed horrible. And the thought of doing it just to say I'd done it seemed crazy. At the same time, quitting meant complete failure. I'd always been able to do something I'd put my mind to. But here I was looking at defeat and with my mind in a war with itself.

It was a challenge that didn't require much figuring, just keep walking, and I wasn't enjoying the walking at all. Had I put my mind on figuring out how to enjoy the walking, I might have done better. But I didn't. Instead, I decided I didn't like walking across the country and would accept failure and try to figure out what I did want to do.

The third day, I got off the small roads and walked 27 miles, mostly along a four-lane, multi-access road, with the wake from tractor-trailer rigs blowing my hat off. I checked into a motel and the next day took a bus to Sheffield, Alabama, and to Muh's house.

Muh lived by herself in a solid little brick house perched a hundred feet above the Tennessee River. There was a steep bluff between her house and the river. From her sitting room you looked out on the river, which was wider and bigger than any river in Vermont. Barges and tugboats worked on the river, laboriously pushing their loads upstream. I slept out in Muh's sunroom, facing the river, and could hear the throb and pulse of their engines all night.

I wish now that I remembered what Muh and I had talked about because then, maybe, I would know a little more about her. She took me to numerous luncheons with her old-lady friends, the sort of perfunctory, perfume-rich encounters which are utterly meaningless unless you have enough sense of self to be curious about other people. I was trying desperately to understand myself and had no energy or perspective to be interested in these old people, all of whose lives stretched way back before World War II into a world of segregation and Jim Crow that is, quite literally, unimaginable today. After a couple of weeks with Muh, I went up to visit my uncle Jimmy in Nashville. By this time, Jimmy was in recovery from alcoholism. Along the way he'd lost his marriage and family and his law practice, and he owed the IRS a lot of money. I was vividly aware of these facts but only dimly aware of the real personal costs that lay behind them.

He lived in the bottom unit of Metro Manor apartments in downtown Nashville. He showed me into the place with the sort of bemused candor common to recovering drunks. On one hand, it was a big step down in the world for a guy who had been one of the most prominent lawyers in Alabama; on the other hand, sobriety demands honesty and its sister, an inclination not to apologize for the facts of life. I felt like pretty much of a failure myself. To me, Metro Manor seemed great. It was clean, easy to find, and close to Jimmy's new law office.

"I don't really have much to offer you, but you can have my car and I can walk to the office," he said. It was a little Datsun B210. I'd never driven in city traffic before and so I set out timidly exploring the area around Metro Manor apartments and gradually expanding into the whole city. It was a wonderful experience for me.

The whole concept of city traffic confused me. I had grown up driving on dirt roads. In my childhood, the two-lane paved roads had little traffic, and if we did have to go somewhere on the interstate highway, the passing lane was just that, an empty lane which you could use for passing if you came on a slower vehicle, like a farm truck. I'd heard people talking about city driving and so I expected some sort of clear demarcation, an obvious indication, maybe even a sign, that this was the feared and hated city traffic.

I was eager to get out and experience this thing called city driving. It took a week for me to realize the obvious; all there was to city driving was more— more waiting, more speed, more confusion, more cars and lanes. I learned this the best way anyone could, by myself in Jimmy's little Datsun. There was no such thing as a wrong turn. If I wanted to go somewhere and I missed the street, I just went around the block and tried it again. I didn't bother with a map because I could navigate back into the city as long as I didn't lose sight of the skyline.

That week was one of the best visits I've ever had with anyone. Jimmy really had nothing to offer in the way of the usual bullshit that people throw at you when you visit, so at night I went out to dinner with him and his girlfriend in her much nicer car and during the day I roamed around Nashville in his little Datsun.

There was one life-changing experience. One night he asked me if I wanted to go to an AA meeting with him. I was curious. This was a little before 12-step programs became the rage for any sort of ailment. One by one the alcoholics told their version of the same sad story. Alcohol took control of their lives and, in order to keep drinking, they did things from the brazenly heinous to the stupidly mundane until one way or another their lives fell apart and they ended up in this musty church basement, confessing their failings to each other.

I'd witnessed this sad trajectory in Jimmy's life and taken from it my cue to never start drinking. What surprised me was the air of acceptance. As the alcoholics told their stories, the honesty was as palpable as the sadness, and there was an air of optimism too. Every day was a new day for these people, and they had reason to expect that it would be better than the previous day.

You could come into this room after totally screwing up your life—and not just screwing up your life but damaging irrevocably the lives of the people you loved the most—you could come in here and tell these other people. They sure wouldn't tell you that it was all right because they knew from personal experience that what you had done was very fucking far from all right, but they wouldn't kick you out either. The acceptance of imperfection and human failure, acceptance without condoning, was very powerful to me.

I got an immense sense of relief from this knowledge. I didn't feel I needed to use it right away but the thought that I could go somewhere, confess all of my life's failings, this put a base under me—as a position of last resort.

This didn't solve the question of the purpose of life or what I wanted to be, but I did know where I would start from if my whole life crashed and burned.

In the next year, I worked briefly running a log skidder, spent a couple months driving a horse-and-buggy sightseeing carriage in Nantucket, and took a lonely road trip as far west as Roswell, New Mexico. And in between I lived at home. I was miserable when I was gone and miserable when I was home. Wherever I was and whatever I was doing, it was as though there was something holding me back or separating me from life. As soon as I left home I wanted to go back, and as soon as I was home I wanted to go somewhere else.

I liked parts of logging—being in the woods, learning to run the skidder—and it had its moments of beauty. One day I pulled the last hitch onto the landing through a light snowfall. The sun had set, leaving red streaks across the sky, and the last light was disappearing so the outline of the trees and the mountains beyond them were soft and indistinct, like a painting. The exhaust smoke held solid above the skidder, blue gray against the cold, gray sky.

I looked back over my shoulder as we walked down from the landing. It was a good day's work, real work, a beautiful scene, and I was part of it. I knew I should feel lucky, but instead I felt doomed.

Was this all there was? An endless repetition of pointless, if occasionally beautiful, days?

We were up on the side of a mountain in Danville, Vermont, and from my perch inside the frozen cage of the skidder I could look over and see the White Mountains of New Hampshire. Every day I thought about the kids my age over in Dartmouth College in nice, warm dorm rooms, with girls, learning things. What I learned was that I didn't want to run a skidder for the rest of my life. I didn't really want to be in college either, but it seemed like it would be an improvement from logging, so I spent the next month half-heartedly applying to colleges.

Eventually I thought maybe I should live in a city. This prospect held some fear for me, not as much for the city itself as for the repudiation of everything I had believed was important up to this point. Cities, Jefferson said, add to the health of a country as sores add to the health of a human body. Reading this from Jefferson was comforting to me since it affirmed what I liked and gave me an excuse not to experience what scared me. But I had been miserable in so many things I thought I would like that this seemed like something I should try.

Ruth and Bill had a friend who lived in New Orleans. He made me promise that I would give it at least six weeks before I gave up in disgust, then he hooked me up with a friend who owned a tree-trimming business and another guy who rented me a room in his apartment.

In those days you could buy an Amtrak ticket that let you ride any route you wanted for a set price. One hundred fifty bucks got you the eastern third of the country. You could ride as many trains as you wanted, but you had to make out the itinerary beforehand and you only got to get off once before your final destination.

I booked a ticket from Montpelier, Vermont, to Washington, DC, to Miami, back to Washington, and down to New Orleans. I must have been on the train for almost a week. In America, trains go through the back side of cities and towns. Arriving by train is the least inspiring way to come into a city, and as soon as the train cars slowed to a creaking pace as we approached New Orleans, I felt I had made a mistake. Why would anyone want to live here with all this dirty concrete?

These days a kid with my confusion and lack of direction would probably be doped up on some antidepression medication. I don't know if that would have helped me or not. As soon as I got anywhere or started a new project, I would realize that it wasn't right and not what I was looking for. It sounds simple and stupid from a distance looking back. Obviously, I was looking for something in myself and I wasn't going to find it by looking in the world. And yet, even at the time, I recognized this, but I would become convinced that there was a solution, and usually I determined that the solution involved being somewhere else. The solution, like going to New Orleans, would come over me with a sort of dread and gradually build into a conviction that this was what I had to do if I wanted to live.

I spent a lot of time trying to imagine the life I wanted to have. For an 18-year-old country boy from Vermont, New Orleans should have been a paradise of interesting things to do. For me, it was just an opportunity to probe deeper into a self-absorbed search for the meaning of life. If the meaning of life is a wall, then New Orleans was my chance to stand at the bottom of the wall and beat my head against it.

During the day, my work was pleasant enough—chainsaws and trees and working with a tree-trimming crew made up mostly of guys from across Lake Pontchartrain. They were easygoing, part Native American and part African American, mostly quite short, and one guy, who was several years younger than me, already had two kids. I was the only one who wore a watch and so they would ask, "What time it is, brah?" And from that day until this, every time I ask someone for the time, a little voice goes off in my head repeating that phrase.

When I wasn't working or exploring the parts of the city I dared explore on the buses and trolleys, I either read or focused on what I wanted to do. I had a special way of approaching this problem. As long as I wasn't working, whenever in the course of my day an idea would occur to me about what was wrong with my life or some insight into the puzzle of why I was so unhappy, I would focus on it. If possible, I would lie down immediately—on a park bench, on my bed in my room, wherever—as soon as I could get the opportunity. Left foot over right, legs stretched out, hands folded behind my head, I would contemplate the problem.

Sometimes I focused so hard that when I got up my vision was shaky and I didn't have good balance. I would work the question, whatever it was, over and over in my mind until I came to a satisfactory resolution of the particular aspect of the problem I was trying to understand. This was also how I went to sleep every night and how I got up every morning. It was a point of responsibility for me to fill every possible minute trying to answer this question, Jim Heller's old question, What's the purpose of life, Rob?

It took the form of asking how I could be happy or what I should be doing or what any person should be doing. I tried to reason my way to an answer, convinced that, like the other problems I had solved—building, physics sort of problems—I could just figure out the answer. Even to me, even in this state, I could see what a ridiculous way this was to spend my life. But I couldn't stop.

One Saturday morning, when we weren't working, I woke up and as usual started throwing myself against the question. In a fit of rage and desperation, I determined that I wouldn't get out of bed until I had solved it. I lay there methodically working through different scenarios. I imagined myself moving to a different state and what my life would be like, moving back home, going to college. Then I thought about the people I knew and the books I had read in which people seemed engaged and happy with their lives. I pictured myself in their lives; how would that work for me? At 1 pm, after five or six hours of nonstop thinking, I gave up and got out of bed.

When I pondered my life and its purpose, I often came back to James Herriot's books about his life as a veterinarian in England before World War II. My own life had been similar enough to the experiences Herriot described that I could picture myself in his world. He seemed so connected to his life and purpose. Why? How? Where was the line between the tedium of driving between frozen farms and sick animals and the sort of engagement with life that he seemed to have? I broke the problem down. My favorite parts of his books were the angry outbursts between Herriot's boss and the boss's brother. Why was this more compelling to me than the actual vet work where he was saving animals' lives? If interacting with other people was what made his life seem worthwhile to me, why wasn't I happy here in New Orleans with people all around?

I thought of the relatives I had visited, their mundane lives, going to work every day—how did they do it and why? What made it seem worthwhile to them? I thought of the Tintin comics I loved. *There* was a world, a world that seemed fulfilling. How could a comic book world seem more fulfilling than my real life?

Before I got to New Orleans I had been on a Russian authors kick and I had finished reading *War and Peace*. As near as I could tell, I had melancholia, like Pierre. I don't think at that point in my life I had ever heard about a kid being depressed. I thought depression was something suffered by middle-aged housewives who should have had careers, but certainly not young people. For Pierre, the war came along, and that wasn't a solution I wanted. It had to be possible to find purpose without a war.

Fantasy played a big part in my mental efforts. I imagined myself in a different life and then tried to examine how I felt about that life. Was I happy? If I felt a sense of purpose, where did that come from? I wouldn't say that I was scientific, because this was a completely subjective inquiry. I was looking for clues to what might make life worthwhile to me by examining how I thought I would feel in some other, imagined existence.

What I wanted to know was where it was happening. For some people, "it" would mean the best parties, hottest women, loudest music, and most alcohol. Mardi Gras was literally taking place on the street outside my window, but I ignored it. For me, "it" meant something different, a place where I would be engaged in life rather than feeling as though I was watching it go by without having a real stake in it. It, whatever it was, seemed present in Herriot's life. I wasn't certain about my relatives or other people I stayed with.

It was difficult to resist the temptation to look for signs, the absurd notion that the universe might have a plan for me but would only reveal that plan in cryptic code. But I resisted. I wasn't looking for a sign, some prophetic signal about my purpose. I wanted a reason. Something that made sense. Something internal that seemed more significant than "because I'm interested in it," which was the only explanation I had, the only one that seemed to make any logical sense and still didn't seem to be enough.

The persistent continuous sensation of not feeling right with myself, as though something was wrong internally, compelled me to try to answer the question, What is the purpose of my life? Obviously, this was an indulgence many people don't get to enjoy, a bourgeois opportunity created by lack of necessity. I could see that I was happiest in those brief periods when the urgency of a task or situation dragged me out of my contemplation and forced me to engage with the world, but knowing this didn't help.

I engaged in this search as the person I was—a white, North American male. It never occurred to me to conduct this search, an identity search in some ways, in terms of my identity in the culture. Many people—brown people, women, gay people— have to explore not only where their place is in the world, an existential search, but also where they fit into a society that does not necessarily accept or respect who they are biologically. I never thought about that. I felt the hard stare, the mild disgust, and occasional opprobrium of people who couldn't understand what I was doing or why, but these judgments were directed at my choices, not my biology. If I ever resolved my existential struggle, it is not even enough to say I assumed that society would accept me; it never even crossed my mind that it wouldn't.

It is ironic to recognize this now, years later. Had I understood then the privilege of my position, not only would it have made the quest seem more absurd and indulgent, but it also would have given me insight. I didn't appreciate how much fitting in and being accepted by society came as a given from my skin color and gender. Personally, I didn't feel that I fitted in or that I could adopt my expected societal role—college, job, whatever other people expected of me—without resolving for myself my place in the universe. This made me feel like something of an outcast and not voluntarily, since the meaningless pressed with "considerable vitality," as Einstein remarked, but it was an existential struggle in the most general sense, not in the specific sense of being obstructed and oppressed by someone else.

On an intellectual level I understood prejudice and discrimination. Had I been able to see how many people, just because of their biology, struggle to be treated as meaningful beings by the culture—thinking about this question in terms of actual, tangible oppression—might have been illuminating for me.

As the end of my promised six-week stay in New Orleans came to an end, I needed to decide what to do next. I narrowed it down to going home and making some maple syrup, which would at least get me involved in doing something, or staying away from home and starting a new life. In this last option I found two interesting places—northwestern Montana and Alaska. I was leaning toward Alaska, and while wandering around New Orleans I bought a copy of John McPhee's book

Coming into the Country.

I pictured Alaska being like Vermont, a place where my skills at building things and improvising solutions to fix things would be useful. At first, as I read McPhee's book, I thought it sounded like the perfect place for me. But gradually another image grew from my reading. Alaska was also a place where people went to extract wealth and then leave. I was looking for someplace to stay and be part of. Getting money and then leaving was the opposite of what I wanted. So I crossed Alaska off my list. Montana or home.

I pondered the merits of each and came to the conclusion that I couldn't choose. And if I couldn't choose, then it couldn't make much difference. My ceaseless pondering about the purpose of life left me with one obvious, logical conclusion: It didn't matter where you were or what you did. It mattered how you lived your life, but not where or what. And if this were the case, I should be able to live a full, content life either by going back to Vermont or going to Montana. But how to choose? If I really believed it didn't matter, I could flip a coin and decide based on that.

I thought about this for a little while—heads Montana, tails Vermont—but I couldn't see any logical escape. What was I afraid of? I flipped, heads. An awful dread filled me. The idea of going to Montana, which had seemed like salvation while

I was imprisoned by my promise to stay in New Orleans for six weeks, now seemed terrifying. What if I was wrong? On the other hand, what if going back to Vermont meant doom and failure? I flipped again, tails. I knew I shouldn't have flipped a second time. It called everything into question. There was only one way out. I had to flip again. Heads. It was done.

I took some of the money I had made and bought an Amtrak ticket from New Orleans to Whitefish, Montana, by way of Chicago, Denver, Salt Lake City, Boise, Portland, and Seattle.

This was my second long train ride and I'd learned a couple of things. Some of the seats near the bulkheads at the front of the car had extra leg room, but don't take one if the bathroom is located there. I could prop my pack under the footrest and make a pretty good bed, provided no one sat with me. I provisioned myself with some fruit and canned food.

The sun came up massive and red through the morning fog as the train rolled into Illinois. I'd been sleeping on and off during the night. I'd look at the towns, the dingy little frame houses rattling as the train rolled by. What if I was somehow sentenced to live in one of those houses in one of those towns forever? How would I make myself happy? It couldn't be that life would be pointless because lots of people had that life and some of them, surely, were happy, but from the train it looked horrible and hopeless.

I looked at the sun over the muddy corn stubble. Montana was a distant, scary, but exciting concept. I didn't think about it or what I would do when I got there. I just looked out the window, reclining in the seat, left foot over right, wondering where I fit in. When I dozed off, my head rested against the window, and when I woke up, all my teeth hurt from the vibration.

We had a layover in Chicago. I walked around the city a bit. By the time I got on the train west, it seemed like days since I left New Orleans. This was a western train with a double-decker observation car. The purpose of the train propelled us west with its glorious motion, clacking and gently rolling while I stared out the window, my mind drifting between sleep and daydream but always coming back to the same question: What did I want to do and why? And when I followed an idea into a dead end, along would come another town and people whose lives, terribly drab from my perspective, still seemed to have meaning to them. Through Iowa and Nebraska I'd think about what it must be like to be them going home to their families at the farms and ranches we were passing.

By Denver it seemed like I had been on the train for one long, long day, or a month—I didn't care. The passing of day and night became irrelevant, but as the train pushed west and started to struggle uphill, I woke from my trance. A long string of boxcars was parked on a curve to block the wind and snow. We were in the mountains. I hadn't seen mountains in almost two months and I'd never seen mountains like these.

The mountains in Vermont don't end, they just become hills and then lesser hills. You can drive from Vermont to the seacoast in Maine or to the flat land of Ohio and it is always a gradual transition, one topography morphing gently into another.

The train had been pulling through the Great Plains, but now I was looking out my window at a mountain that started abruptly, almost as though it had been piled there by an enormous earth-moving machine. It looked as though I could walk over and touch the exact spot where the flat land stopped and the mountain started. I stared at it in disbelief. We'd been heading straight into the mountains, but because of the corner in the tracks, I could see the plains stretching away behind us on one side of the train and the mountains on the other.

For a day I put aside my self-absorption and looked out the window in amazement. I've always been a lover of land; why, I don't know, but looking at the land go by is fascinating for me. This was like nothing I'd ever seen. As the train labored through the Rockies, I moved from side to side in the observation car. As some rocky, arid peaks passed over the train, I promised myself that I would come back someday and live in these amazing mountains.

By late night we were rolling through Utah. I slept a little and woke to stare out at the desert landscape illuminated by a half-moon and the dim, shadowy mountains.

I went back to pondering my purpose. I don't know what happened that night, but I felt as though I found an answer. It wasn't an answer that I can remember or maybe that I could even articulate at the time, but it was more satisfactory than anything I had come up with in a year and a half of looking. Strange to say, although I don't remember what I resolved, I remember exactly that I was sitting toward the front of the car on the south side and I can remember clearly the small plain with jagged mountains in the distance and a couple of faint lights from a ranch. I felt a sort of peace and drifted off to sleep again only to wake up in the beautiful high desert.

For the next several days I felt no need for obsessive thinking about the point of my life and I just watched the western landscape roll by. Inevitably, the train got to Whitefish, Montana, and I got off. For a 19-year-old kid, I was very skilled and would have been a useful employee to almost anyone, but I knew nothing about how to get a job. I walked around for a couple days, made a few timid inquiries, but my heart wasn't in it. Whitefish was a place like other places, full of people going about their mundane lives. I'd walked, driven, taken the train, lived in New Orleans and Nantucket, and visited relatives and friends in Alabama, Nashville, Pennsylvania, Ohio, Missouri, and Oklahoma and it all seemed the same, pointless.

Through the pointlessness of it, there were still things I wanted to do. A week earlier I had desperately wanted to live in Whitefish, and now that I was here it seemed just the same as everywhere else. I took a bus to the airport in Kalispell, about 40 miles away, and bought a plane ticket home. On the plane ride home, I decided that I had to choose a project and however wrong it felt simply push through until the end, if for no other reason than just as an experiment to see if it changed things.

I need to explain something that probably isn't obvious. I didn't quit doing all the things I quit because I was lazy or even necessarily because I was homesick or bored or disillusioned, although these last three all played their role. The underlying motivation was a sincere and deep feeling that somehow I was being untrue to myself. I was driven to find a purpose, compelled by a sense that somehow I needed, or ought to be doing, something and unable to find what it was.

In many ways, a life of mundane and dreary tasks was enormously appealing, but it seemed like giving up. It wasn't that I wanted to be famous or rich, but I felt that there must be something with more meaning. When I contemplated starting a project and finishing it, and there were many projects I really wanted to do, I saw them all as a diversion from finding my purpose, and in that way I felt that it was dishonest of me to indulge myself. So by deciding to start and complete a project, I felt that I was engaged in an experiment. I knew I could finish the project. The question was whether by putting aside my quest for a purpose and simply delving into a distraction I could break myself out of the dead end I seemed to be stuck in.

I'd always wanted a canoe, and as I flew home I sketched out a design. It was going to be small and maneuverable. I hadn't figured out yet that because a small canoe draws much more water than a large canoe, you can often get into more secluded, low-water places with a bigger canoe. I planned my canoe to be eight feet long and I figured I could bend the ribs using forms like I used for oxbows. I wanted it to be durable so I could explore ponds and places where the bottom was likely to scrape, so I decided to cover it with an old inner tube from a tractor tire.

I set to work as soon as I got home, first wandering around in the woods until I collected enough ash wood for the ribs and then driving to tire repair shops until I found a discarded inner tube that was large enough. It took about a week or a little more. I didn't allow myself to think about the point of my life; I just lived it and made my canoe. The frame was crude and the inner tube skin heavier than I expected and it was tippy as all hell, but it floated and I paddled it around the beaver pond.

While I was working on the canoe, I was moderately happy; as soon as I was done, the same feeling of pointlessness settled over me. I was out of ideas. I still filled my idle moments with contemplating my purpose, but it was like going round and round on a hamster wheel. A year or so before, when I applied to colleges, I and been accepted to St. John's College in Santa Fe. I deferred for a year because I knew I didn't want to be in college, but as far as I knew they were still expecting me in the fall. I didn't think I would go, but it was the only thing I had on my horizon.

So, the spring turned into summer, with me living at home and feeling half alive, even when I was doing things I wanted to be doing. I would go fishing in my little canoe, but I wasn't really into it. I'd work my oxen, but what was the point. Then, in the middle of the summer one night, on public television, I chanced to watch *Cat on a Hot Tin Roof,* with Tommy Lee Jones and Jessica Lange.

It's a complicated play with tangles of dishonesty and sexuality, family relationships, and alcohol, but at the time I saw it more simply. In Brick and his inability to act, I saw myself, or what I thought my future would be if I didn't leave and make a new life for myself. The feeling came on with such compulsion and dread that I decided I needed to leave immediately. We were in the middle of cutting hay, it was a bad time to go, but I felt certain that staying home was the most cowardly act.

I had a little money left over from my work in New Orleans and I'd been doing odd jobs for people. I bought another plane ticket and about a week later landed back in Kalispell, Montana. It must have been early to middle of July and it stayed light until almost 10:30 at night. I walked and hitchhiked up to Whitefish, no more sure how to go about making a life there than I had been the first time.

On the way there I meet three brothers from California, all of the same mother but by different fathers, who were getting together to hike in Glacier National Park, so I rode up there with them and hiked for several days. Then back to Whitefish, already knowing that I didn't want to stay there and didn't know how to start a new life even if I wanted to. In a couple of days I was ready to go home. I had just enough money left for a train ticket, so I bought the ticket and spent the night leaning against my pack a little way down the train tracks from the station. There were some hobos there and a crazy guy who kept trying to tell me he'd been in the Olympics, but all in all it seemed relatively safe.

The train came through early in the morning and I didn't want to miss it. I didn't sleep much, running over my life failures in my mind and keeping an eye on my pack.

I got on the train exhausted and depressed, but the tracks cut right through Glacier National Park—the other side, the side I hadn't hiked in—and so I determined to stay awake until we were through the park.

In the seat behind me was an Indian guy with brown skin and a big white turban around his head. I judged that he must be some sort of important religious person because with him was an attendant, an American. As near as I could tell, the Indian guy didn't speak English, he just sat serenely behind me.

I stared out the window for several hours until we were through the mountains and then I drifted off to sleep. I don't know what happened or when it happened, but I came home in a different frame of mind. My worry about what I would be or do was gone, utterly vanished. So vanished I didn't even think about whether or not I needed to think about it.

I got home unashamed to be back and delighted to engage myself in whatever I wanted to do. I can't explain my attitude any better than to use the cliché that I was living in the moment. I worked my oxen on the old horse-drawn mowing machine I'd had for several years, but I didn't worry that I needed to get it working better before I used it. Nor did I worry that it was a waste of time because I would probably never use it again. I enjoyed cutting hay without thinking about whether I wanted to have my own farm to cut hay on someday. I checked, and apparently St. John's was expecting me as a freshman that fall and I thought, "What the hell, all the paperwork has been done, why not try it?" Maybe I would love New Mexico and stay there forever. Maybe I wouldn't like college and I would come home. Everything seemed possible and nothing seemed inevitable.

I hadn't reached any sort of mental conclusion, despite years of searching. I thought, in a sort of silly way, that maybe the Indian guy on the train had sensed my existential turmoil and cast some sort of spiritual assistance to me without my knowing it. But I didn't care one way or the other. Whatever it was, it was, and whatever came next would be what it was too.

I lasted in this state through the rest of the summer and was feeling this way when I entered college in the early fall. I don't know what to say about that period except that it faded but never went entirely away. It comes back occasionally, just a whiff, the way a breeze will momentarily bring you a scent and transport you to another time.

I've struggled with the meaning of life since then, particularly after college, but never approaching the intensity of that two-year period. In a way, that was my most focused effort on anything, ever. In other ways, it was incredibly misguided and wasteful. I don't know what I learned or if I learned anything. I was compelled to look for the meaning in my life and I knew rationally that fundamentally the meaning couldn't be different in Montana than in Vermont or New Orleans, but I didn't believe it and had to look on my own.

Those two years of soul-searching were the most formative of my adult life, but I can't say what I learned. I've recounted the experience and yet I can't even define how it changed me. Did I just need time to grow up? Would I have gotten to the same place in my mind no matter what I did? Could I have gotten there faster and with less sadness and pain? Do you have to search even if it is impossible to find what you are looking for? If I had spent that time doing something more structured and with other people, would I be happier than I am now, or less happy? I don't know the answers to these questions.

When physicists examine atoms, they smash them together and then try to determine what was there by tracing the debris from the collision. Life is kind of like that. You don't really know who you are, but you do things, and afterward you look back and realize, "Oh, I was the person, the seeker, who chose to ride around the country on a train looking out the window and puzzling the purpose of my life."

Most of the foregoing essay is a simple account of what I did. I want to add a small footnote that occurred to me as I reread this chapter. When I rode the train and looked out the window at the drab houses filled with people living normal lives, I wondered what made their lives meaningful and how, if I were to suddenly trade places with them, I would make my life meaningful. The answer— inasmuch as there is one, and it is an answer I didn't understand at the time, which is why I bring it up here—is other people. People's lives are meaningful because of their interactions with other people.

This isn't exactly an answer to the question Jim Heller posed because it doesn't address the larger meaning. Then again, it is an answer because it addresses the meaning people find. The people living in those forgettable little towns the train passed through, the reason they were happy—and surely many of them were—is because of their relationships with other people. That, in the end, is why people do things.

17- Handshake

I remember exactly when I became convinced that the firm handshake was just a gimmick. I was 18 and at my aunt Peggy's house. Peggy needed a hayloft built in her barn. It was a simple project and I'm not sure why we didn't go to the local lumberyard for materials. Probably the reason was that I had never built with regular planed lumber, and so I suggested that we buy some rough-cut lumber directly from a sawmill.

We ended up at a typical rural sawmill, where the owner was also the primary worker and employed a couple of other men. I don't remember the man's name now. He wasn't huge, but he was several inches taller than I was and dressed in tan coveralls.

Peggy lived in Glenmoore, Pennsylvania, just few miles past the last stop on the Main Line. You can forget, as you're passing by Bryn Mawr and Haverford and the other Main Line colleges, that many places in rural Pennsylvania have more in common with the South than the North.

Anyway, like my father, this sawyer favored the South in his speech and general demeanor; that is to say, he was both courteous and threatening at the same time.

He extended a hand in greeting, and it is to this

day probably the most physically powerful hand I've ever shaken. It was thickly swollen with muscles developed by years of rolling logs and lifting boards and had calluses nearly as hard as the oak we were buying. I remember thinking that if his arms matched his hands—and it was a near certainty that they did because his hands didn't get that toughened on their own—then he probably could have grabbed one of my hands in each of his and dismembered me without effort.

His grapple of a hand closed slightly and gently encased mine. His eyes were emotionless little slits permanently formed that way after years of squinting into blowing sawdust. We shook lightly a few times and I was forever cured of the notion that real men have a firm handshake.

This was a real man in every sense by which you could judge from a casual meeting—hardworking, tough, strong, honest, everything that is supposed to be represented by a firm handshake. Furthermore, he had a hand that was capable of delivering not only a firm handshake but quite possibly a lethal one, and yet he felt no obligation to crush my hand to make a mock point about who he was. Contrast this with the salesman or business executive who, fresh from the gym, tries to flatten your hand with his lotioned palm and stares into your eyes as though this animalistic ritual would convince you of his character.

In our culture, it is considered important for a man to give a firm handshake and look the other person in the eye when doing so. It is supposed to be a sign of a man's strength of character and integrity that he has strong hands. That he will look you in the eye while shaking your hand proves that he has nothing to hide and is honest.

These are frontier values. The firm handshake is supposed to indicate the quality of the individual as opposed to, say, judging the individual based on family and tribe. I am deeply in favor of judging individuals rather than groups, but what reason is there these days for thinking that just because a man's hands are strong or he looks you in the eye that he is honest and hardworking? Maybe it was true many years ago when the majority of people did some sort of physical work for a living, but now? And these days, women, forced to compete in a man's world, often grip your hand as firmly as a man does when they shake it.

I bring this up because there are many customs, silly and anachronistic, which are also pervasive and powerful. Even now, 30 years after I had this realization, when some guy tries to convince me of how good he is by how hard he can grip my hand, it is hard for me to resist the urge to squeeze back.

18- Bill and Machine Repairs

Bill around 1985

My father wanted to own a farm ever since he was 12 and went with a friend to stay with the friend's grandparents on their farm outside of Memphis. He achieved his dream and lives on a sidehill farm that is the Yankee equivalent of the Memphis farm.

Bill's small farm, like pretty much every farm, has a fairly vast collection of old machines. I'll just list some of the more important machines: three tractors, a dump truck, a backhoe, a bulldozer, hay balers, hay rakes and mowing machines, lawnmowers, snowblowers, rototillers, wood splitter, wood processor, log truck, chainsaws—and this is without mentioning barn plumbing and wiring, compressors, and so on. There is also a 50-

yard-long line of broken equipment that is used for parts.

The machines are, without exception, old and prone to breakdowns. My father manages to keep them running most of the time. But here is the point: He is not a natural mechanic. There are some basic principles of mechanics and physics that he still doesn't understand even after 50 years of troubleshooting a fleet of dying machines. As you've probably deduced, he is hardheaded, determined, and persistent. But his success is due to more than stubbornness, and that's what I want to explain.

When it comes to mechanical repairs, in place of knowledge he imposes will. When that is not sufficient to fix the problem, he applies more will and, if necessary, backs it up with increasingly big hammers until he gets his way. In the face of a perplexing mechanical problem, he often advances with an intuitive insight based on a misunderstanding.

Now, I'm not saying my father is always a successful mechanic. Machine breakdowns are an ongoing trial for him, but more often than not he manages to get things going and keep moving forward.

Half of his success is probably due to what people used to call sheer cussedness—being too tough to give up. This is a formidable quality. Most of human history has been, as it continues to be for most other animals and also still for many humans, a struggle for survival never completely beyond the reach of hunger. The survivors of this evolutionary battle, from whom we are all descended, were the ones who persisted doggedly despite bleak prospects. Bill obviously got an extra dose of this determination.

But the reason for the other half of his success as a mechanic is his misguided intuition. To explain this, I have to contrast his approach to a mechanical problem with my own. I am a mechanically inclined person, at least more so than Bill. For the most part, I understand the basic mechanical and physical principles, and when a machine breaks I begin with my understanding of how the machine works and try to advance from there to uncovering why it has ceased working. This is, as far as I know, the same logical strategy employed by my father.

The difference is that I actually understand how the machine works, while Bill's understanding often associates unrelated causes and effects in a system that makes sense to him but could not work in reality. No matter, he forges forward because he must, because he is determined to solve the problem and fix the machine. Often, what he perceives as the cause of the problem, I recognize as being an impossible location to discover a solution either because that part is functioning fine or because it would not cause the symptoms we are seeing if it did malfunction.

I am not a great mechanic. Even though I

understand the way machines work, I don't have great intuition on what has caused them to break. I have to figure it out every time, slowly and tediously. And although my understanding is usually correct, that doesn't mean my diagnosis is. Machines, even relatively simple machines, usually have multiple interacting systems. There are many potential causes of a breakdown that are logically consistent with how the machine functions. I work my way along methodically, often taking wrong turns, inspecting parts that could have been the cause but in fact are functioning fine. When a machine breaks, anything could be wrong, so you start by eliminating possibilities, and pretty quickly you get to possibilities that can't be eliminated without a little work. And then sometimes my logic is faulty or I have misunderstood how the machine works.

My method is superior to my father's because it is based on a better understanding. And I think Bill would agree that I am, although far from good, a better mechanic than he is.

However, Bill's method is much more successful than you would ever think it should be. He and I have been repairing machines together since I was 12 or younger. Time and again I have seen him approach a mechanical problem, use his misguided intuition, and head down a blind alley. I know, because I understand how the machine works, that the solution is not in the place he is investigating.

He forges on undeterred, and before he can be completely convinced that he is looking in the wrong place he discovers something that redirects his intuition, misguided though it is, and he's off again, following this logically incorrect, but to him promising, lead. He doesn't follow this new lead to the solution; he follows it, of course, to what he sees as another lead, but eventually he does get to where he needs to be to fix it.

Meanwhile, I have been methodically and tediously eliminating causes—causes that in the real world of physics and mechanics could actually have been the source of the problem. Of course, I make mistakes, both in my understanding and also because there are many possible causes that have to be examined.

Bill not infrequently solves the problem first. He has kept old, worn-out machines running on his farm for 40 years now. I think that generally speaking, and especially when it is a complex problem, I usually beat Bill to a solution, but not always, and this is what is interesting. I have seen him be successful so many times, even though I knew he started out with a logically incorrect diagnosis, that I have to conclude that sometimes, often, taking action, even incorrect action, is a better strategy than trying to figure it out.

19- How I Knew Louis Was Smarter than Me

From my limited observation point inside this skull looking out (and what is a man, really, but a variant on a crab, holding ignorance and fear inside his skull-shell, capturing experiences with his senses, and then returning to the safety of his thoughts to chew over his prize), I'd say that when it comes to pure mental horsepower, the ability to absorb, categorize, and process information, I'm about average.

I have a couple of unusual mental skills, but these advantages are offset by slower than average processing power. My brother, Louis, has always been faster with repartee and faster to grasp a concept than I am. But these too are mere mental flourishes; real intelligence is the ability to see across systems and frames of reference. Here too, I'm afraid, Louis has the edge.

One Christmas I came home from college and discovered that the shower curtain bar (we only had one bathroom) had been bent and then straightened and propped in place, so it was precarious and prone to falling off. When the curtain fell, it brushed against your naked body with a horrible cold wetness, and the ensuing struggle to get away resulted in water on the floor and even more cold interactions with the curtain. I tried to remember to get a shower curtain rod when I was in town but I kept forgetting, and no one else seemed able to remember either.

When I returned home for summer vacation, the new shower curtain rod that greeted me was a maple sapling. My brother—he would have been 10 or 11 at the time—had peeled the sapling and pounded it very firmly into place so that it held the shower curtain with a rigidity that communicated a certain degree of anger and frustration on the part of its builder.

What Louis had seen was that despite the fact that the existing shower curtain bar was metal, a wooden one would be perfectly adequate. This was not a huge cognitive leap, but Louis had seen what had completely escaped me, the woodworker of the family—not only the woodworker but also the one who usually got his materials from the forest. Just because we always replaced the flimsy shower bar with another cheap, metal one, we didn't have to do it that way. Three decades later, the shower curtain bar from the forest endures.

This is a small example of an easy mental leap, but that makes it a good illustration of the point. Real intelligence comes from being able to look at one system—in this case, the habit of using a purchased metal shower curtain bar—and jump outside of that system to find a solution in another system. And often the more mundane mental habits are the hardest to get over. I hadn't been able to see or solve the shower curtain bar problem even though I was, one would have thought, much more suited to coming up with a solution than Louis. He crossed between systems more easily than me, and this is the mark of superior intelligence.

20- Bill, Gordon, and Ducks

In strangely parallel situations, both my father, Bill, and my friend Gordon, without meaning to in either case, showed me an aspect of what it means to be a human being.

When I was 10 or 12, a logger came to visit and to look at an adjoining piece of land from which he thought he might want to cut the timber. This guy was also a duck hunter and so he brought his shotgun, and on the way to look at the prospective logging site we detoured along the back side of the beaver pond. I was trailing along behind the group and was startled when his shotgun blasted off. He'd shot at a duck, a wood duck he thought, about 50 or 60 yards out and he was pretty certain that he'd hit it. He'd seen it on the water and then it had disappeared.

We all peered through the dead trees and cattails at the water where the duck was supposed to be. After five minutes with no more evidence of the duck, the guy was ready to move on. My father said no, he was going out there to find the duck. At first, I couldn't believe my ears. The swamp, as we called the beaver pond, held some creatures that were, at least to my young mind, terrifying. There were leeches as long as your hand and giant snapping turtles. The scariest was the dark, shallow water and whatever unknown monsters it might conceal in its muddy bottom.

Bill removed his wallet and started wading toward the spot where the duck had been last seen. I thought there was a good chance it would be the end of him, but he floundered out in the waist-deep water and muck, picking his way over sunken logs and around cattail mounds. He couldn't find the duck and eventually he came back, much to my relief.

There was, of course, nothing in the swamp that could have seriously injured Bill. The majority of my fear came from not knowing what was under that dark water.

Twenty or so years later I tried a little duck hunting myself. Every night in the fall, hundreds of ducks would fly into the beaver pond below our house. Beth Ann had always wanted to prepare duck à l'orange, which she had often served when she used to work as a waitress but had never actually cooked herself. I thought I had discovered a limitless supply of organic duck meat and a type of hunting that would be endorsed by my wife. What could be better?

I outfitted the canoe with a chicken wire covering and stuck cattail reeds through the chicken wire to camouflage the boat. I'm a lousy wing shot, but after some clean misses in the air I got better and feared I might have wounded a duck.

After that, I decided to shoot only clean kills, and for me that meant shooting on the water. It also meant I could aim for a head shot and protect most of the meat—unsportsmanlike, but more humane.

Several evenings later I had four or five duck carcasses in the refrigerator when Gordon called and said he would like to go out duck hunting. It was a nice evening and we had barely settled into the reeds when we heard a strange rasping sound. It was a rhythmic but intermittent sound and seemed to come from the cattails behind us. A little prodding and poling the canoe deeper into the reeds and we glimpsed a duck scuttling through the pond weed and reed mounds. It was wounded and apparently unable to fly but able to swim along quite quickly through the reeds.

We pushed our way into the mass of cattails in a couple of different places, trying to get close enough for a shot to save the poor bird from a prolonged death. The reeds were much too thick for us to get very close and the duck knew that its advantage lay in staying low in the thickest stems.

After 10 or 15 minutes, with dark getting closer, we faced the prospect of leaving the duck to die overnight. All the ducks I had shot at had flown off, but a lingering guilt made me think I might be responsible for this poor duck's condition. We were at a standstill, every rasping breath of the duck bringing fresh guilt to my conscience, when Gordon resolved the situation by stepping out of the canoe. The water was three or four feet deep, the bottom soft mud, and the cattails so thick that he had to swam-crawl through them, but the duck was no match for him and eventually he cornered it against a particularly thick patch of reeds. It was badly wounded in the wing and the lung and we put it quickly to death.

When Gordon stepped out of the boat, it reminded me of Bill but also of the fact that a human being is an animal that is willing to step into the unknown. These are trivial examples, and perhaps that is why they are revealing for me. There was nothing truly dangerous in either case, just the unknown nastiness of dark, swampy water, but the casualness with which Bill and Gordon stepped into the water, my fear of it as a child, and, as an adult, my greater understanding of human nature made me realize something.

The human being is probably the most fearless creature that has ever walked the face of the earth. With a shrug we enter the unknown, and, despite being somewhat fragile as creatures, relying on tools, intellect, and determination, we overcome and destroy whatever resists us.

I say this not as a criticism nor as praise. It is what we are. No one criticizes the *Tyrannosaurus rex* for being a voracious predator. Unlike the dinosaurs, however, we all have choices about how we act, and everyone needs to choose which parts of their nature they want to restrain or encourage.

The human animal has some impressive features, and this is one: When push comes to shove, it is willing to, and assumes that it can, take on the unknown. Many, many people have made this assumption and been wrong and then dead, but for better or worse this assumption is a part of us and has been right often enough to let us dominate the earth.

A human will step off into muddy, dark water because it wants to find a wounded duck or launch a reed boat into the Pacific Ocean without knowing where it will end up or set out for the moon in a spaceship.

The Caveman Corollary

People, including but not limited to my wife, always tell me that I am an angry man. I aggressively defended myself against this accusation for years. Of course, I could see that my father was an angry man, as was my brother. But it is not just our family. Virtually every man I know is, under the right prodding, willing to reveal extreme anger about something.

So, yes, goddamn it! I'm angry for no obvious reason and so's every other guy I know. Watch them. The ones that don't admit it are just lying.

Why?

In the modern world, people only do really crazy shit when they are drunk, high, or incredibly angry. But thousands of years ago, before we invented drugs and alcohol and there was only anger, what was its use?

A human being is essentially a frail animal. We've got good endurance but no claws, horns, thick skin, not even thick hair. All we've got is the big brain for making tools, and for most of human history the toolmaking wasn't all that great.

So if you're living in a cave with your wife and kids and extended family and you've got a spear and a rock and a saber-toothed tiger is at the mouth of the cave, what is going to propel you outside that cave to do battle with the beast and save your family? Anger, that's what. You need to exist in a state of nearly permanent rage, ready at the spur-of-the-moment to do the craziest sort of shit imaginable, like running out of a cave in the dark wearing a loincloth and carrying a stick with a sharp rock tied on the end to attack a cat five times your size sporting teeth as long as your forearm.

It turns out that this theory also explains another perplexing fact of modern life. Why is it that many women, often even the most militantly feminist of women, seem attracted to angry men? Under this theory, the answer is simple. For tens of thousands of years, the women who survived were the ones who were attracted to men crazy enough to attack lions and bears and tigers with only spears and rocks. These were the angriest men. Their children survived, carrying on the genes for extreme anger and attraction to extreme anger. And now we have the world we live in.

21- Important Books

There are four books (so far, 2020) that shifted my perspective as I read them. These aren't the most important books in the world or the best written, just the four that had the most impact on me.

The Gift of Good Land — **Wendell Berry**

Someday you will read Keats's poem "On First Looking into Chapman's Homer," and ever after revelatory moments will be different for you. You will say to anyone else who has read and loved the poem, "It was like Chapman's Homer," and they will know, more intimately than you could ever express or show, exactly how you felt. So it was for me when I first read Wendell Berry. I felt, as Keats wrote, "like some watcher of the skies when a new planet swims into his ken."

A friend at the newspaper, Dan Gilmore, loaned a copy of *The Gift of Good Land* to my father, and Bill thought I might like it. I was in ninth or tenth grade and I took it to school because I always took a book to read in my free periods. In those days at U-32 High School, they let us more or less choose our classes, and, naturally, I opted for as few classes as possible. I spent the majority of my (excessive) free time playing tape-ball basketball in the halls, playing Ultimate Frisbee in front of the school when the weather was nice, playing tackle football behind the school (no equipment of any kind; it was for this that I got my first and only detention), hiding in the library and reading old *National Geographic* magazines and trying to figure out where else I might want to go someday. In case all of these diversions failed, I took a book to read.

On this day, for whatever reason, I couldn't find anything to do other than read, and so I made my way to the art area, which was the homeroom area for my teacher-advisor, Pat Pritchett. I found a comfortable spot on one of the unused pottery wheels and started reading.

Wendell Berry was talking about all of the things I was interested in—farming, the woods, and building things. I'd read how-to books and the Foxfire books and novels about people living hardscrabble existences, but this was different. Berry was making arguments about politics and democracy intertwined with observations about working horses or cutting wood.

I had always lived a divided life. One part of my life was involved in building and farming and logging and interacting with people who were also doing these things. The other part of my life was reading and thinking. The two didn't really mix when I was a child. But here was Berry combining these interests in beautifully written essays. Every page was an argument giving intellectual weight and value to rural occupations, such as shoveling manure or felling a tree, that I enjoyed.

I know it sounds strange in modern Vermont, where small farmers who went to Ivy League colleges make a living producing artisanal cheese, where slow-food promoters and vegans are everywhere and sometimes find common ground with hunters, ATV enthusiasts, and right-wing property-rights advocates. Hell, today I have vegetarian friends who are also gun nuts, but to my life at that time, it was revelatory. I lived in a two-part world, and Wendell Berry joined the two parts together.

It didn't mean that the people I talked to about farming and hunting and fixing machines were suddenly going to talk to me about how much they liked reading *Far from the Madding Crowd*. What it meant for me was that the two parts of my life made sense to me.

The lack of connection between the two sides of my life hadn't ever really bothered me. It was slightly inconvenient when the two groups collided, but usually they didn't. My two closest friends, Benji and Lee, were easily able to bridge the gap from one side to the other. But all of a sudden I realized that there were two sides and that I had been instinctively keeping them separate without even knowing it. And then *The Gift of Good Land* came along and put them together.

When you learn the meaning of a word, you start hearing or reading that word more often. You know the word existed and was certainly as prevalent in conversation before you learned the meaning, but having learned the meaning you see it everywhere, so you know that in the past you must have been just skipping over it. That's the way this was for me. All of a sudden something made sense that hadn't been bothering me before, but now I understood that I had been skipping over it. I felt exhilarated.

In two or three days I had finished all of *The Gift of Good Land*. The essays thrilled me when Berry described some farmer—usually a farmer who worked horses—and how that farmer had managed to stay small and be productive and profitable using old technology. Then he would go on about the farmer's importance to his community and democracy and the Jeffersonian ideal of independent farmer citizens. He didn't forget to land a few sharp points about venal corporations destroying the environment and democracy. And he did it all with a graceful acuteness of logic and prose.

When I was 18, miserable and returning home after my first cross-country road trip, I drove through Kentucky. I knew Wendell Berry lived in Port Royal, near the Kentucky River, so I looked at my map and headed up a road that went through

Port Royal and paralleled the river. When I saw some horse-drawn equipment next to a barn, I stopped my car and asked at the house across the road from the barn if Wendell Berry lived there. The woman who answered the door—his wife, I suppose—said he was up in back working his horses.

He had some sort of foreign-exchange student with him, a college kid—German, maybe, I wasn't sure of the accent. The kid's European sense of manners and propriety was offended that I, a complete stranger, would simply show up. He expressed this in his limited English, but Berry, American rustic intellectual working his horses, seemed unruffled. We talked for a little while, I don't remember about what, and then I went on my way.

The One-Straw Revolution — Masanobu Fukuoka

The One-Straw Revolution was the second and least important of the four books to really alter my outlook on the world.

Masanobu's theory of farming was "Do Nothing" farming, by which he meant establishing a farm where the various plants and animals were in a sort of self-perpetuating balance with each other such that minimal effort on the part of the farmer would be sufficient to maintain the balance and the farmer could live on the resulting productivity.

I've never been much good at gardening. I considered my inability a character defect for years. Every spring, flush with enthusiasm for life and growing plants, I started a garden, and for me this meant ripping up the soil with a machine, creating some mounds or trenches, and depositing seeds. Gardening takes a light touch. A little weeding every few days, maybe some gentle trimming—you're really just making it a little easier for the plants to do what they naturally want to do. After preparing the ground and planting the seeds, I usually lost interest. By July, when I checked on the garden again and found the weeds and vegetable plants twisted together in a battle for sunlight, I would give up in shame.

Fukuoka's concept is of man in control not through force but by gently and thoughtfully organizing the pieces of a system so they work more efficiently and sustainably with each other. This concept I found very compelling. I am naturally inclined to see the world the way Teddy Roosevelt saw it when he said that "it is only through labor and painful effort, by grim energy and resolute courage, that we move on to better things." In other words, I see life in terms of conflict and struggle, overcoming obstacles and prevailing over adversity.

Not true, said this gentle Japanese farmer. Life

is lived better through a thoughtful arrangement of the pieces rather than through struggle. Discovering the right arrangement might be a struggle, but it is a struggle to understand, not a struggle to overcome—a struggle to find a suitable order among pieces, including yourself, so that they can all prosper, rather than a struggle to prosper by overcoming something else. At its heart is the belief that things are generally what they should be, only a little disorganized, as opposed to a belief that nature must be controlled and reshaped to benefit us.

A similar dichotomy exists in the book of Genesis, as Wendell Berry points out, in which there are two creation stories, one where man is the steward of nature and the other where he has dominion over nature.

Fukuoka, like Wendell Berry, took a dim view of what we call progress. What more could a human being want than to take care of the garden he lives in? Modern advancements, in Fukuoka's view, rather than freeing us and improving our lives, chained us down and put us in an adversarial relationship with the planet and other life forms that we are ultimately dependent on for our survival. The life of a Do Nothing farmer was as good as it could be—lots of leisure time to spend talking with friends, plenty of rest, good food, and a schedule dictated by the motion of the earth around the sun and the changing seasons.

For a while after college I toyed with the idea of trying to establish a Fukuoka-inspired farm in Vermont. I am still under the influence of Fukuoka's and Wendell Berry's thinking, but when I was 28 and Louis and I took our cross-country road trip, I abandoned the notion that their solutions had much relevance in the modern world. I saw just how huge the modern industrial economy is.

We have created a global industrial beast. We are as dependent on this creature as we are on the planet that supports it and us. A world of eight billion Do Nothing farmers working their horses and hand planting their rice might be a better place, but it can't happen. Our future existence depends on making the modern industrial economy function in a sustainable way.

Man's Search for Meaning — Viktor Frankl

While *The One-Straw Revolution* is the least influential of the four books that have changed me, *Man's Search for Meaning* by Viktor Frankl is the most important.

I first read *Man's Search for Meaning* in high school. The story of Frankl's imprisonment in the German concentration camps in World War II was shocking and especially compelling because a girl I had a crush on was fascinated by the Holocaust. I paid extra attention to the book in case I got a chance to impress her during class.

My high school English teacher introduced the book by telling us to read the narrative about Frankl's experience in the concentration camps, but he also said we could skip the second part of the book, called "Logotherapy in a Nutshell," because that was, according to this teacher, "just something Frankl cooked up to help market the book and sell more copies." Naturally, I didn't read the part where Frankl describes the theory of psychology he created before the war and then, when he was captured, tested against life in Auschwitz. In fact, I more or less forgot about the book altogether.

The most memorable part of that class was when the girl I had the crush on managed to twist a wood screw out of the leg of the table where we were sitting. She handed it to me as we were leaving class and said, "You wanna screw?" I took the wood screw but doubted the sincerity of the rest of the offer, a mistake I forgot about until 20 years later when a friend described one of his early sexual encounters to me.

Although he went to a different school and several years older, he met this girl and, to hear his side of the story, she explained to him that she was eager to explore her body with someone. She was not a stunning beauty but pretty and enthusiastic, her skin stretched tight with sweetness, optimism, and potential.

Fortunately, my memory, probably in an attempt to protect me from the pain of irretrievably lost opportunity, has forgotten most of the details my friend told me, but I do remember that they spent a few impassioned weeks culminating in taking showers together. And now, after that digression, let me get back to Frankl and finding meaning in suffering.

The two-year period between high school and college was the most miserable, so far, in my life. But after college, I lapsed back into another period of melancholy, although not as severe, and it was during this time that my mother came home with a copy of *Man's Search for Meaning*. She had been at the library and had chanced to see the title and thought it sounded perfect for me. I was moderately pissed off at her intrusion into my personal depression, and the title of the book implied that she thought I needed help in my search for meaning, which, although true, still irritated me. But a book is a book and I figured there was no harm in taking a look.

It wasn't until I was a little way into the book that I realized I had already read it and remembered the high school class. A good part of my sadness was caused by separation from my girlfriend Aliza, who was Jewish, and so, inspired for a second time by unfulfilled love, I took to the subject with renewed interest.

I was crippled by indecision. Would Aliza and I get back together if I did this or, instead, should I do that? Trying to configure your current actions to ensure some future outcome, especially an outcome dependent on other people's choices, is a loser's game we are all playing to some extent, but it had almost consumed me and controlled me to the inevitable point of paralysis. The story of "Death in Tehran," which Frankl recounts, is in some way central to his philosophy and it spoke directly to my situation. It is an old story. Here is a version:

In the morning, a prince is walking in his garden when he encounters one of his servants, who is upset. The servant says that he has just seen Death and begs the prince to give him a fast horse that he can use to flee to Tehran. The prince agrees, and after the servant leaves, the prince walks back to his house, where he meets Death. "Why did you upset my servant?" asks the prince. "I didn't mean to upset him," says Death. "I was just surprised to see him still here when I planned to pick him up later tonight in Tehran."

The book, which in high school had been engaging but forgettable, now carried the truth I was looking for. This time, I read beyond the description of Frankl's time in the concentration camps to his introduction to logotherapy. It really is a remarkable book—on the one hand, a graphic and personal account of his struggles as a prisoner, and on the other hand, a logical analysis of his prescription for living a meaningful life. I think I gave my last copy away, but for years I made sure always to have a copy nearby, not only to hand it along to anyone else I thought might benefit from reading it, but as a pillar to lean against when I felt overwhelmed by life.

I loved "Logotherapy in a Nutshell" so much that I read several more books that Frankl wrote where he described his theory of psychology in greater depth.

In short, happiness and worth come from having meaning in your life, and there are no situations in which you cannot have meaning because, even stripped of everything and suffering the most abject deprivation, one can still suffer well and find meaning by suffering well. In other words, there is an awful lot you can't control, like where you are going to meet Death, but in all circumstances you can choose how to act and you can make those choices based on what you think is meaningful. Since he tried his theory on himself in Auschwitz, it is impossible to argue against Frankl's conviction.

Finding meaning is a matter of personal will. It is there, inherent in every life, and the logotherapist's job is to help the patient uncover and realize his or her meaning. So, when you think your life sucks, accept the hand fate has dealt you and choose which part to make meaningful. If all you have is unrelenting suffering, then you can choose to suffer with dignity and courage. (I think Frankl would say that unrelenting suffering is hard to imagine. He wrote that some of the moments of purest happiness in his whole life were in front of the fire in the barracks when the other prisoners had gone to sleep and he had a few minutes of peace and comfort to himself.)

And yet, the book that did and still does provide me with the best path I have found doesn't work for everyone. When you are searching for answers, you know when you have found what you are looking for and when you haven't. Of all the friends going through a tough time to whom I have given a copy of *Man's Search for Meaning*, I don't think it has connected with any of them. This seems, I suppose, fitting. Life and meaning are individual experiences. You don't know what is going to work for someone else.

The Alchemy of Finance — George Soros
I came to this book early in my self-education about investing. I read a reference to it in an article somewhere and thought I would give it a try.

Soros has a theory of markets and human behavior and history, which he calls reflexivity. If you're curious, you should give it a try yourself because my two-paragraph description of a theory it took another person a lifetime to develop doesn't do it justice.

Soros's theory, in short, is that markets, far from being efficient allocators of capital, are often driven by feedback loops where the actions of the participants start influencing the market to the point of changing the underlying economic fundamentals. He used his theory to make billions of dollars, and so one might think that people would take him more seriously.

Had Soros toiled away in a university economics department, writing papers and seeking historical examples to model his theory, maybe one day he would have been accorded intellectual acclaim from other economists, and when his theory was proven to be spectacularly prescient in the 2008 financial crisis, he might have even been given a Nobel Prize.

But the human mind is full of contradictions. When a person gets rich or famous, people hang on every trivial word about subjects completely unrelated to their area of expertise. At the same time, let someone like Soros get rich in one field—speculating—and then attempt to have a serious opinion in another field—history—and the important and serious people in that field eschew him as non-serious, a dilettante in their field. The established serious people in the field feel threatened by this successful newcomer and they do their best to ignore him and his ideas. For most established academics, protecting their turf is infinitely more important than seeking truth. I'm not sure why Soros wants his theory to be taken seriously, but it is evident from the repetitive way he presents it in this book and others that he would like people to pay attention.

Anyway, as a theory it is pretty obvious. No one invests in markets without understanding that the madness of crowds has the power to destroy or make a market.

Well, I shouldn't say that. Everyone investing in the financial markets in any sort of direct way knows that markets are often irrational. However, you can't build a career, convince a client to part with money, or look smart to your boss or at cocktail parties by admitting what you don't know.

So instead of admitting their ignorance, money managers and academics created an edifice they call Efficient Market Hypothesis, which is sufficiently dense to have inspired a few Nobel Prizes and, more to the point, creates an intellectual cover for money managers who can point to the theory as cause for their success when the market goes up and, most importantly, as an excuse for their failure when it surprises them by going down. Efficient Market Hypothesis is pretty good most of the time, while things are normal, and so it endures. Unfortunately, to make money speculating in the financial markets, you need to avoid the really terrible times and have your timing close to right for the good times. At this, Soros is the greatest the world has ever produced.

But as is often the case, the main idea of his book, the theory of reflexivity, is not what I found most compelling. The theory of reflexivity is interesting and you won't find it exactly anywhere else. Soros withholds comment on how he implements the theory in daily trading moves, and that seems disingenuous given how much he wants people to take him seriously. But the magnificence of his book is what he calls the real-time experiment, where he documents, somewhat sporadically, his own investment moves.

Here you get a master on display. He buys something, tells you why, changes his mind, covers his position, changes his mind again, and goes back in. His mind is global and he understands what financiers in London will think of some decision by the Japanese government. He understands this not as an economist who tries to distill all of these questions to a universal mathematical equation; no, he understands the questions as a human being, an outsider, an outcast. Just as the slave must know the master's mind better than the master because the slave's very existence depends on anticipating the master's moods, so too Soros, who learned currency trading as a Hungarian Jew in the shadow of the Nazis, has to understand why each market participant makes the choices he makes and how the other participants will react. But beyond that he must be honest with himself so that when he misjudges, as inevitably happens, he needs to be able to recognize his own mistake and reverse it.

In the real-time experiment you get a window, albeit a small window, into the mind of a master. In this case, it is a master of markets and everything contained within markets, which is to say, economics, culture, chance, individual personality, and, not to forget, politics. Here is a man buying $100 million worth of Japanese yen and then a few weeks later admitting to himself that he made a $100 million mistake. Far from wanting to jump off a bridge and give up in despair, he takes it in stride, noting his mistake and the reasons for it, and taking his loss and going the other way.

How can he do this? Well, one explanation is that he is a man from Mars. During World War II, the group of Hungarian Jewish scientists who immigrated to the United States and worked on the first atomic bomb were jokingly said to be from Mars. They all spoke heavily accented English and were so unbelievably intelligent that people said they couldn't be human and must be from Mars. Soros is of a slightly later generation, and I think he mentions somewhere that math wasn't his strongest subject, but he does seem to have a similar sort of almost superhuman intelligence about the financial markets.

A more plausible explanation and the one he advances (in another book, I think) is that he always had a theory—not just the theory of reflexivity but specific theories formulated for individual market situations and based around the overall concept of reflexivity. He points out that his theory was often incorrect but, nonetheless, having a theory gave him an advantage over the other market players. He was willing to modify his theory or abandon it for a new theory as conditions changed, but he was always operating within the structure of a rational theory.

A theory, especially a scientific theory—and economics desperately wants to be a legitimate science—needs to be provable. A theory is tested against observable phenomena and used to make predictions about future events. If a theory fails either of these tests, it must be changed or considered false. But here is Soros saying that in financial markets there are no permanent, immutable laws and that the fundamental nature of the market can be changed by the participants. Therefore, the theories must keep evolving to stay abreast of the market.

Although the market can exist for long periods in a state of more or less equilibrium, where a theory like the Efficient Market will adequately predict results, it is not a stable system. Very few people are reassured by the idea of living in an unstable world. Almost no one wants to run millions—and eventually billions—of dollars based on a theory whose first principle is that you can't know what comes next. Soros was willing to take this scary proposition and not only invest his own and other people's money but also to lever up his investments so the price for being wrong would be even higher.

You can't really call arrogant a guy whose theory of investment is based on knowing that he's going to be wrong a lot. Audacious sounds too flippant. Maybe it is just plain old guts, but that doesn't do justice to the intricate intellectual work Soros put into being wrong.

22- Two Lessons from Land Rover Bill

I hate working on cars. One approach to hatred is to embrace the task you hate and learn to do it well. Until I met Land Rover Bill, this was my approach to car repairs—put them off as long as possible, but when I absolutely had to do it, I tried to do a complete and thorough job.

When I first met Land Rover Bill, he rolled out from under a Land Rover and carried on a 15-minute conversation with a perfect English accent. He was working on Land Rovers in a shop in northern Vermont. I figured he was just a wayward Brit. Turned out that he hailed from the distant climes of Long Island. He was definitely a wayward soul but the accent was just an act, although the rest of his eccentricities were as genuine as the large Jackson Pollock painting hanging in his house.

Of all repair jobs, I hate brakes the most and I can draw a straight line from that hatred to my experiences working on old Land Rover brakes.

Any brake job of any significance meant bleeding the brake system, and this seemed to always result in a broken bleed nipple and then replacing the whole slave cylinder, although usually not until I had removed the slave cylinder and clamped it in a vise and tried to heat or beat the bleed nipple into turning loose. The expense of a new slave cylinder, especially after all the wasted labor trying to get the old one to work, fed into my conviction that the way to overcome my hatred of working on brakes was to do it right, which meant new parts.

But Land Rover Bill showed me a whole new approach. When he encountered a frozen bleed nipple, he opened his toolbox and produced a little dental tool. He would carefully slide this tool past the O-ring in the slave cylinder, creating a small gap for the air to escape. Yes, it was an unorthodox method requiring a good deal of dexterity and the procedure had to be executed carefully in order to remove air rather than introducing more air. But it was very fast and effective, at least when done by Land Rover Bill, and that slave cylinder with the frozen bleed nipple, despite being half worn-out, was probably going to last as long as the rest of the car anyway.

My assumption was pessimistic. When something broke, it needed to be fixed properly, and that meant correcting anything that wasn't in perfect functioning order because sooner or later all those weak links would break down. Land Rover Bill was much more optimistic. Everything was always in a state of greater or lesser disrepair; that's life. When a machine broke down, he looked for the exact cause of the problem, which, because he was a marvelously intuitive mechanic, he could usually diagnosis very quickly. Then he tried to solve just that one problem, ignoring and avoiding the other worn-out parts and future problems.

In one garage where Land Rover Bill worked, whenever they wanted to put out their cigarettes, they would throw them into a 55-gallon drum full of gasoline drained from gas tanks they had repaired.

The cigarettes didn't burn the gas because they were smothered and drowned before they could ignite it. Of course, one hot, humid day, with gas fumes hanging heavy over the 55-gallon drum, someone threw a cigarette into the drum and the gas fumes above the liquid gas were thick enough and sufficiently mixed with air to ignite and the drum caught fire and burned the garage down.

This is a basic piece of chemistry. In order to have a fire, you need oxygen. The oxygen has to be sufficiently mixed with combustible material in order for it to burn.

Wood doesn't just burn, it has to be mixed with oxygen. Since wood is a solid material, it doesn't mix well with oxygen, but when it gets hot it starts to break down into its component gases, then the gases mix easily with the surrounding air and burn. The heat from the burning gas causes more of the wood to decompose into gas, and the fire can become self-sustaining.

23- Fossil Fuels

The next time you buy a gallon of milk, look at that eight-pound jug in your hand and consider that filled with gasoline instead of milk, it would be a couple of pounds lighter but it would contain enough energy to push your 3,000-pound car for 20 or 30 miles at 60 miles per hour. And remember that approximately 25 percent of the energy released by burning that gas would go toward moving your car; the rest would be wasted as heat out the tailpipe.

Then, sometime when your car is parked, put it in neutral and push it for a few feet yourself while contemplating that when your car is moving at 60 miles an hour, the bulk of the energy used to move the car (as opposed to the energy wasted out the tailpipe) is used to move air out of the way, not to accelerate the car or overcome the friction of the wheels.

Then pause to contemplate the fact that until 200 years ago, everything that got done, got done by muscle power, either animal or human, with the only major exceptions being waterwheels and wind power. That gallon of gas is equal to approximately 400 hours of physical work by a human being. In other words, if you labored for a year of five-day weeks and eight-hour days, the value of your physical effort would be approximately five gallons of gas and whatever it cost to buy a machine to do your task. That gallon of gas might as well be a miracle or a genie in a bottle for what it is able to do.

24- The Wisdom of

. . . Molly Porter
"Whatever the energy is that controls the universe, it is an energy of irony."

. . . Phil Wheeler
On why politicians appear honest but aren't: "They know to save the lies for things that really matter."

. . . Rich Green
"The two most underrated pleasures in the world are a good shit and a bad fuck."

. . . me
"You almost never get in trouble for what you don't say."

. . . Lee Frantz
From his time working drug interdiction in the Coast Guard: "Once you pull your weapon, you can't put it back."

. . . Hilton Dier
"Necessity may be the mother of invention, but

desperation is the father of craftiness."

. . . David/Freddy Laflin
"It's a fascinatin' world."

. . . Gordon Grunder
"Everything that is good about capitalism happens in small businesses."

. . . Frank Spencer
"Eat real food."

. . . Louis Porter
"For some people, taking away the rights of other people is the most enjoyable thing."

. . . Gary Miller
"For every editor who hates your writing, there are 15 more editors who hate your writing."

. . . Seth Bagen
"The world is like a room full of shit. You pick a corner and start shoveling."

. . . Beth Ann
"You have to make time for the good stuff, even when you don't have time."

25- Patience and Learning

There are many small, simple, powerful, but difficult little tricks for making life work smoothly. I don't know many, and for some reason I resist learning them, but here are a few I have gleaned:

Sometimes, on my road trip with Louis, I felt utterly hopeless and without direction when we would camp for the night. But the next morning, even though our circumstances were no different, I would feel better and more optimistic. This seems simple and obvious when you read it, but at night, or anytime when you are despairing, it is difficult to convince yourself to be patient and that a good night's sleep will improve things, but it does.

When I was building furniture, especially in the early years when each piece was a struggle, at the end of the day I would look at the joints I had been scribing and cutting, then re-scribing and re-cutting, and think that they were good enough. The thought of redoing them again was utterly demoralizing, and I would tell myself that I needed to manage my time and move forward with the next step of the project. But the next morning I would quite happily redo the same work I hadn't been able to face repeating the night before.

George Washington's trick of counting to 10 before you say something when you are angry—and 100 if very angry—is obvious, simple, powerful, and damn near impossible to do.

When you are feeling down and nothing seems worthwhile, force yourself to learn about something. I don't remember exactly the context in which I first heard this idea; it had something to do with the concept in Judaism that learning is a sacred act.

Years ago, I got a good chance to test this idea. I arrived at my aunt Peggy's house and there was no one there. I was depressed and on my way back to Vermont, failing, after yet another road trip, to find any direction for my life. Since there was no one around, I was lonely, and that just added to my sense of hopelessness. I decided to test the idea about learning, and so I set out foraging for information through the woods surrounding Peggy's house. This was useless information to me. I really didn't care what grew in the woods around Peggy's house, but it made for a good test of the idea. If learning in and of itself was beneficial, then it shouldn't matter that I was learning about something of no importance to me.

The trees were different trees than I was familiar

with, but I knew enough to start making some assumptions. I tracked the old stone walls and plotted the location of the nearby highway. Every time I felt hopeless, rather than fighting it I just looked for a new way to add information to my growing store of useless knowledge about the environs surrounding Peggy's house. The effect on my mood was so profound that I was almost startled. It took about an hour to completely change my outlook. I'm not saying this relieved my underlying condition, but in that hour and for a while afterward the sense of hopelessness was gone, purely because I had learned something.

When I was riding the train across the country and feeling miserable for reasons I didn't understand and couldn't figure out, I would occasionally force myself to go to the bathroom and wash my face and hands. This and brushing your teeth are about the extent of hygiene that is possible from a coach seat on a train, but it made a huge difference in my mood.

26- Happiness

"Love is a rose but you better not pick it," wrote Neil Young, and then Linda Ronstadt sang it so beautifully that it seemed like her song. Things have to find their place. Happiness is a rose also. When I gave up on trying to be happy, I became much happier.

Everyone wants to be happy, and a person with a little leisure time in which to contemplate life usually starts to think about how to make himself happier. This is especially true when you are young and the new responsibility of being in charge of your own life weighs heavily on you.

"Happiness is overrated." I heard this line from my sister Molly, who attributed it to one of our brother Louis's early girlfriends, a depressive sort of girl, and so the line seemed even bolder given that she didn't have much extra happiness to be careless with. Does happiness come from meaning, from love, from purpose, from money, from fame, from family? Who knows? All I know is that trying to be happy is the least likely way to become happy. The unhappiest people in the world seem to be those earnestly struggling to figure out what makes them happy. I've been there, and from that sad perch I've noticed that the people with the least reason, seemingly, to be happy are often the most cheerful.

Turn your back on the entirely logical and also, by definition, entirely self-absorbed quest for happiness. Happiness is the byproduct of life, the unguaranteed byproduct, the thing you can have but never hold, the faint star; you know when it is there, but if you try to make sure, then it disappears.

To relinquish the quest for happiness is an act of humility because it is surrendering the control of your most fervent and final desire. Accepting that you cannot willfully attain happiness means accepting that you are not in control of this key aspect of your life—an admission of powerlessness. Of necessity, this realization forces your attention outward.

The final personal objective is always happiness because once happiness is obtained, you want no more. If you cannot by force of choice or effort or concentration induce happiness in yourself, and happiness is overrated, then what? You have to die or make something else your objective. If you accept that you cannot obtain happiness by struggling or calculating to obtain it, then you are forced away from the realm of personal gratification toward something else, something outside yourself.

Happiness is a gift; it either comes to you or it doesn't, and you can't coax it, so forget about it and concentrate on something you think is meaningful or interesting and let happiness take care of itself. When you think it might be there, give it a quick sideways glance, take a little longer to savor the moment, then get back to the task at hand.

27- What Is Love?

I was walking in the woods, consoling my broken heart after college and my breakup with Aliza, my mind drifting aimlessly from one thought to another. I started imagining what scenarios would possibly give me a legitimate excuse for getting back in touch with her. We had ended eventually with the conclusion that not talking with each other for a while was the best choice, and I couldn't think of much that would justify breaking this decision until it occurred to me that the death of one of my parents would be a momentous enough event to necessitate a phone call.

I can't remember what precipitated this thought; perhaps a relative had died and that started my mind on this morbid train of thought. At any rate, it caused me to realize just how ridiculous my mental state was. I stopped at the top of Low Road, where years before I had cut a dead beech tree so big that there was still a sunny spot made by the hole it left in the forest canopy.

I had to ask myself, Was I in love with her or did this debilitating "love" really just mean I was a desperately dependent and obsessed failure of a human being? I leaned against a hemlock tree that was reaching into the sunny spot and started sifting through my brain, looking for examples of true love.

I knew I loved my parents and my siblings, even my oxen, but those relationships were all complicated with an element of dependency or at least a connection that was not voluntary. I thought about friends I loved, male and female, but I could go months, years, maybe the rest of my life without seeing them, and while that thought might make me a little sad, it didn't make me feel utterly despairing and hollow the way my separation from Aliza did.

Maybe what I felt for her wasn't really love at all, just the pathetic longing of a person unable to be whole by himself. I searched for other examples of love, something I was absolutely certain I loved not because of what it could do for me but just for what it was in and of itself. Trees, that's what I found. I really loved trees and wood. They were always interesting to me and I was happy around them. Unlike human relationships, love for trees was a one-way relationship. Plus, they had to stay where they were and couldn't leave you, but I knew without a doubt that I loved trees.

This wasn't a successful conclusion to my contemplation, and I pushed myself off the rough hemlock bark and continued my way down the hill. If I could be sure only that I truly loved trees, then what kind of relationship would I have with humans? Would they all be desperate, dependent relationships?

At St. John's College, Aliza and I had to learn ancient Greek and the different Greek words for love. Fittingly, I can only remember eros and philos, but there were a couple more. Eros, from which we get the word "erotic," had to do with sexual love. The other Greek distinctions about love I lumped together in my mind as one thing, Love. I saw the Greeks as having love with lust and the rest of love without lust. This is a good example of being unable to understand a culture or language outside your own. I simply transplanted my understanding of love onto the Greek words.

In English we don't have a lot of synonyms for love. We have a lot of words for crazy—mad, insane, berserk, lunatic, and so on—but only love for love. Certainly, there are as many people in love as there are crazy people; why such a deficit of words? We have lots of ways of describing love—obsessive love, infatuated love, platonic love, even the phrase "in love" is different than love—but they are all modifications of love.

I don't know the reason that such a useful and adaptable language as English would be so limited when it comes to words for love. I'll hazard a guess that it has something to do with Christianity. The English-speaking cultures have been predominately Christian, and Christians are called on to love each other, their enemies, and especially to love God. Christian culture sees a hierarchy of love, with love of God as the highest and all other love is just a lesser version of the same thing.

Naturally, when you look at love this way, there has to be a distinction between sexual love and love of God, and so we have the word "lust" and other words, including the word "erotic." No one is expected or encouraged to lust after God. The priests of the Catholic sect go all the way, unifying every love into one love of God, and in this attempt they take vows of celibacy so no form of their love will be directed elsewhere. This is a good test case and they seem to be spectacularly unsuccessful in this attempt to reduce their lives to one pure form of love.

Things seemed different to the ancient Greeks. They saw different kinds of love, different enough to give them different names. Eros was one kind of love, but there were others as well. When I ignorantly categorized their words for love into my understanding of love, dividing it neatly as an English speaker into love and lust, I was missing the whole point.

Love is not one thing, or if you want to call it one emotion, then you should recognize several different species of this emotion. This is difficult to understand because we only have one word for love and have elevated love until it is the highest objective and so it shades out any competitors.

Even erotic love is considered lesser than true love, although, as the priests have shown, erotic love often wins in a contest with a supposedly purer love.

Love your parents. Love your kids. Love your spouse. Love your neighbor. Love your enemies. Love is the way. Love is the purpose. Do what you love. Love your job. Love that movie. Love him like a brother. Lovin' life. Stay connected with the people you love. Love you! You can even say, "Well, he died doing what he loved," as a way to somehow mitigate or even justify a person's death. Really, that's all the same love?

The Greeks are right. There are different kinds of love. These aren't different degrees of love or different purities of love. They are all capable of producing feelings so strong that they must be called love, but they are far from the same. Whatever the cause of our linguistic deficiency, it is confusing to have only one word for such a multiplicity of emotions.

I loved trees, I loved Aliza, I loved my family. The only word for these emotions was love, but they weren't the same emotion even though they were equally powerful.

And so, when you are in love with someone and the relationship is bringing you peaks of ecstasy and fulfillment and also despairing emptiness, it is love, but it is not the same, nor should it be, as the love you have for an old friend whose character you admire and whose advice you trust, nor is it the same as the love you have for your parents or the feeling you have leaning against the roots of an old hemlock tree and looking down into a forest full of beech and ironwood and maple and fir.

28- Exercise

I woke up with a hurt neck this morning, an injury from sleeping; one of the joys of growing old is that you can hurt yourself while unconscious. It got me thinking about the days when I used to exercise every day.

My first round of regular exercise followed immediately after seeing the movie *Rocky*. I was probably 10 or 11 and I started doing push-ups, sit-ups, and occasionally drinking a glass full of raw eggs. I doubt this phase lasted more than a month, although, as with everything when you are a child, it seemed much longer, and my body quickly responded to the exercise.

By today's standards, I was a pretty fit kid, lean, accustomed to a lot of daily work, like shoveling out the cow and horse stalls and splitting wood. Exercise for its own end rather than as the result of work never occurred to me before I saw *Rocky*. But there are many doors in your mind that once opened, can't ever be completely closed. Rocky opened the door not only to the joys and benefits of exercise but also to the idea of your body as an object whose image you could modify through exercise.

I was never fat or even pudgy, but when I was 19 I saw a picture in *National Geographic* of a fisherman in Gloucester, Massachusetts. He was shirtless, holding a large fish, and his belly was a bit extended. In the roundness of his belly you could see the faint definition of his stomach muscles. I'd always had a solid set of stomach muscles, maybe they go back to those original, *Rocky*-inspired sit-ups, and when I saw this picture I thought I saw my future—a potbelly gradually overshadowing my muscles. I happened across this picture not too many years ago and was surprised at how trim the fisherman looked. No one would call him fat.

There is a double point here. That picture represented the beginning of the second round of exercise in my life, and by seeing it years later I can tell how skewed my body image was then. The fate of looking as fit as that fisherman is hardly something to be afraid of and yet at the time it seemed horrible to me. This is the two-edged sword of exercise and body image; it is hard to have any perspective on yourself.

Lots of other issues more important than this picture spurred me to exercise. I had struggled to lose weight. In my case this was unnecessary and I failed at it repeatedly, and I'm not entirely sure where the motivation came from. Around the time I saw the picture of the fisherman, I decided that if I wasn't able to lose the few pounds I mistakenly thought I should lose, then I would at least turn them into muscle.

I also saw this as a personal test. I didn't feel in control of myself or of my life and being unable to force myself to lose weight was an example of this lack of control. I realized that in some sense I was fighting nature to try to lose weight, so exercise was a compromise. I wouldn't try battles that were seemingly unwinnable, but where I did have control, I would accept no compromise.

The exercise plan I came up with was simple: push-ups, sit-ups, chin-ups, pull-ups, and a little bit of running or hiking every day, no exceptions. By no exceptions, I meant no exceptions. I started out with a moderate number of each exercise. I would go down to the barn and do chin-ups and pull-ups on the roof trusses. I couldn't do very many—five or six at a time to start—and so I would keep doing them until I could no longer pull myself up and I would keep pulling as far as I could until I fell off.

Pretty quickly I worked up to a set of 16 chin-ups, 12 pull-ups, two sets of 50 push-ups, and 100 sit-ups. In between, I stretched.

Somewhere along the way I decided that 16 chin-ups was enough; I don't remember why exactly, but it coincided with another important decision. I placed my emphasis on exercising every day rather than adding more exercise routines or more repetitions. In retrospect, this was a good choice. I'm not saying it was a healthy decision mentally—moderation in the number of repetitions was a good call—but I balanced it with extremism in my every day commitment. My daily exercise became the grounding point of my life, like a religion or a meditation. I knew I was okay because I exercised every day. An insecurity underlay this motivation, but the limit on adding to the amount of exercise kept it mostly in check. I remembered my initial motivation: exercise was not to lose weight, it was for control and discipline.

I'm sure physical therapists would say that exercising to that extent every single day is bad for you, and they are probably right. But every day, pulling out that set of exercises, tired or not, had a tempering effect on my body. I could take a bad fall running in the woods and get up with no muscles pulled. I could throw hay bales all afternoon and have no sore muscles the next day. I was young, too.

In the first few years of exercising, I often went a month or more without missing a single day. Eventually something would come along and, for whatever reason, I would end up missing a day. I felt horrible guilt over this because I had let myself down in my commitment to do it every day. But I had another rule: no doing more the next day to make it up.

A year after I started exercising, I went to college, but I had designed my exercise program to be able to be done anywhere so there would never be an excuse for not doing it. All I needed was a flat space for push-ups and sit-ups and a tree limb or a door jamb for chin-ups.

At first I exercised in my dorm room. St. John's College had a rudimentary weight room, but the thought of exercising in public seemed to me to betray the purity of it. I wasn't exercising for other people. I was exercising because it was a touchstone, a way I knew I was in control, and doing it around other people I thought might complicate that. For the same reason, I never listened to music while I was exercising. I meant exercise to be about exercise.

But the dorm-room floor was hard, and when I did sit-ups I developed blisters on my ass, and then when I didn't stop doing sit-ups I got cuts and scabs. I tried doing sit-ups on my camping pad, but it quickly became apparent that I was going to wear out the pad every couple of weeks. I needed the pad for camping and didn't want to buy another one. They cost $12.50, as I remember.

So I succumbed to going to the weight room. It was a shabby weight room in the basement of the science building and often I was there alone. I kept my same exercise program and ignored the weights.

And it was here that exercise taught me another lesson: If you are in one place regularly enough, everyone passes by you. I usually went to the weight room before dinner, around 5:00 or 5:30, and I went every day for 20 minutes to half an hour. The weight room was probably the most out-of-the-way place in the whole school, but sooner or later I crossed paths with everyone, from the dean to a freshman kid so uncoordinated he simply couldn't learn to jump rope.

Eventually I chilled out a little bit about missing days of exercise. I still exercised nearly every day, but when I missed a day, I understood that it was not necessarily a personal failure.

Self-consciousness is a crippling burden, both in the narrow sense of being uncomfortably sensitive to how you appear to others and in the broad sense of being aware of your existence and mortality. So humanity limps along under this burden, using whatever crutches we can to make the journey easier. For me, exercise was a good crutch; other people use alcohol, music, money, you name it. My recommendation is to pick crutches like exercise that are relatively benign and have ancillary benefits.

29- Vegetarianism

There's an old saying, "Life and Death walk hand in hand." It is as true as ever, of course, because every living thing dies, but it is much less apparent, at least in our modern American lives. There are things worse than death, but not many, so we've pushed death as far away as we can.

When you grow up on a farm, as I did, you're an active participant in the dance of life and death, a conductor witnessing and directing the cycle of life. Which is an embroidered way of saying I grew up eating a lot of meat, much of it killed and butchered by my own hands. At some point, any thinking person asks if it is wrong to live on the blood of other animals.

I've lived much closer to the killing that inevitably precedes meat eating than most Americans. Most people, most of the time are so separated from the consequences of creating the food they are about to put in their mouths that it is irrelevant to them whether it is meat, vegetable, or plastic. This is unfortunate on one level and contributes to the atrocity that is our industrialized, factory-farm food system.

On another level, it is entirely normal. We all have a separation between what we are doing and what made it possible. Having decided that hunting is morally acceptable, if I shoot a deer in the morning and then in the evening fry up the backstrap with some onions and garlic, while I'm happily chewing away on delicious venison tenderloin, I'm not thinking about how that deer bolted away from the crash of my rifle. How the sound alone was terrifying for the deer. How it fled, confused, its legs quickly weakening, how it probably sensed "that long black cloud . . . coming down" even if it couldn't rationally know what was coming. I'm not thinking about standing over its wrecked carcass and looking at the intricate machine whose parts all look perfectly fine except for the small, sometimes almost invisible, hole in its chest where I directed a bullet that caused utter havoc and disorganization to this otherwise marvelously functioning creation.

No, I'm thinking about how good it tastes, and even if these other thoughts come into my mind, I brush them aside to be dealt with later. We humans do this all the time, thousands of times a day, for trivial and weighty subjects. Whatever you are doing right now is what you are doing right now. Whatever this current action is, it was made possible by previous actions—my own, in the case of me and the deer, or somebody else's, in the case of a person buying a hamburger. We understand the cause-and-result connection perfectly on a rational level, but for the most part we live our lives in the moment of what we are doing. Whatever faculty allows us to separate what we are doing from what it took to get to where we are, it is a strong and necessary tool.

Once we decide it is morally permissible to kill for food, then, as unpleasant as the killing may be, it is just a matter of minutes to disconnect that unpleasantness from whatever comes next. This is a horrifying truth about humans. It is why Nazis could herd Jews into gas chambers and then go home to hug their own kids. It is why soldiers in a war can intermingle acts of brutality with acts of kindness.

I'm not saying there are no psychological consequences to violence, just that the ability to switch between frames of reference is extremely strong and clear. If the television is showing pictures of starving children while you're eating dinner, it becomes difficult to enjoy your dinner, but as soon as the channel is changed, dinner resumes. We do live in the moment. Throwing away the rest your dinner isn't going to help the starving children, neither is remembering the brutality of shooting a deer while I'm trying to eat it.

When people are putting food in their mouths, they are thinking about eating and not thinking about where it came from, whether it is fast food French fries, venison steak, or locally and sustainably grown arugula and carrots. After all, if we spent our lives always thinking about something other than what we were doing, our minds and our bodies would become irretrievably separated from each other.

My point is twofold. It is very natural, whether you are a hunter or pulling into the drive-up window, to separate the eating from whatever made the eating possible. This is why the thinking that goes into the decision in the first place is important. Vegetarians deserve credit for taking the time to think about their actions and responsibility for them. The important choice—is it moral to live on other animals?—is going to happen in a separate realm from the eating.

Because most vegetarians, if they were meat eaters, would not be directly engaged in procuring their own meat, their argument—their moral argument—is that they don't want their actions to be indirectly responsible for the death of animals. Animals are going to be slaughtered for meat whether or not they eat them, but they don't want to participate in that system.

As a protest against the horror of factory farming, this makes sense to me. But as a general argument, the problem is that by becoming a vegetarian and not participating in the meat growing and slaughtering system, one doesn't remove oneself from the larger system of destroying animals.

Farming and trucking vegetables and grains; growing more calories per acre of land, as crop raising does compared to meat raising; foregoing animal products, like eggs and cheese—all of these actions still eliminate animals from the world. Fewer animals are raised for food, so instead of being killed these animals simply never come into being, but many animals also are destroyed to make way for other food. Life of all kinds supplants other life.

We have canine teeth, as meat eaters are fond of pointing out, because we evolved in the cycle of life as omnivores. This is a weak argument, at least on first cut, because it assumes we should not try to rise above our animal natures. If we are by nature occasionally given to violence, meat eating, wars, wife beating, theft, as we indubitably are, so be it; that's the way we evolved. I don't accept this argument.

On a deeper level, although the canine teeth are not necessarily a justification for eating meat, they are evidence that life exists on other life. We can choose what role we want to play in this cycle, but we can't opt out of the cycle. We evolved to play a meat-eating role and perhaps we want to leave that behind, but we will not live without living on other life and, directly or indirectly, some of that life will be animal life.

I remember a steer and a morning. The steer had been free—summers in a pasture that grew nice grass but wasn't suited to other crops, and two winters wandering in and out of the barn. He was not quite grown but had already lived longer than most steers.

Life is palpable on a warm March morning in Vermont when sunshine and the sound of melting snow combine with the singing of returning birds.

The steer stood, blinking sleepily, absorbing the morning warmth, each long hair translucent and the light illuminating his dark, red fur. You don't know what goes on in an animal's mind, but you think you know. He and I felt the same—lucky to be alive. There was only one terrible difference between us. I knew what was coming.

You can't look at a young steer about to die on a beautiful morning and contrive justice from the event. But neither can you pretend that there is any alternative. It is as wrong as it is inevitable.

Directly or indirectly, life displaces life. The choice, the ethical question, is *how* you want to be part of the killing that is inextricable from the living, but not whether. The obvious distinctions, meat or no meat, are comforting and easy to draw but betray the real choices. You can say, "Not this steer, not now." You can choose not to eat meat. But if you're alive, you can't opt out of the cycle.

Even plants draw sustenance from the decaying remains of their vanquished competitors. A forest, especially a young forest, is a place where trees are starving each other to death. The field that grew the grain, the truck carrying it, the roads, the cities where the food is destined—these are all animal and other lives usurped and extinguished. Is the eater of the bread less to blame for the death of those animals than the eater of a steak?

The important ethical choices are shared equally by all eaters. How do you want to participate in the displacement of life that your life requires? These are difficult choices that must be made in a thousand different situations throughout a lifetime. I see no other logical resolution, and yet, killer, meat eater that I am, when there is blood on my hands, a little voice wonders, "Really, are you sure this is right?"

30- Why Hunting Is the Best of Everything

I'm just not much of a hunter. My bad eyesight doesn't help, but somehow it is not in my character, either. I'm a builder and a contemplator, driven mostly by a creative urge, but a predator needs to be mostly an observer.

I've pretty much always hunted alone. It's habit now and I guess I like it better. When I was a boy, my father let me have a gun at age 10 or 12. Since Bill took a rather open view of fish-and-game regulations, viewing them rather like speed limits on roads—as good recommendations for the general welfare but not demanding perfect compliance—I could hunt whenever I wanted as long as I ate whatever I killed, which he imposed as an inviolable law.

But I wasn't allowed to hunt with other kids. Bill was right. A responsible kid is very unlikely to shoot himself, but when you put two kids together, that's when accidents and mischief can happen. So I spent a lot of time in the woods with my gun, by myself, fruitlessly hunting.

My brother has a theory that everyone something they are good at doing but don't want to do. I have the inverse theory: Everyone has something they are not good at that they like doing.

So it goes with siblings. Both of us love to hunt and neither of us is any good at it.

Now, it has to be said early on and as a disclaimer that very many hunters demonstrate the worst of everything. They are cruel, wasteful, dangerous, utterly without connection to place, and they give hunting a bad name. So understand that by "hunting" I mean hunting when it is done properly. Because hunting is a heightened version of life, when it is bad it is a heightened version of bad living.

But when it is good, it is the best of everything.

Hunting is a blood connection to the land. The first thing non-hunters always say to you is, "Well, if you like chasing animals through the woods and trying to catch them, why don't you just take a camera?" And this, of course, shows that they don't even understand the first thing about what makes hunting important. Instead, they have an urbanized view of challenges and goals, competition and scoring, which misses most of what hunting is about.

There is absolutely nothing wrong with stalking through the woods with a camera, shooting pictures, but it isn't hunting precisely because you aren't trying to kill something.

Hunting is a life-and-death struggle. The struggle is tilted entirely in favor of the hunter, who is very rarely in any sort of threat from his quarry.

Guns have exponentially increased this advantage, but it is nature's way. Look at a cat and a mouse or a fox and a mouse or a lion and a gazelle. Predators are evolved to take very small risks when they go up against their prey. Nature has no use for fairness. Balance, yes, but not fairness.

And so when a hunter goes out into the woods looking for a deer and armed with a rifle that can kill a deer from 300 yards, it is a continuation—an exaggerated continuation—of a habit that was in us long before we were *Homo sapiens*.

Hunting is about survival. When you hunt, you are directly engaged in an activity that sustained humans for all those millions of years before we started farming. There are very few blood connections to the land. Not everyone is susceptible to a land connection. Many people are urbanized to the point where they live lives suspended above the land—complete, healthy, engaging lives that are totally dependent on human structures and never meaningfully attached to a place or piece of land.

Hunting and farming, gardening, herding, fishing, these are blood connections to the land where the person's existence, the fodder for their thoughts as well as their bodies, comes from their interaction with the land. For most people, this is a fleeting connection—a few days in the woods, the chickens they keep out back that are in no way critical for their survival but connect them to the land nonetheless.

Connection to this timeless game of survival, the cycle of life, is what makes hunting special. As a hunter, you are a participant; you have blood on your hands in the game of life that is inescapably a blood game. It is not for everybody, nor is hunting the only way to be connected to the land, but when you immerse yourself in the woods with a weapon and the intent to kill, you become part of a river extending back to the earliest humans. Killing is unnecessary. Most hunts end unsuccessfully and this in no way diminishes the connection. But without the intent, the honest intent on which you will act given the opportunity, you are just an observer.

It is a fine line. Watch a house cat observing birds feeding, sniffing at a mouse hole, rotating its ears while walking across the lawn and you see that every hunter, like every prey species, is mostly an observer. But catch a glimpse of the cat's flashing eyes and you know there is intent. The cat is a hunter.

The intent makes all the difference. It is a different game when it is a blood game. Your thinking and perception change. You're connected. Not like the Bushmen, who hunt to live as their ancestors always have, whose existence and even language is seamlessly woven into their environment; but for an afternoon or a few days you have a foot in the same stream, the stream of being purely alive on earth.

You matter. The wind matters. Your body matters. Your smell matters. Whether you can hike over the ridge or stand for an hour in one spot matters. And, above all, the land matters. Are the deer down in the softwoods or up in the oaks? Every undulation in the land makes a difference when you are hunting. And when you pause to look around, what you see is the uniqueness of every square inch of earth, the interaction of chance and struggle. The arched-over cherry tree grew on that spot because a seed fell there and the soil was favorable enough for it to compete with the maples all around it, and then later loggers crushed it as a sapling when they came to cut the bigger maples, and so it grew bent over but was able to survive because some of the maples were gone. And now, leaning, sitting almost, longer than you meant to because the trunk is conveniently angled and comfortable, you hear the small precise sound of a deer's pointed hooves poking into leaves as it takes three steps and then stops, looking around always, its whole life timid and tentative, taking three steps, looking and listening and always smelling. Your heart races for a minute, knowing it is a buck, until reality overcomes imagination and the slightly baby-faced head of a fawn emerges from behind a little hemlock. Had it been a buck and had you shot it, you would have imposed your action, struggle and chance again, on this place. But instead, you watch for 15 minutes as the deer, knowing something is wrong but unsure what, drifts cautiously away until you see it one minute and then, turning your eyes but not your head to look at a noise you knew was a squirrel before you looked but couldn't help looking anyway in case it was the buck, when you look back you can't even see the fawn although you know it hasn't moved because the leaves are too dry not to have heard it, and then a tail twitch reveals its position as it takes three steps and disappears completely. That night, your brother asks if you saw anything and you say, "Just a fawn by that big, bent-over cherry tree up on the ridge," and he knows and you know without saying more that he knows where you mean because he too has stopped there. You ask if he saw anything. "No, nothing. Just a partridge. This is

Hunting with my brother

Photo by Ruth Porter

such a waste of time. I don't know why I do it." And you know this means for a certainty that he will be going out the next morning.

Hunting is not just a connection to the land, it is also a connection to the past. People of a certain type are inclined to view guns as evil instruments of death, which they most assuredly can be. And seeing guns this way, they are horrified, mystified, and disgusted that other people cherish their guns. (This view is helped along by gun culture and especially gun shops that exude certain fetishism that, while not overtly sexual, certainly has undertones.)

For the hunter, the gun is also a talisman, a witness, the only material connection between past hunts and the current hunt and, even more powerfully, between past hunters and the hunter holding the gun now. People without a blood connection to the land have no way of understanding how a gun, a mere tool—and a dangerous tool at that—could be held with such reverence. It is no different than any other artifact connecting someone to the past: a piece of furniture from a dead relative, a musical instrument, or a special book. The difference is the gun's connection to hunting, to having been there on the land, in the hands.

Hunting is not just a connection to the land and the earth. It is also an internal journey. The challenge of being in the moment is the toughest existential challenge, and it is every moment when you are hunting. Convince yourself that you know the future and that there are no deer here now, and you've lost the thread.

This was taught to me, written on the ground. I'd been hunting for several hours, starting low in the swamp and working my way up over the top of Blackberry Hill. I walked like a deer—three steps and then pause to look and wait, three more steps—through the brush and up the sidehill to the cliff over the Eureka Quarry. Then I picked my way to the top of the hill. There were several inches of snow on the ground and the going was fairly quiet. I paused on top of the hill to look down at the village a mile or so away, with the beaver pond stretched out below. The glacier stopped here too, and the hillside below was incredibly steep and strewn with huge broken pieces of granite, churned and dumped by the glacier as it stopped for a moment of glacier time before resuming its advance.

There was no point in trying to hunt down this slope. The deer love it and go there to sleep, where they will get the early sun on a cold morning, but it was brushy and noisy and impossible to see far or walk quietly. Not that I hadn't tried in the past, but all you hear is the crash of a deer jumping away and, if you are lucky, you may see a white flash of a tail disappearing behind a rock or brush.

So on this day, I skirted the slope to the east, hoping to cut tracks and see if any deer had crossed out of the bottom land and up to the hillside. None had. I hadn't seen a fresh track all day and I was struggling to believe there were deer anywhere and doubted that I would see any.

I swung wide away from the hill, still determined to hunt my way out, but I wasn't in the moment anymore. I'd gotten too focused on the deer instead of the hunting, but I forced myself to push on, moving slowly and taking my time, even though I'd lost the connection. This was a barren section of woods, open and vulnerable from the ridge above. The deer I had seen always walked the edge of the ridge. In fact, there was a pretty good trail there where they could jump over the ridge on one side or fade into the brush of the hillside on the other.

I stopped to consider my next move midway through a small thicket. I didn't feel like hunting anymore and wanted to walk home. I should have either turned and walked for home and enjoyed the walk or continued hunting, but I was reluctant to give up on the hunt, and so, after a few minutes of mental tug-of-war, I decided to walk quickly to a new area around the other side of the hill where I was sure there would be deer.

On my first step I heard the thump that means a

deer has been startled and jumped away. A few more thumps and it was gone. I walked 75 feet through the saplings, and there were the tracks, like a lesson in a book.

It was a big deer, broad beamed, and its hooves dragged a little in the snow as a buck's often do. He had been walking directly toward me at a slow walk, stopping occasionally to nibble a fern or twig. Here, where I was certain there were no deer, so certain I decided to throw away this moment's hunt in favor of hunting somewhere else in the future, right there in that moment the deer had been there, but I wasn't.

THREE

31- Terry and the Gravel Pile

I've never had a mellow character. When I was a teenager, I thought of myself as a relaxed, easygoing sort of person, laid-back, like a surfer dude, although growing up in Vermont I'd never met any surfer dudes. I thought this because that's what I wanted to be, but wanting something doesn't make it so. One day I rounded the corner of our house, deep in thought about some project, and my head collided with the open edge of a metal window. It was a good knock and it bled a bit, as head cuts usually do.

I let forth a stream of curse words, blaming the stupidity of the window and life in general. My mother, when she determined the injury wasn't serious, made a comment about my needing to chill out a bit, to which I replied that I was the most laid-back person in the whole family. In the conversation that followed, she told me that I had a rather dark, intense character, "Black Yankee" was the term she used, and she suggested that if I looked up at the world instead of walking around with my head bent in thought, I would see the next window that happened to be open in my path. I protested with such vehemence and anger that I pretty well proved her point for her.

Not wanting her to be right and sincerely wanting to be an easygoing sort of person, I spent years trying to cultivate a degree of mellowness into my being. Part and parcel with this was a belief that human relationships are never improved by violence. This is why the incident with the gravel pile was so shocking and eye-opening.

I'd just turned 28 and was working for my friend Terry (who also is not known for his mellowness of character) in his landscaping business. We had a nice job building some stone walls and a sunken terrace at an old farmhouse halfway up the side of a hill. The place faced south and west. It was fall and there were just the two of us on the job, although there were some carpenters renovating the house. It was a particularly beautiful and idyllic job site. The leaves were changing and we had a spectacular view of the Worcester Range.

After about a week of work, I felt a rising tension between us. There was no obvious cause, just tension.

Then one day we were standing by a pile of gravel, discussing and probably disagreeing about some part of the job, when one of us pushed the other. I can't say who pushed whom because neither of us remembers (we're still friends 25 years later), but one of us saw that the other was slightly off-balance and took the opportunity to push him over. A wrestling match ensued on top of the gravel pile, down the gravel pile, on the driveway, and down the nearby embankment. At some point, each of us came close to pinning the other, but in the end it was a draw, with each of us exhausted. When we recovered our breath, we wiped the blood and dirt out of several minor cuts and went back to work as though nothing had happened.

But something had happened; our relationship had immeasurably improved. We didn't discuss this until several years later (we hadn't discussed the rising tension either), but we worked through the rest of the job and several jobs after that in a spirit of friendship and camaraderie. I was reluctant to accept what had happened because it contradicted who I wanted to be and what I wanted to believe, but the fact is our friendship improved through violence.

32- Close Calls

I've had a few close calls in my life, probably fewer than a lot of people, and most of mine involved dangerous situations logging. According to my brother, Louis, humans are the only animal, other than some types of ants, more likely to be killed by one of their own species than by an animal from another species. This doesn't speak well for us or for the ants. Fortunately for me, and I suppose I am the exception, none of my close calls have come at the hands of other humans.

One winter, when I was about 14, my father and Rick Barstow and I were logging. Bill was running the tractor skidding the logs and Rick was felling trees. I was limbing and generally trying to help out where needed. On this particular day, Rick was felling some nice red spruce trees on a steep bank. I stood uphill of him and watched him cut the trees. When he got several of them down on the ground, we would both work on limbing them and getting them ready for Bill, who would be returning with the tractor. We had already cut some trees on this bank, and the snow, which about three feet deep, was covered with spruce limbs.

As Rick finished the back cut on one tree, it started, slowly at first, to fall. From my perspective a little way up hill, it looked as though the tree was falling right toward me. I wouldn't have made much progress going uphill through the snow, so I started down the hill, aiming my steps at the larger limbs so I would not sink into the deep snow and get stuck.

Something about my perspective from partway up the steep bank must have thrown my eye off because the tree hadn't been falling toward me but across the hill below me, just where Rick had aimed it. Three or four steps into my downhill sprint I realized this and that I was running directly under the falling tree. Stopping would have been impossible and, anyway, it would have left me right where the tree was going to land. There was nothing for it but to get under it and out the other side. As I went by Rick, I heard him bellowing, "Run! Run!" He had a big grin on his face after the tree fell and I was safely out the other side. "What the hell were you doing?" he asked. "I thought it was falling uphill." I explained. He grinned some more and we went to work limbing.

But the effects lasted longer. The next time I started to fell a tree myself, I couldn't tell which way it was going to fall. Every time I looked up at the treetop, it looked as though it was leaning toward me. Sometimes, after cutting a felling notch in one side of a tree, I would convince myself that it wanted to fall the other way and I'd cut a notch in the other side. This creates an extra dangerous situation in which you have very little control over which way the tree eventually falls. Sometimes I hooked a come-along winch to the tree to pull it in one direction or the other because I simply couldn't decide which way it was leaning.

For at least a year I had trouble felling trees. Running under the falling tree and my subsequent phobia over cutting trees taught me a couple of good lessons. First, things are often not as they seem. You can look at a tree that is not falling on you and be sure that it is. A rational check on your perception is a good thing to keep in mind. I learned to keep an eye on how a tree's branches are moving relative to its neighbor while I am felling it. This still relies on my sight, but I am judging how one object—tree limbs, in this case— is moving relative to another object rather than relative to myself. (You have to watch out for clouds drifting by because they can make it seem as though the tree has suddenly started to move.)

The second point is that a good fright can literally rearrange the way your brain sees things; something that looked one way to you now looks different. I lost the ability to see which way a tree was leaning until they all seemed to be leaning toward me.

When I'm driving and I check twice in both directions before I pull into an intersection, that habit comes from having made mistakes when it mattered, like thinking that tree was falling uphill toward me when it actually wasn't. The human organism is a magnificent creation of nature, all the more magnificent for being able to doubt itself, and that doubt is often well placed.

It is also an organism capable of doing things without knowing it is doing them. I've cut a lot of dead trees for firewood, and dead trees tend to have many partially rotted limbs, which are, for good reason, referred to as widow-makers. Occasionally when you are felling one of these trees, it will start to go down more suddenly than you were expecting, and usually this is accompanied by lots of cracking and some falling branches. The only thing to do is get out of the way as fast as possible.

It happens like this: You're crouched beside the tree, making the back cut and squinting through the flying sawdust at the treetop for any sign of movement or falling branches, when all of a sudden the deadwood in the tree shudders and breaks and the tree starts to fall before you expected. Without any conscious thought you start to run as fast as you can away from the tree. If you're smart, you've mapped out an escape route beforehand and cleared any underbrush you might trip on.

I've had this happen any number of times, and the part that never fails to amaze me is that after the tree has fallen and I walk back toward it, I find my chainsaw, usually 20 or 30 feet from the tree. Sometimes it is lying upside down. It may or may not be running, obviously dropped as I fled. And I have absolutely no memory of having pulled it from the cut, having run with it, or having dropped it.

I remember that I ran, that's all. And yet, some other part of my mind, some part that was never filtered through my consciousness, thought to pull the saw from the cut, thought again to run with it rather than dropping it immediately, and then, at some further point, decided either that the saw was too much of a burden or that it was sufficiently out of danger and dropped it. Sometimes, whatever part of the mind this is has chosen to switch the saw off, sometimes not. These are actions—deliberate actions, actions that required a calculation—that took place 10 or 15 seconds earlier and of which I have no memory.

When you do something dangerous, you can often divide the event into two important parts: before shit happens and when shit happens. *Before* shit happens is the most important, *when* shit happens is the most interesting. People naturally tend to focus on interesting things rather than important things, but if you are going to do something dangerous—for instance, taking down a tricky-looking tree or climbing a ladder—it pays to put a lot of effort into the "before shit happens" part of the equation.

Small things make a big difference. Planning an escape route for every tree you cut is an inconvenience, but on the one tree that goes wrong it can be lifesaving to have a clear path and know where it is. Stepping from a roof onto a ladder is somewhat dangerous. It is also relatively quick and takes only a couple of seconds. So taking four seconds instead of two seconds to transition from the roof to the ladder is a 100 percent increase in the amount of time you have to prepare and make the move carefully. Taking these extra two seconds may not increase your safety by a 100 percent, but it does gain you a lot. You have that much more time, 100 percent more, to make sure your footing and grip are good, and it only takes two seconds.

I am surprised by how often I see other people, parents with kids and the kids themselves, unable to distinguish between different types of dangerous activities. Riding a bicycle on a busy road with no shoulder can get you killed. Falling off the monkey bars at the playground might break an arm. These are two totally different risk groups.

I think that doing risky things is an essential part of human development and thought. We evolved in an environment full of risk and injury. Taking risks exposes you in a personal way to your human fallibility. It is not hard to imagine that if our president George W. Bush and his draft-dodging vice president Dick Cheney had had some actual experience of war, as Bush's father had, they would have been both more cautious and more effective in the wars they started.

33- How I Met Your Mom

At the end of the summer of 1993, I drove from California to Oberlin, Ohio, with my girlfriend Jennie. She stayed there for her sophomore year of college and I continued back to Vermont, very sad that we were breaking up and completely uncertain about what to do with my life. I hadn't been home for more than a couple of weeks when, on a bulletin board, I saw a sign that said "Room for rent, Middlesex, $230 a month."

The woman who answered the phone gave me directions and explained that the place was on top of a hill. She said to walk around back to the side farthest from the parking lot. The driveway was steep and badly washed out, but there was a flat parking area on top with several cars, at least one of which looked like it hadn't run in a while. The house, an old farmhouse that had been added on to and converted into a duplex, was correspondingly dilapidated.

I could see an open door, so I walked through long grass past a broken lawnmower toward what I assumed was the back side of the duplex. As I approached, a fluffy dog bounded out, followed by a barefoot woman with very long hair, wearing shorts and some sort of fringed shirt jacket—Beth Ann. I followed her up the steps into the kitchen, which had a door on either end so that as I entered I could look straight through the kitchen and out the open door on the other side and off into the hills.

There was an old wooden picnic table in the kitchen. We sat there and discussed the terms of the rental, which I remember as being none, other than the requirement to pay your rent every month.

I had my choice between the two available rooms. One was small, over the kitchen, but warmer. I took the other, which didn't get much heat from the worn-out furnace but faced off to the north and Dumpling Hill. From that angle, Dumpling Hill looked very much like the small mountain, Monte Sol in Santa Fe, which I used to climb every day as part of my exercise program during my four years in college. The place seemed perfect to me, but I didn't know then how much it would affect the rest of my life.

As I left, after agreeing to the flexible terms of the rental, Beth Ann remembers thinking to herself, "Who the hell was that?"

I lived there for four months and spent many hours sitting at that picnic table or, as it got colder, in the rocking chair next to the woodstove, discussing my ended relationship with Jennie and Beth Ann's troubled relationship with her boyfriend.

What I remember most about those conversations was how different she seemed from people I went to college with. Despite four years of seminars studying classics, many people at St. John's College were often more interested in saying what was expected of them than in trying to understand something for themselves. It took me a while to recognize this, but by the time I graduated, it frustrated me.

Beth Ann wasn't from an educated background and yet she was interested in the way the world worked and capable, even eager, to devise her own understanding of things rather than accepting the world as other people told her it was or should be.

Not long after I moved in, I came home and found a note from Beth Ann on the picnic table. Written in her bold, curvaceous script, it said "Cluster flies have arrived!" In the fall, the leaky old farmhouse was a magnet for these disgusting, slow-moving flies as they looked for warm, dry places to park their bodies for the winter. Beth Ann's note, with its mixture of enthusiasm for the cycles of nature and resignation about the irritating, new housemates who would be sharing our space, caused me to pause, puzzled by sentiments I understood but never would have expressed that way. And yet it has stayed in my mind ever since, a very different formulation of a worldview very similar to my own.

Living there changed me in some ways more than college, and it wasn't just Beth Ann; it was the house and the people living there. That house was where I first became comfortable with who I was. But I felt I had to move on to something. Louis and I talked each other into a road trip, and on the last day of 1993 I cleaned out my happy little room and moved my belongings back to my parents' house.

Beth Ann's sister, Johnene, was visiting and they were out celebrating New Year's Eve, so the house was still and lonely. I threw my sleeping bag on the floor of the empty room and watched the Big Dipper pinwheel over Dumpling Hill. Beth Ann came home sometime after midnight. She told me later that she paced back and forth in the hallway for a long time before she dragged her sleeping bag into the room beside me. I had wondered if we would get a chance to say goodbye.

"I just wanted to dream with you," she said, "if that's all right."

34- Marriage

We did not have or plan for a church-sanctioned marriage. This gave Beth Ann's mother a little unease and she asked us to talk to John, her pastor. He was a kindly seeming man and his advice to us was that in the eyes of God, "marriage" occurs between two people when they become committed to each other, an act that is ceremonially recognized by the church and legally recognized by the state but actually takes place between two people.

At the time, I saw this as gentle but skillful

guidance, the sort of explanation that allows everyone some peace of mind without having to alter anyone's actions. I was grateful to Pastor John for what I took to be diplomacy and semantics in the best sense of both words. But over the years, and by observing other people, I have come to think that what he said was deeper and a true description of human beings.

I think that a commitment between two people happens on a biological level. Marriage is society's way of formalizing this commitment. (Whether the eyes of God see this commitment, I'll leave to God and the priests.) The commitment happens on an animal level but not, I think, a purely sexual level.

I don't mean to separate this action from reason or rational choice or even an irrational but nonetheless deliberate choice, but we are a pair-bonding species similar to wolves and geese. What happens in the minds of wolves or geese when they pair-bond? On what level does the commitment happen? It is decisive. Is it deliberate? We presume that they do not reason, but then again, many people don't reason when it comes to choosing a mate. Whatever takes place in the mind of a goose or a wolf is probably pretty close to what happens in our heads. Everything that comes after this commitment, what we call marriage—the blessing by a priest, the marriage license, the party, the drunk relatives—this is all the human veneer over the animal.

(Lay aside how our pair-bonding compares to other animals and moral judgments about our relative monogamy or the duration of our connections. We're clearly a pair-bonding species even if the particulars of our habits make us seem, by comparison to other animals, less well suited to long-term commitment than some of the lower beasts.)

Marriage is a set of guidelines, sometimes useful, that society imposes on the pair-bonding feature of the animal *Homo sapiens*. And the animal obliges and then sometimes shrugs them off the same way a dog sheds a collar or a horse throws a shoe. Society slowly but continually adjusts, adapting marriage expectations as the animal encounters new circumstances. The pair-bonding feature endures, the expectations about the related obligations evolve.

When you start looking at marriage as simply the ceremonial extension of a biological feature, it alters your view of human relationships. The animal pair-bonding is the primary feature, and it is what it is—intrinsic, compelling, durable but often impermanent, widespread but not universal, encompassing a wide variety of couples, and occasionally inexplicable to people outside the bond. Marriage is a shell, one we have crafted because, unlike the wolves and geese, we are a linguistic and legalistic creature that needs definitions and laws, and marriage fits over the pair-bonding feature imperfectly and sometimes is nothing more than a shell housing no pair-bonding at all.

In this country, we've lately been modifying the marriage shell to accommodate couples who have pair-bonded but are of the same sex. It is an overdue modification and one that is spreading rapidly because it involves a change in definition, not behavior; the pair-bonding of same-sex couples has been happening forever but it has taken a while to adapt the meaning of the word "marriage."

Here is how the pair-bonding theory of marriage changed my view of relationships: People are attracted to each other. Sometimes it is a casual connection, and sometimes they become "a couple." Whatever that step is, the step when two people become a couple, that is pair-bonding. It doesn't mean that they will get married or that they should—or even that they want to—because people are subtle and recognize that marriage comes with other complications and expectations, both personal and social. But the coupling aspect of our nature is pair-bonding and it is biological.

Wolves and geese supposedly mate for life, although I'm not sure exactly what this means. Does the female wolf never say, "That's it, I've had it with your shit," and storm out while the male wolf watches her bushy tail disappear over the esker, thinking to himself, "Damn, I knew I should have kept the caribou-meat flatulence out of the den." Maybe some scientist knows. What we all know about people is that our pair-bonding is often serial.

This intermittent aspect of our bonding offends our desire to appear logical and consistent; probably this is why marriage used to be imposed as a life sentence—society's attempt to force the human animal to live according to rules. The reality is that humans usually have several or many pair-bonded relationships. When a pair-bonded relationship ends, a connection on a biological level has been broken.

It is accepted in our society that when a marriage ends, it is emotionally difficult for both sides, even when it is a bad or an unhappy marriage. And everyone knows that a breakup is hard, but what we don't typically acknowledge is that on a biological level, a broken marriage and a broken relationship between a couple are probably pretty much the same thing.

Obviously, some marriages and some pair-bonded relationships are more significant than others; plus, marriages carry additional emotional freight piled on by society. But when you start seeing the pair-bonding feature as the underlying cause of connection, with marriage just the socially imposed shell, it changes how you look at coupled but unmarried relationships. They become more serious because they are a feature of our nature and not just a modern indulgence made possible by a permissive culture.

There have been and still are all sorts of rituals and rules governing the association between men and women that might lead to pair-bonding. More traditional societies discourage interaction between men and women that might allow coupling to happen before it can be formalized with marriage. This is an often brutal attempt to impose law on irrepressible natural features of the human animal and there are many examples of how unsuccessful it can be; *Romeo and Juliet* comes to mind.

Perhaps some of these customs were designed to ease the process of creating compatible couples. Certainly, nature seems to dispense the pair-bonding motivation without much regard to compatibility. But for the most part, the traditional rules about who gets to become part of a couple seem to have been designed to empower men, subjugate women, and severely punish same-sex couples, so it is a good thing they have been mostly rendered obsolete.

This freedom means that in our culture, people form relationships and pair-bond, when they do, in a more or less unrestricted fashion. It doesn't mean that pair-bonding is any less important or innate than it ever was or any less uncomfortable when it comes apart. So be advised, our culture, ridiculous in its fear of small injuries and unintentional insults, when it comes to pair-bonding, allows you to take whatever risks you choose.

What happens—whether or not you're married—when you've pair-bonded, been part of a couple for long enough to pass beyond the easy stage to an inevitable point at which you disagree over things to such an extent that it calls the pair-bond into question and yet you don't want to break up?

I always thought that Tolstoy had it exactly backwards in the beginning of *Anna Karenina*, where he says that all unhappy families are unhappy in their own way, while happy families are all alike. Unhappiness in people, and especially between people, seems to me to be startlingly similar, while happiness seems rather personal. But however you think about that question, it is very true that unhappy people spend much more time thinking about their lives and relationships than happy people do. And it follows that people who are struggling with their marriages are the ones who think about marriage. So too with me. Most of my thoughts about marriage arise from the travails, not the successes. This distorts your understanding of marriage because you put your effort into examining what hasn't worked rather than what has worked.

In my observation of both my own marriage and other people's, it is an almost universal fact that each partner feels they do more than the other. When things are going well, no one cares or bothers to keep score, but when things start to get rocky, each side has the same complaint, which is some version of "I'm doing it all." Or, for those more tilted toward blame than self-pity, "You're not keeping up your end."

Naturally, this complaint results in conversations, then arguments, then rules, and eventually, if you're persistent enough, marriage therapy. Usually the result of therapy is the same; things get better for a while, then they get bad again, kind of like the weather.

When you push hard enough—I'm speaking from painful experience here—you always come to the same conclusion: It's the other person's fault. Yeah, sure, you weren't perfect, but you did pretty well and they weren't trying as hard. When you talk to your friends who are having trouble in their marriages, it is pretty much the same story.

If you pause for a minute to hear what your spouse is saying—I'd say it takes 5 to 10 years of relationship before you are ready for this, and many people never get there—you can notice a conceptual similarity between your complaints and theirs. The details are completely different but the general idea is identical. "You're not doing your share. This isn't what I thought I signed on for. You don't hear what I am saying."

So if you find yourself in this spot, here is the best, most practical solution I have come up with: Life isn't fair and neither is marriage. Fairness isn't the savior of marriage. Making fairness the goal is destructive. Fair doesn't exist in marriage any more than it exists in life. Feeling sorry for the unfair deal you got in life, however true that may be or at least appear to you, doesn't make your life any better, nor does feeling anger about the unfairness of your marriage improve your marriage.

Maybe humans are genetically programmed to expect someone to be taking advantage of us. Maybe it is impossible to see someone else's point of view because it is just so much easier to see your own. Maybe the inner malcontent in all of us has to find someone to blame for our personal dissatisfaction. Maybe a cultural myth deludes us into thinking that another person will fulfill us. There are a thousand possible explanations, but the end result is the same: two people end up blaming each other.

Think of alternative numbers systems. We generally use a decimal system that runs on a base of 10. It is hard at first to imagine a different number system, but the remnants are all around us. Our measurement of time has features of a sexagesimal system, with a base of 60. Twelve has the same relationship to three; it is four times three and so on, in whatever system you use—sexagesimal, decimal, or base 12, dozenal—but the different systems have different advantages.

Base 12 and base 8 (octal) systems divide up nicely into fractions, which make them very convenient when measuring things. Try dividing 11 centimeters (base 10) in half and you have 55 millimeters, in half again and you have 27.5 millimeters. A half millimeter is basically invisible to a middle-aged carpenter like me. Divide 11 inches in half four times and you have 11/16—tough but doable for an old guy with bad eyes. Divide in half again and you have 11/32 of an inch. I can't see that well enough to mark it, but 1/32 of an inch is still a lot bigger than a half millimeter.

Even in the example above, I am using the language of a decimal system; 16 refers to a system that starts repeating at 10, so to us, 16 means 10 plus 6. Imagine a system where 16 had its own identity. It is easy to do if you think about 11 and 12, which are really oneteen and twoteen but instead have their own names. Imagine a number system going all the way to 20 or even 60, with a separate name and character for each number. The point is that the underlying relationships are all the same, but the ways of understanding them are quite different, so different, in fact, that it takes a moment or two just to wrap your head around the idea of a sexagesimal system.

Imagine then how difficult it is to understand someone else's perspective on what is fair and unfair. The relationships between numbers are fixed; the events in our lives are constantly changing, seen from different perspectives, processed through different brains, and, ultimately, people come to different conclusions.

No one who is married has a universal perspective from which to judge. All we know for sure is that both sides feel deeply aggrieved. Marriage, at least when it is not going well, seems unfair, just like life. After you give up on changing the other person or making a deal with the other person to make things "fair," what's left is to either leave or accept them as they are.

If you accept that your partner is not going to change, then the things about them that seem unfair to you become more like the other problems in your life—the weather, gravity, your job. You make the best of it. If it is insufferable, you move to a different climate.

Assuming you stay choose to stay married, relinquishing the hope of changing your partner means accepting their frustrating characteristics. It also allows you to see them as they are rather than as you wish they were. I'm sure this sounds like a dismal view of marriage, especially in a society that promotes marriage as an act of personal fulfillment. "Relinquishing hope" is probably not a phrase uttered by many marriage therapists or therapists of any kind, but I see it as a freeing, rather than a discouraging, attitude.

When marriage is working badly, you witness the person you love and also your own better characteristics worn down by the friction of coexistence. Each day, you descend into petty bitterness, keeping score of your virtues and their faults. The worst of this is when you see little flashes of what you originally admired, and in those flashes you recognize not only the deterioration but also that you have contributed to that deterioration.

When things are going well, you are partners in marriage, working together, dealing with the inevitable difficulties, sharing the triumphs, contributing your different abilities to make a whole that is greater than the parts. If this well-functioning marriage is achieved through years of trying to modify your behavior in return for an equal modification from your partner so that neither of you is doing the things that bug the other, then it is always a precarious balance. If, on the other hand, in exchange for accepting rather than trying to change their irritating behavior you arrive at a comfortable place, then it is also a stable place because staying in it is a matter of your choice.

I think I can summarize this view of marriage

succinctly: You have the ability to make your spouse's life wonderful. You don't have the ability to make them reciprocate.

This was a thought that occurred to me and, I confess, scared me a little. I couldn't see, based on my experience, any flaw in this simple formulation, but it felt disempowering. My assumption, an assumption that had been reinforced by marriage therapy, was that you improved your marriage by discussion, explanation, and open-minded listening, which resulted in intentional behavioral changes. This assumption implied a level of control; if you could just explain your feelings sufficiently, then everything would work out. Except it didn't or hadn't. I felt as though Beth Ann and I went around and around, an infinite repetition of the same disagreements acted out on different stages but always with the same underlying themes. What if that's the way it is not because we were particularly incompatible or because we weren't listening or trying hard enough but simply because people don't really change that much and almost never according to someone else's description of what ought to change?

I decided, in the interest of experimentation and also for lack or a better option, to give the idea a try. I wish I could say that this decision was as logical as it seems when I write it down.

Unfortunately, that's not the way it was.

We had our life and our marriage, and most of the time things went along fine. As I mentioned earlier, when everything is going well, you don't really think about your marriage, much less experiment with it. But whenever we'd have an argument, with the usual recriminations and "I said . . . you said," I'd also hear a little voice in my head saying, "Instead of trying to be fair and demanding what is fair in return, why don't you just try to be as nice as you can be, forget about everything else, and see what happens."

There are, and I had, two obvious responses to this idea. First, I didn't want to be taken advantage of and, second, if you give yourself over to being nice, where does that leave the things that you want or are important to you? I didn't have an answer for either of these questions, but in the interest of experimentation I decided to try anyway.

This was not a controlled experiment. I'd toy with the idea—try to think about my actions in terms of being unconditionally nice for a few days then forget about it or, worse, fall back into stewing over whether something was fair.

It's been years, by the time of this writing, that I've had this idea playing in my head and that I've been playing with it in my own life and marriage. I have no certain conclusion, but the high points in our marriage seem longer and higher and more peaceful; the low points, by contrast, seem darker, more terminal, but shorter.

The act of being nice without expecting any certain sort of treatment in return can be a sort of self-reinforcing circle. I should say that by being nice, I don't mean saccharine actions and comments but, in my own case, restraining from a sarcastic comment or, even more powerfully, staying observant about the myriad small inflections and attitudes we load onto our speech and actions. These subtle communications are at least as important as the words we use. You can say, "Yes, I see what you are saying," and by your tone let the person know you understand but perhaps aren't completely clear or certain. Or you can say the same thing and let them know that you understand what they are saying and consider them foolish for saying it. Either way of inflecting your statement is completely reasonable, but the second version is derogatory.

The trick is to make choices, subtle and obvious, that you genuinely believe will make your partner's life better without worrying about the consequences to you. This is often the way people treat each other when they first get together because as long as there is no real commitment, there is really no consequence to you for being nice and not worrying about whether or not there is some sort of reciprocation.

There are obvious problems with this as a marriage theory. For one thing, you could easily be in a relationship with someone who was willing to soak up all of your good intentions and never reciprocate at all. There's no guarantee. You can leave; that's really your only alternative. Since leaving is the nuclear option in marriage, a relationship theory that proposes leaving as your only option if you're discontent is a deficient theory.

Second, without the years of disagreement that preceded this experiment, it is unlikely that either Beth Ann or I would have had as clear of an idea about what the other one wanted and therefore how to make things nice for them or the motivation to put in the extra effort it takes to go out of your way to be nice to someone else.

Third, it has to be acknowledged that for most of history, women have been subjected to abusive marriages with no alternative other than to make the best of it. I think of Beth Ann's mother being told by her priest to go back to her physically abusive husband because she "must have done something wrong to make him mad." Leaving has to be an option.

With all that said, I consider this a very successful experiment with respect to our marriage and one that has implications in other areas as well. The ability to give, genuinely and without expecting in return, has great power, and the power is almost inverse to the gift, so the smallest gestures, when they are genuine, seem to carry as much or more weight than large acts of generosity.

There is in this experiment something of the conundrum I find in almost all human activity. We seek, for some reason, a unilateral answer. So if I determine that it works well as a marriage theory to try to make my partner's life wonderful without expecting anything in return, then this seems like it needs to be a universal law. But obviously it can't be. There are situations and people, probably many of them, where this theory doesn't work.

Perhaps our minds, able only to contemplate one thought at a time, are structurally drawn to universal solutions, however illogical that may be. One has to choose and then reassess and choose again. There's no rest. This theory of marriage means you are never done. You never arrive at a place where things are settled. Instead, you act and your partner acts in a sort of unspoken dance, the result of which can be mutually beneficial or destructive and about which you only get to choose half of the actions; the other half is beyond your power to control. There is no rule and no guarantee about tomorrow.

There is one other aspect of marriage, one that's not specific to marriage, that you don't think of until you've been together for years and that gets better with the years. I think of it as the long traveler.

It becomes obvious after a few decades of life not only that we are hurtling through space on "a long, strange trip," but also that you have a connection to the people you've shared the trip with, friends as well as enemies. The more and the more intimate the experiences you've shared, the greater the connection. Since people generally share the most intimate life experiences with the person they're married to, it follows that the long-traveler connection in a marriage, especially as it grows in years, is usually irreplaceable by any other connection.

This is like the compounded return on an investment. It starts slowly. Time is an essential feature. At some point, you realize that there are aspects of your relationship, the shared experiences on this mysterious passage called life, that you could never duplicate with another person.

35- A Sense of Style

Until recently, when it came to clothing I didn't think of myself as a person exhibiting a sense of style. I go for the durable and drab. Practicality is my goal—no bright colors or words or advertising for other people, products, or issues. I see clothes as serving a function and, as is the case with most functional items, the less fuss, the more efficiently the function is fulfilled.

It is true that I wear a hat all the time, and during the warm months this is a cowboy hat, which, living in Vermont, is an attention-getting fashion choice. I can't entirely explain this affectation. It started with a Greek fisherman's cap when I was 13 or 14 and from that day to this, I have always had a hat on my head.

In the summer, even in Vermont, a brimmed hat is an extremely convenient and practical choice, especially if you work outside. Frankly, I'm dumbfounded that all people don't wear hats given how effective they are at keeping sunlight off your face. I also wonder if my inability to recognize faces translates into an unconscious need to make myself recognizable to other people. If only they would do the same and start wearing easily identifiable headgear.

Despite my hat, the rest of my wardrobe is, or so I thought, bland, quiet, and unassuming. I persisted in this ignorant and indulgent belief until almost quite recently. Beth Ann and I were talking about our first encounter, and I pointed out that it was strange for a person who loves clothes and fashion to have been attracted to and ended up married to someone with no sense of style.

"You have a very clear sense of style," she said. "It was one of the first things I noticed."

I protested that I didn't have a sense of style, I simply chose practical clothes. She laughed the sort of laugh that in a certain type of marital discussion can lead to accusations of condescension and passive-aggressiveness and in a different conversation opens a window of understanding. One of the many benefits of loving someone and knowing them for a long time is that you gain a subtlety of insight into another perspective that is impossible in a casual friendship.

I knew from her laugh that what I had said was not only laughably ridiculous to her but also that she considered trying to convince me a fruitless undertaking.

"You mean when you saw my clothes, you thought I had some sort of fashion sense?" I said, slyly substituting fashion for style.

She ignored the sophistry. "It told me a lot about who you were. I thought, 'Hmm, that's interesting,'" she said, refusing to reveal more.

And then I knew that I had been an idiot all those years. To Beth Ann, who is less focused on language than I am (although no less versed in linguistic tactics), there were other forms of communication. I could think, foolishly, that I wasn't communicating with the rest of the world by what I wore. In fact, my inclination never to wear words or slogans (a preference shared by Beth Ann, although we didn't know that when we met) might have seemed consistent with my belief that I wasn't saying anything with my clothes, but that was not the case.

Every choice is a statement and it is heard by those who are paying attention. Walking around thinking that this wasn't the case was like being one of those people talking on a phone headset, spewing their one-sided conversation into the air as though the rest of us didn't exist and couldn't hear them.

The world is full of sentient creatures observing. There is no escape or hiding place. We are always communicating; every gesture, every choice says something. The words, our unique human language, are just the most obvious and overt form of communication, and even here the subtle inflections and tones carry as much or more meaning than the words themselves. A person like me, focused too much on the words, misses the other communication, but it is there, even if I don't think I'm participating.

36- Way of the Rustic Furniture Maker

Cherry and yellow birch cupboard

When I was seven, we drove from Rutland, Vermont, where I was born, to Adamant, Vermont, to look at our new house and walk the land. I saw many large smooth-barked trees. I assumed they were young maple trees whose bark had yet to turn rough, as it does on old maples, and I made the additional wrong assumption that the soil must be very fertile because these trees were able to grow so big before their bark got rough and furrowed. These were, in fact, beech trees, the most beautiful tree in the Vermont forest, but we didn't have any beech trees in the woods I played in at our house outside of Rutland and so I had never seen one before. To have been so focused on the different types of trees at age seven, I think I must have had a natural inclination toward them.

On the ride home, as I lay in the back of the car (in those days, a kid could lie on the floor in front of the back seat or in the way back and be mesmerized by the vibration and hum of the transmission and wheels), I made elaborate plans for treehouses— never to be realized, alas—thinking about how I would make a rope ladder that could be pulled up to keep other people out.

So I think I was always a builder, but the quest to bend an oxbow sent me wandering the woods and in this way I filled out my knowledge of trees, not just their names but how they smelled when you cut them, where they grew, the color of their wood.

Until I built my mother a writing cabin, pretty much everything I built was symmetrical. I used a lot of logs in my building because I could just go into the woods, cut a tree, and pull it out of the woods with my oxen or a tractor, and so I had an unlimited supply of free building materials. Like most builders, I always looked for the straightest, most uniform logs. I built a couple of barns, little sheds, countless animal feeders, pretty much anything we needed on our small farm.

In retrospect, one of the things that surprises me is how unschooled and untooled I was. Most of what I learned about woodworking I learned by getting wood from the woods and building something. Other than that, my primary sources of education were the Foxfire books and Eric Sloane's books *An Age of Barns*, *A Reverence for Wood*, and *A Museum of Early American Tools*. I had some hand tools, primarily a drawknife, axes, a hand adze, and a couple of big augers that came from a guy who sold old tools out of his basement.

"As the twig is bent, so grows the tree," and this has remained true for me. I have always gone ahead with limited preparation or knowledge, even when I was making furniture full-time. This may have pushed me to be more innovative and original in what I built, but it was also very limiting.

When my mother, Ruth, asked me to build her a little writing cabin, I was 24. My brother, Louis, and our friend John Ruskey and I were about to head to Wyoming to canoe down the Green River. I'd just seen a picture in *National Geographic* of a beautiful rustic church in Peru, where the roof was supported by many twisted, white-washed tree trunks. The effect was so magical and fascinating that it bumped me out of my belief that everything should be straight and symmetrical.

I conceived the idea of framing Ruth's cabin with bent branches that would make the vertical line of the wall and then have a natural bend that would bring them together for the roof peak. John and I spent a couple days walking barefoot through the May woods, tramping on wild leeks and looking for the right branches. We didn't find many, but I did notice a lot of heavy, curved cedar limbs. I changed plans and decided to build her a cabin with a curved roof.

Writing cabin frame

For light I wanted to use some old single-pane windows that had been removed from the house, but these presented a problem. I wanted the eave of the roof to be at the height of the top of the windows, otherwise the small cabin would look too tall, but this wasn't high enough to fit a door under. I thought about having a door you had to stoop to go through, a hobbit door, but I didn't like this solution, which seemed less like a solution than a design concession.

Because the roof was going to be framed with these curving cedar limbs that were going to push out quite forcefully, I needed one continuous piece of wood as a rafter plate on the top of each side wall. In other words, I didn't want to frame in a high spot for the door because then I would lose the strength of one continuous piece of wood. Then I remembered a red pine tree we had seen, with a peculiar crook in its trunk. We cut this tree and I framed it into the wall so that the crook provided a high spot in the frame into which I could put a door.

Writing cabin

In a sense, this was the beginning of rustic furniture for me, although I was still a couple of years from making my first piece of furniture. Most of my building up to this point had been an act of creating my design from wood. This is what most woodworking amounts to. You take a tree, cut it into boards, and shape these boards into something. Straight trees make the best straight boards. It is all an act of taking a natural material, a material shaped by life forces, and imposing order on it; for wood, the order is boards with straight lines. The design exists before the material, and the material is forced to conform to the design. Nothing wrong with that, but the cabin door problem opened new possibilities to me.

Here was a design where the peculiarities of the material assisted in solving the design problems. There was more of a give-and-take between the material and the design. And it was asymmetrical. I knew I had crossed a line in my mind and it opened a whole world of design possibilities.

I started building rustic furniture because I needed money. Granted, for most people, rustic furniture is not the first thing that springs to mind when they find themselves short of cash. It happened for me like this:

First of all, I (obviously) didn't know what I wanted to do with my life. I met a girl named Jennie. She was at least as frugal as I was, but relationships are what they are and almost immediately I needed more money than came in from the sort of serendipitously occurring odd carpentry jobs that had sustained me up to that point.

I agonized for a little while about what I should do with my life, but it was such a well-worn path that I knew I wasn't going to get anywhere I hadn't already been. I had four years of college studying classics, mostly philosophy, and so I determined to reason my way to a profitable and productive vocation. Rustic furniture is what I came up with.

I had an idea that such a thing as rustic furniture existed because I had seen one picture of a rustic bench in a magazine. The logic that rustic furniture would lead to money goes like this: I already had some tools. Wood for buildings or conventional furniture had to be purchased, but wood for rustic furniture was available for free on my parents' land. I had noticed, when I built other things, that people responded favorably to my sense of design. I loved trees and wood.

This logical conclusion did not immediately lead to money in my pocket, but I did start building some pieces. My first creations were walking sticks, a chair, and a swing. I had a job clearing some land and, in the process, I cut a small ash sapling that had been crushed down when it was just a sprout. Maybe a deer or a hiker stepped on it. As a result, it had struggled back toward the light with a pretty curve in its trunk and a ball of wood had grown over the injury. It was shaped and sized perfectly for a cane, and after I looked at the ball of wood on the end for a while it began to resemble a fist. I got my chisels and pocketknife and brought the fist out of my imagination and into existence on the end of the cane. I followed that with canes carved like fish, a rhinoceros, and others I can't remember now.

I made a swing from an apple branch that was curved almost into a U shape and a chair based on an African design I had seen.

Then I set out to sell my wares, Jennie accompanying me sometimes. Naturally, I expected my brilliance as a woodworker to be recognized and rewarded by the first shopkeeper I walked in on. I started with the ski towns of Stowe and Waitsfield. The owners of the little craft shops and art galleries were, for the most part, friendly and understanding when I showed up unannounced on their doorsteps. They were also uninterested in what I had made. Most people who run a little craft shop know exactly what sells well to the people who walk through their doors. They've survived by efficiently and repetitively making those products available to their customers. But I didn't know this. I thought they were looking for good, unusual stuff, when in fact what they wanted were things they knew they could sell.

They would select a carved walking stick or cane from my collection and say, "I like these. How much do you sell these for?" I didn't see the canes as "these." They were individual carvings. Sometimes they came out really well, sometimes they weren't as good. I had thought I would sell the good ones for more. The laborious sanding (I was doing it all by hand), the way I had carefully used two different types and colors of wood to inlay for the eyes of the carving—this wasn't what the shopkeepers noticed. They wanted to know how much that model was and if they could get more if it sold. I didn't know. I wasn't certain I could find another tree bent that way. When I tried to explain this, they lost interest rapidly and sent me on my way.

So it went until, after several expeditions, I gave up on the tourist towns and decided to try Burlington. I wandered around for a little while. Jennie was with me and eventually we came on a store with a rustic interior decorated with beams from an old barn. Inside were some hand-stitched moccasins and other handmade crafts.

The shopkeeper approached and made an admiring comment about my walking stick, which gave me the perfect opening to pitch him my work. In a few minutes I was hustling back to the car to get the rest of my wares, unable to believe my good luck. The storefront was connected to some alternative community in the wilds of the Northeast Kingdom. They got income from their crafts, and this store was how they sold them. They understood that handmade things were all different and were happy to have my work alongside their own.

I talked with the guy for a little while and Jennie looked around the store. When I asked about his commune, he said it was based on the Bible, on families, and honest work with their hands, and he made a comment about the "right for men and women to love each other desperately." Well, the world is full of freaks and he had a right to his religious convictions. As for the comment about desperate love, it seemed odd, then again true to my experience and observation, so I let it go.

I'd been home for a couple of hours, still floating on my good fortune, when some neighbors stopped by and as I explained to them how I had finally found a place for my woodworking, the woman said, "You mean in that store run by the homophobic, misogynistic cult?" I dug out the little pamphlet that the shopkeeper had handed me as I left and which I had thrown away without even looking. Sure enough, the hate was slightly veiled but perfectly apparent.

I couldn't support these beliefs with my work and so I decided to go the next day and take my work out. What's more, I figured that I had given woodworking a pretty good shot. I'd put a fair amount of effort into making things and more effort into trying to find a place to sell them. Not only had it not worked out, but the only place that wanted what I had was a fundamentalist cult whose beliefs were repugnant to me. I was disappointed but not particularly despairing. There was a whole world of things to do. I'd do something else.

The next day, before I left to get my stuff out of the store, a friend told me that she thought there was another craft store opening in Burlington. I told her I thought I was done with this woodworking experiment.

The guy at the cult store was reasonable. He'd probably been through rejections before and mine didn't leave any room for how I felt, but I was polite, which was probably more than he often got. Immensely relieved that it hadn't turned into an ugly scene, I thought, what the hell, why not walk up the street and see if I could find this other store.

The store was a new branch of an established craft store named Frog Hollow. Although they usually had a jurying process to accept craftspeople, they were eager to fill their new store. The whole day seemed charmed. I'd gone to Burlington to retrieve my work and give up on the idea of making a living by woodworking and instead I ended up with my work in a much nicer store than any of the others I had been in.

I bumped along making walking sticks, wooden spoons, pretty much whatever little wooden creations came to my mind. Frog Hollow, in the persons of Wendy and Connie, the two women who had welcomed me the first day I walked into the store, was accommodating and allowed me to price the pieces I brought in according to my own discretion, which is to say mostly by guessing.

Then I had the idea to make a large, rustic wooden bed. I suggested this idea to Frog Hollow and they liked the idea and said it would be their window display for April. This must have been in the late fall.

The applewood bed on display in Frog Hollow

I got the idea for the bed while out prospecting in a cattle pasture for dead apple branches that were shaped in a way that would work for wooden coat hooks. This was an idea I got from an old Eric Sloane book, and the hooks seemed to sell reliably for four or five bucks apiece. This particular apple tree had been girdled by cattle, who are not normally very good bark strippers since in the front of their mouths they only have teeth on the bottom jaw. Nonetheless, some of the more creative individuals learn that they can pull bark off trees by scraping their bottom teeth upward along the trunk in the manner of an old-fashioned steam shovel mining a gravel bank.

This tree had died a little bit at a time over years and, as a result, its trunk was a variegated mess of old scars and spots where new wood had overgrown the damaged sections. Then it had given up the ghost altogether and the bark eventually slipped off but not before dyeing the surface of the wood a marvelous patina of browns and blacks. I cut the whole tree and several more like it and carried them back to my makeshift workshop in my parents' mudroom. I still needed wood to make the bed rails, and for this I found an old, dead elm tree 12 or 14 inches in diameter. I felled it and, using a chainsaw, slabbed off a piece a couple of inches thick from either side. With my materials gathered and drying in the mudroom, I procrastinated for a while and then, in February, I started working on building the bed. I needed more space, so I moved my operation to Ruth and Bill's porch.

On nice days I would take my chisels, mallet, and handsaw, leave the apartment Jennie and I rented in Montpelier, and work on fashioning a bed out of these gnarled pieces of applewood. It was laborious work and I had no idea what I was doing.

I built it like a barn, cutting square mortise and tenon joints and constructing the frame first and then building a headboard made from branches into the frame. This was an ass-backward procedure and resulted in horrendously sloppy joints, especially in the headboard.

I quickly began to despair of the whole project. I'm utterly certain I would have given up had I not promised to have it completed for the April window display at Frog Hollow. With the head- and footboard assembled and pinned together with wooden pegs, I started on the rails. I planed them by hand, fighting against the interlocking grain of the elm wood. Then, with a belt sander, I ground off what I couldn't plane down. It was depressing work made more so by the pronounced bow the slabs had taken on as they dried.

Still, there was no turning back and no giving up because Frog Hollow was counting on it for their window display. I covered the whole creation in several coats of a linseed oil wood finish and bought a futon mattress to rest on the slats.

The effect was impressive. The mattress softened the dark scarred wood and made it look inviting. The oil gave the wood a polished and ancient appearance. It looked like something you might find in a castle. I was still horrified by the gaps in the joints, especially in the headboard, but nobody else seemed to notice. I set the bed up in my parents' living room and what people saw was the idea of these rough but beautiful pieces of wood tortured into a bed shape. No one noticed or commented on the joinery.

It had taken me more than a month to build the bed but I made the April 1 deadline, a habit I managed to maintain throughout the rest of my furniture-building career. The bed wasn't going to fall apart but the joinery was too sloppy for me to feel much pride. I recognized that other people liked it, and given that it was huge and had taken a long time to build, and with some encouragement from my aunt, who lived in New York City and probably had a distorted view of what things cost, I decided to try to sell it for $3,000. This was a punt as much as anything else. Why the hell not. I had nothing to lose, or so I thought. Frog Hollow, as always, went obligingly along.

A couple of days after I set the bed up in Frog Hollow's window, they called to say that people loved it. Two weeks later a guy from Boston who owned a trucking company bought it. I was amazed, horrified, delighted all at once. The bed finished its run as the April window display and then I delivered it to the guy's house in Boston. I felt like a fraud and a genius at the same time. I had taken an old, dead, worthless apple tree and turned it into something other people felt was beautiful and valuable. At the same time, it was very crudely accomplished and I knew I could do much better.

Around this time, I rented a garret over an old carriage house across the street from our apartment to use as a workshop. I started immediately on my next bed, a simpler creation built from peeled pieces of spruce wood, mostly straight pieces, with a curved piece of cedar for the headboard and a sunray pattern under the arch. It was a simpler and much easier bed to build. I was cutting all of my joints into square tenons with a handsaw and coping the shoulders of the joints with a chisel and mallet. The joinery on this bed was much tighter. I put it in Frog Hollow and it sold quite quickly for $1,600.

You might think that at this point I would have started to feel as though I had found my path in the world. I was making things out of wood, something I had done my whole life, and it looked as though it could turn into an actual living. A smart person might have devoted himself to perfecting his craft, increasing his output, and figuring out a more logical marketing strategy than simply making the next idea he took a fancy to. He might have even gotten interested in furniture and read about the history of American furniture and paid special attention to rustic furniture.

Instead, I thought, "This can't be all there is. I don't even like furniture." I was increasingly proud of the pieces I made, and my skills were improving by leaps and bounds as I devised new ways to do things and gradually bought new tools, but I couldn't see myself making furniture for the rest of my life. It seemed that there had to be something somewhere more interesting and meaningful. This was, I had to admit, by far the best way I had come up with to make money, but I had never really valued money except as a means to an end.

In the fall, Jennie went to college and I moved my workshop to a bigger, heated space a little way out of town. It wasn't a perfect shop. The unheated front portion was occupied by a septic tank pumper truck, but my shop was cozy, with some nice windows. I worked more or less regular hours and, after I finished working, I often sat for half an hour just looking at what I had built. I'm not sure why. I wasn't planning the next steps. I was just soaking it up and getting a feel for how it looked. I wasn't happy but I kept plodding along with projects. Then I got a call from Frog Hollow that forever scarred my woodworking.

The guy who had purchased the applewood bed had found a bug in the wood. He wanted his money back. Frog Hollow wanted me to call him. He said his wife had seen a little pile of sawdust beside the bed and when she examined where it came from, she saw a little bug drilling its way into the wood. "She screamed so loud the neighbors thought I'd shot her," he said. His Boston accent was a little thicker than I remembered. He'd said he was "in the trucking business" and I began to wonder what he actually did for work given that his neighbor's first thought was that he'd shot his wife. Or maybe he was just inserting the concept of shooting into the discussion to make the point that he wanted his money back. Either way I had to agree that I didn't mean to sell him a bed with bugs in it. Fortunately, I had sold enough other pieces to have enough money to pay him back for the bed. A couple of days later, he showed up about 8:00 at night at my new shop space with a scary-looking sidekick. We unloaded the bed, I gave him a check, and he went away. What didn't go away was a bone-deep fear of having something go wrong with a piece of furniture.

In the library, I took a crash course in powder-post beetles, the annoying creatures that like to set up house in deadwood. I thought that by using deadwood I was saving a live tree and also getting drier wood. I didn't know I was also getting a wood condominium inhabited by little beetles and their eggs and larvae.

I set up the applewood bed in my parents' house, and they are sleeping on it to this day with no further problems. Powder-post beetles do like applewood but they don't reinfest finished wood. I lived in fear about the other pieces of furniture I had sold. Were powder-post beetles going to start coming out of everything? But they didn't so, gradually, instead of letting go, I turned the fear over powder-post beetles into a generalized fear that something, anything, would go wrong with furniture I had built.

I kept building furniture all winter and it kept selling. It still took me almost a month of hard work with a handsaw and chisels to build a bed, and I wasn't feeling as though furniture was my calling in life. When Jennie wanted to go to California after her first year of college, I followed her. When we broke up, I came back to Vermont, unsure what to do next. Then Louis and I took our disastrous cross-country road trip.

Part Two

I've talked mostly about the story of how I got started building rustic furniture. Now I want to focus on the furniture itself and what I learned about building and designing furniture.

After our road trip, somewhat re-enthused for building furniture and determined to stay put for a while, I resumed building. My first shop after the road trip was Jim Picone's basement. That's where, with my friend Lee Frantz's help, I built my first butternut bed, which Frog Hollow sold to a Japanese businessman, who had it shipped to Japan.

Then Roy Haggett's old welding shop came for

sale. This gave me a big, open space for working and storing wood. I'm amazed when I look back over my portfolio of pieces. For the first few years, every piece seemed to teeter between failure and completion. Gradually, I improved my techniques and invented ways to make most of the difficult steps easier.

Butternut wood bed

I didn't start out with a theory about furniture or any specific knowledge about furniture in general or rustic furniture in particular. I'd seen the picture of the church in Peru and a picture of a rustic bench and that was it. Fairly early on I tracked down the maker of the bench, a guy named Barry Gregson. He was, although I didn't know it, one of the preeminent rustic furniture builders in the Adirondacks. When I met him, I knew too little about woodworking or furniture to learn as much as I should have from the meeting. His chairs were remarkably comfortable, fashioned out of wood with the bark on and mortised with round, through tenons.

Bark on furniture is a tradition in the Adirondacks, and had I been paying better attention I would have remembered that Barry told me to check out the Adirondack Museum in Blue Mountain Lake, New York, and their rustic furniture show. In my arrogance and guilelessness, I was not interested in other people's traditions or even their designs and techniques except insofar as they could help me solve my own woodworking problems.

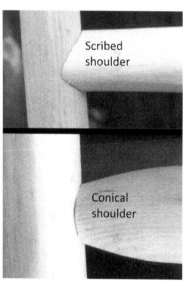

I took two important ideas from Barry. First, I saw that he scribed some of the joints so that where two irregularly shaped pieces of wood came together, one piece fit around the other as though it had grown there.

A lot of rustic furniture is joined with round tenons, created by a tool like a giant pencil sharpener. The cutter creates a round tenon and a conical shoulder on the tenon. This is a solution to the problem of how to join differently shaped pieces of wood.

For most woodworking projects, from building a house or a cabinet, you start with boards that have straight, flat edges. The edges go against the fence of a woodworking tool, and that provides a point of reference for the cut. Mostly the boards are joined perpendicularly or parallel to each other. Occasionally, there are angles, but the angle cuts are almost always straight cuts. When curves are imposed on the wood, usually the starting point is a straight board onto which a regular curve is traced and cut or cut to conform to a jig.

When you build something out of naturally shaped pieces of wood, there is no straight line to serve as a frame of reference. Take two round sticks and join one perpendicularly to another and, unlike two traditional boards, you get a messy connection unless you are willing to scribe one to fit around the other. This is what Barry was doing, at least on some of his joints. The other joints were done with round tenons and conical shoulders so the otherwise messy connection of the two round pieces was somewhat neatened by the conical shoulder of the tenon.

I liked the look of Barry's scribed joints and decided to try to make furniture where all of the joints were scribed so your eye would flow from one piece of wood to another without being interrupted. This was a brash and limiting choice. Scribing joints is very time consuming, and putting furniture together this way necessitates an order of operations.

If I were building a bed, for instance, I would build the headboard without the posts. After all of these joints were scribed and fitted, then I could fit the post on and scribe the ends of the headboard stretchers to fit the posts.

Do the stretchers and the posts first, as I did on the applewood bed, and it became impossible to get tight joints on the pieces in the headboard. Plus, these joints all have to be fitted a little bit at a time.

Big cedar bed going together

In other words, put the joint together loosely, scribe some marks, take it apart and cut to your marks, put it back together, scribe some tighter, better marks, and so forth. There is no such thing as taking a pile of irregularly shaped pieces of wood, measuring them to fit each other as you would do with boards. There's just no reference point from which to measure or mark. You are always starting with an approximate cut and gradually working it into shape.

But with a bed or most other pieces of furniture, eventually it has to end up the right size; otherwise, the mattress won't fit. Plus, when you are dealing with curved and angled pieces of wood, as you adjust and improve the fit of your joint, you also move along the curve or angle, changing the length or position of the piece. Making rustic furniture, in some ways, is on the other side of the moon from building something where you rely on your measurements. You have to come up with a strategy for coaxing all of the pieces together. Insisting on scribed shoulders, as I did, just makes this process that much more difficult.

During the first few years I built furniture, each piece was a struggle, during which, at least once, I would feel the despair of thinking I couldn't complete the project. Usually this came after several days of fitting and refitting joints and still not being able to get things right. Then the next morning I'd push on and rework the joints I had thought couldn't possibly get any better, and I got them fitted better.

There is a lesson here and it's not the necessity of persistence, although that is important. I was being a dumb ass. I was developing a way of building furniture with scribed joints and square tenons. The result was furniture whose rustic appearance was more than a façade. This is all fine, but like any zealot, it is hard to keep your eye on the original intention and easy to get sidetracked into slavishly following the rituals. In this case, rituals I had created, like cutting my clunky square tenons by hand, were limiting rather than enhancing my work. My goal, at least the aesthetic that gradually developed, was to create furniture where the natural shapes of the wood flowed together and didn't look, as much rustic furniture does, like a bunch of sticks screwed together. The square tenon, cut from the end of the piece of wood being fitted, an integral piece, seemed important to me.

A lot of rustic furniture is essentially a rustic façade over a more traditional construction. There is nothing wrong with this, of course, but my nature and my vision for furniture was more fundamentalist. If I was going to build furniture out of naturally curved pieces of wood, I wanted those pieces of wood to be the actual frame and heart of the furniture as well as the decoration. Having a tenon that was an integral piece of the wood seemed a continuation of this open, undisguised approach to building.

I don't really have any design rules, but as close as I come to having a rule, it is this: Don't try to pretend that something is something it is not. Faux anything, at least in furniture and architecture, hardly ever works for me. And so I took this idea to an extreme and stuck doggedly to my square tenons.

I started doing some craft shows and gradually got exposed to other rustic furniture builders, and I saw that no one was making furniture like mine. Rustic furniture runs the gamut from incredibly shoddy creations to utter masterpieces. This is true both in craftsmanship and in design. There are people like me who develop their own techniques and style, and there are people who build things more or less in what they see as a particular traditional style. But because the material is always varying, the solutions to problems are much wider than they would be with more traditional furniture.

Give a bunch of furniture makers specializing in Shaker furniture some cherry boards and ask them to build an end table, and the results will be pretty similar. Give a bunch of rustic furniture builders a pile of sticks, which, by definition, won't be that similar, and the end tables they come up with will vary widely as each builder solves the problems his individual sticks present.

At first, I didn't run across anyone scribing all of

their joints. Then I did a show where there were a couple of guys from the Adirondacks. Their joints were all scribed and incredibly tight, far tighter than I had ever been able to get. They were using a lot of cedar, which is very soft and easier than hardwood to get a tight fit because the edges of the joint conform a little as you squeeze the joint together. And instead of mortise and tenon, they were fastening everything with screws, which also helped pull things tight. Still, there was no denying how perfectly fitted their joints were.

They were cutting their joints with an oscillating spindle sander—basically, just a small, spinning sanding drum. This put me in a quandary. There was no way to use a sanding drum and also use a tenon that was cut integral to the piece of wood being joined. Screwing things together didn't work for me; I was afraid the screws would eventually loosen. And years later, when I experimented with some screwed-together joints on a railing in our house, that's exactly what happened. These guys had a different style than mine. They were making large beds with heavy frames and many decorative pieces laid against the heavier member and screwed into place. The joint was scribed and fitted and it worked well in this application, but it wouldn't have worked as well, for instance, in a rocking chair.

I knew I could use a round blind tenon— essentially, a piece of dowel fitted into a hole in each of the two pieces of wood to be joined together. I had known that going to this kind of joint would speed up my building, but I had held out because I felt there was something more honest about my integral tenons. Integral tenons meant one piece of wood joined to another—no third piece in there acting as an intermediary. Even though the blind tenon had some structural advantages, I held out, zealously protecting the purity of my approach.

The oscillating spindle sander pushed me over the edge. I had to have those tight joints, and so I decided to try the blind tenoning approach. I felt that this was a betrayal of my principles but also that it warranted an experiment.

I didn't want to buy an oscillating sander since they cost a couple of hundred bucks, so instead I had a machine shop fabricate a shaft I could chuck into a horizontal drill press. The shaft was the right size to fit spindle sander drums. Then, using an electric drill to drill the holes, I assembled my first piece of furniture using a round blind tenon system. I can't remember if I did this first on a rocking chair or a bed, but joints were much better than any I'd achieved before.

I'd been so doggedly stuck on the idea of what I was doing that I'd missed a really great way to improve what I was making. But bigger improvements were ahead. Once I accepted the idea of this system of joinery, my next struggle was how to get the holes in each piece of wood at the perfect angle to each other. I had been drilling holes, then chiseling them square for my square tenons, and this gave me some room to modify the angle of the mortise slightly. The round blind tenon fit the round drilled hole almost perfectly, so the alignment had to be very close to perfect too.

Even a perpendicular joint is pretty hard to drill straight by hand. Curved pieces, rocking chair frames that were slightly wider in front than in back, anyplace where the hole had to be at the perfect angle and it was a non-perpendicular angle, these were horrible. I tried setting up two carpenter's squares tilted at the correct angles to give me some guides to direct my drilling, and it helped, but there were some early chairs that had to be pounded together because the angles of the joints were slightly off.

My next improvement was to believe in myself. I thought if I got several old Shopsmith machines, the cheaper models that occasionally came up in the classified ads, I could build a machine that would help me drill the holes for this blind tenoning system.

Since there is no reference point for an irregular piece of wood, no straight edge you can rest against a woodworking fence, I needed a different way to line things up for drilling holes. My idea was to build a table that slid in front of two drill presses. I would retrofit the old Shopsmiths to work as horizontal and vertical drill presses. Then I would place the piece of wood or the partially assembled piece of furniture on this sliding table and clamp it in whatever position made the holes I wanted to drill at the angle I wanted. This way the plane of the table became the reference point and I could slide it along, drilling a series of parallel holes even though the piece of wood was curved.

It is difficult to describe and not important to exactly understand how it worked. The point is that it allowed me to get the right angle consistently when I was drilling holes. I invested two weeks of work and several hundred dollars, which seemed like a lot of money and time, in this invention. It seemed like a big risk, but it worked.

As with the blind tenoning system and cutting the scribed joints with a sanding drum, I should have done it much sooner because it vastly improved what I could do and how fast I could do it. My stubborn adherence to a foolish idea about integral tenons and my reluctance to experiment with a new tool had been a terrible limitation on my ability to make furniture.

Another tool that played a big role in the direction of my furniture design was the pneumatic drum sander. This is a rubber drum filled with air and covered with sandpaper. You can change the air pressure to make the drum softer or harder.

Because the drum is flexible, it contours to the wood and allows you to sand curved irregular pieces of wood. I was able to buy one of these drums for $100 and fit it to an old grinder arbor, so it was a relatively easy adaption to make.

Rustic furniture builders are about as tangential from the mainstream of society as you can get. They are a bunch of independent jack-of-all-trades misfits like me who couldn't even conform to traditional woodworking or found that traditional woodworking didn't inspire them as much as the fantastic shapes of rustic furniture.

Everything about rustic furniture woodworking has to do with adapting the tools and machines to accommodate irregular pieces of wood. Traditional woodworking comes at the problem from the other side. The wood is sawed and planed into regular shapes, boards, which accommodate very well to the straight fence on most woodworking tools.

The wood is the master in rustic furniture. Your goal is to deliver a piece of beautiful, functional furniture from the very irregularities of the wood that would make it unsuitable for regular furniture.

In any kind of modern woodworking, the machines have gotten so good, so precise, so sharp, so convenient to use that a skilled person can produce nearly perfect pieces of furniture. This isn't bad, but it has made woodworking more like machining metal and less like an interaction between trees, wood, and a craftsperson.

Something major has been gained, and it is the stunning precision of joinery and sanding. And something has been lost, and it is the vitality of a sense of struggle. Wood has become simply a material. In a lot of furniture, the wood could be high-density plastic or some other composite manmade material, shaped and fitted by machines.

I thought a lot about this when I was making furniture. What is it we like about wood? Why are we drawn to the figured grain that often results from stress in the tree while at the same time love the straight, parallel grain of old growth trees that had hundreds, maybe thousands, of years of steady, consistent growth?

It is the connection with life, I think. The curves, peculiar grain, knots, and discoloration that find their way into rustic furniture are a direct, tactile connection to the life of that tree. No less, the parallel, almost mathematically consistent grain in old growth western cedar is a testament to that tree's life, the fogs that rolled in century after century from the Pacific Ocean. This sense of life and the consequences of life, as evidenced by the irregularity of the wood that shows up in rustic furniture, is what makes it special and creates a connection between people and the piece.

Drawer pulls made from pieces of wood split out around knots pretty well embody my rustic furniture. First, you take an interesting piece of wood; then, working with the shape of the grain, try to coax that shape into a useable form. There is give-and-take. The shape is never perfectly functional. To some extent, you are imposing function on material, but you are also letting the design be influenced by the individual grain pattern, which is in itself a reflection of the individual tree and even more of a particular struggle faced by that individual tree. The result manifests a coexistence with nature, a sort of acknowledgment of adapting to fit the world and adapting the world to fit you. The best drawer pulls made this way have unpredictable shapes that fulfill a simple function. The best wood is one with a somewhat visible grain so that it is apparent that the handle is not arbitrary but follows an underlying pattern.

After six or eight years of building furniture and going to craft shows, I developed a strategy: always have a really expensive piece with you. At every craft show, the rumor goes around about someone who sold some really expensive creation. Sometimes I ended up talking to the craftsperson and verified the rumor, sometimes not, but always I left with the envious feeling that someone else had made a really high dollar sale. The other side of this transaction is the person who buys the expensive item. There is always someone who wants to be known as the one who could buy the best.

So it happened that I was at the Adirondack Museum Rustic Furniture Fair with a cabinet I priced at $12,000 when a short man walked into my booth and started to talk me up. He was a middle-aged guy with a much younger, tall, blonde woman beside him. She looked bored and I figured her for a girlfriend, maybe just a weekend girlfriend, and when the guy asked me how much it would cost to build a cabinet like the one I was displaying but two and a half times as big, I thought he was just showing off.

I mumbled something noncommittal about the price. I thought he just wanted to impress his girlfriend with how much money he could spend, leave me with an eager expression on my face before walking off. So when I got a call a few days after the show, I didn't return it right away. When he called back a few days later, I started to take him seriously. I got almost a year's worth of work from that guy. I was right that the woman was a girlfriend. She was around the whole time I worked for him and I never heard him refer to her as anything but "the Blonde."

There's a saying about opening a business, that if you go into a town that has a dozen pizza shops and one burger place then you should open a pizza shop not a burger place because pizza is what the people in that town like to eat.

I did the opposite with furniture. When I started

doing more craft shows, and especially the Adirondack furniture show, I saw that pretty much everyone made rocking chairs but fewer people made big beds. I was already making beds so I figured I would stick with beds.

Beds are well suited to rustic work. They are big pieces of furniture, and the ruggedness of rustic furniture works well for a bed. It doesn't matter how heavy a bed is because you want it solid. Lightness is an advantage in a chair. But beds have other problems: they are difficult to ship, hard to display, and everybody seems to have a different size mattress in mind. I learned that the first question to ask when you make a bed for someone is to find out what size mattress they are planning on using. This determines how high the bed rails are from the floor, how far from the rails to the bottom of the headboard. And the next question is whether it is going under a window, in which case the headboard can't be too tall. By the time you leave six or eight inches below the bottom of the rail and then someone puts 20 inches of mattress and box spring on the bed and then tries to squeeze the headboard under a window—even a relatively high window four feet off the floor—at most you've got 22 inches for the headboard. That's not enough to make it look right if you are using thicker rustic wood.

Eventually I made a couple of rocking chairs and

I discovered why all of the other builders make rocking chairs: because people love to buy rocking chairs. A bed is a big deal. You can always move things around and fit in a rocking chair.

Cherry rocking chair

Rocking chairs are sort of the opposite of beds, structurally speaking. A bed stands still and supports a weight that, while not exactly static, is usually pretty still, and any movement in a bed is cushioned by the mattress. A rocking chair moves, and with every rock back and forth a dynamic load is placed on the chair. Wedge your fingers under the arms of a rocking chair where the arms meet the front posts and rock back and forth and you'll feel a slight tightening and loosening as the chair flexes and absorbs the strain of your momentum as it reaches the end of each rock.

When I was a child, there was a rocking chair that we kept in front of the woodstove. Right now it hangs, somewhat dilapidated, in the garage attic, waiting for me to repair it. By family lore it rocked my maternal great-grandfather, Perry King, in Ohio when he was a baby. So it was a special chair, especially for my mother, although I associate it more closely with my father, who often sat there and read in the evening and, when he used to smoke, puffed on his pipe. At least, that's the way I remember it because I associate the brown color of the wood with the color of tobacco.

The frame is oak, but when my parents inherited that chair the seat was broken. They took it to the Rutland Mission, near where they lived, and a man who was drying out from alcoholism repaired the seat with white and brown ash wood that he cut and pounded into little strips and wove into a seat. That seat is still on the chair and his name is still written on a little piece of paper under the arm. He would only take $15 dollars for his work; otherwise, he thought it would be too much temptation to get drunk.

When I was a boy, the tail of one of the rockers broke off. I may have broken it off myself, roughhousing. What I remember is that for most of my childhood, the glaring, jagged break in the end of the rocker offended me. The rockers on this chair are long and prone to breaking because in a curve that long, when it is cut from a straight board, by the end of the curve the grain of the wood is running across the rocker instead of along it. They say the older a rocking chair is, the shorter the rockers, but this is a fairly old chair, so some craftsman, probably in Ohio and much predating Sam Maloof and his famous rocking chair style, decided to build this chair with long rocker tails.

Perhaps it was guilt, if I was the one who broke it, that made the broken rocker bother me. What I remember is how much the design flaw infuriated me. Why would someone make a piece of furniture with a fragile piece so vulnerable to breaking?

So that's what I was thinking when I started to build my first rocking chair. I wanted to use naturally curved pieces of wood for the rockers so the grain of the wood would flow along with the curve, making it very unlikely the rocker tail would ever break. I knew the chair would be subjected to the dynamic load of a person rocking and so I wanted the chair to be very strong.

Now, there are two basic designs for wooden

chairs. There is a frame chair, where the seat and back don't contribute that much to the structure and are supported by a wooden frame. And there are Windsor chairs, where the seat is a relatively thick piece of wood and everything else is attached to the seat, which acts like a base plate and anchor for the whole structure.

The Windsor chair is a happy marriage of design and engineering. On the design side, it is simple, elegant, and intuitive. On the engineering side, the weight of the person sitting in the chair serves to help press the legs tighter into the seat. The traditional Windsor chair craftsmen employ some brilliant and tricky joinery to ensure the rungs are unlikely to work loose from the legs.

Modern joinery and hardware have enabled woodworkers to make chairs that are sort of a hybrid of these two types, where the chair is a frame chair with a seat that is integral to its structure. But for traditional woodworking, nothing beats the genius of the Windsor chair design.

I decided to make a frame chair type of rocking chair. It wasn't a decision as much as an assumption. I hadn't given chairs that much thought, and when I decided to try my hand at a rocking chair, the chair I imagined was a frame chair. It took 5 or 10 chairs to work out my design and I continued to make little adjustments and improvements after that but I got a design I liked a lot.

I kept notes for each rocking chair I built. I'd never done this with any other furniture. I usually had a sketch with some dimensions for beds, but with rocking chairs I wanted a record so I could make improvements. I marked down how far each chair leaned back, the curvature of the rockers, depth, width, and height of the seat.

Rocking chair seat detail

I put more effort into improving and refining my rocking chairs than I had with any other furniture. Some of the big cabinet pieces I built were perhaps more beautiful and certainly more impressive because of the size and complexity of creating a big cabinet with a rustic frame and functioning drawers. But for an evolved rustic design, the rocking chairs were the top for me.

For the last five chairs I built, I had our neighbor, John Dubois, working part-time for me. John had worked with me to finish a big furniture

Harp-backed rocking chair

order and I kept him on to build a set of chairs. I did the designing and rough prepping of the pieces and John did most of the finish joinery, which he was better at than I was. I loved working with John, who is a meticulous craftsman—much better than I am. I hoped I could continue to employ him making chairs and so I spent about six weeks creating a little packet of information describing the chairs and sending this to furniture galleries all around the Northeast. I got absolutely nothing in response. With that, I pretty much gave up. I told John I couldn't afford to employ him anymore. I continued to work on orders that came in from galleries or old customers for another couple of years, but I was done. I was sick of making furniture, and my attempt to find a larger market had failed, so I gave up.

I should have given up years earlier, but it is very hard to change directions when you are self-employed and the work keeps coming in. I wonder, if the money had been better or the rocking chair project had gotten legs or if I'd switched to building small buildings instead of furniture, if I would still be building things for a living and if that would be a good thing.

I'm very proud when I look back at my portfolio of work, and some of the better pieces came after my heart was no longer in it. To have a body of work you are proud of is a nice thing in your life. The things that came after my furniture business—the solar installation business and the hydroelectric businesses—expanded my mind in ways that never would have happened if I continued to build things. Although I was already writing and, in fact, had already started on this book before I quit building furniture, the free time afforded me by the hydro business is what allowed me to finish it.

Cherry sideboard with black walnut drawer pulls

37- What Food Will You Bring to the Potluck?

Grown-ups always ask kids what they want to be when they grow up. As a child, I was repeatedly a victim of this crime, and as an adult, I'm guilty of committing it. The victim doesn't suffer much, so it's probably just a misdemeanor of bad taste. The real pain comes when the question is self-inflicted.

I could go through the reasons why it is an unfair and misleading question, but if you've ever squirmed under an interrogation about your future—and who hasn't—you know on a visceral level that it is unpleasant. Even more painful than posing the question is watching someone else answer it with a short, trite, and necessarily dehumanizing answer. A person is more than one thing and the future is unknown.

You don't get to choose what you are or will become. You get some choice in what you do and almost total choice in how you do it. Who you are is the result of what you do and how you do it—mostly how you do it—but it is a result, not a choice; a thousand complicated systems in you and the world interact and there you are, the result, like the weather, of something important but unpredictable. It is liberating, if scary, to relinquish control (illusory anyway) over what you are.

As a person still unable to answer the question, What do I want to be when I grow up? I understand that it is difficult not to keep asking the question. Let me suggest what has been a relief to me—reformulating this question by replacing "be" with "do." What do you want to *do* when you grow up?

This shifts the emphasis from identity to occupation. Let identity take care of itself. Don't think about what an occupation means about who you are.

Think of "do" in terms of a potluck dinner party with your friends. You bring food that you think other people will enjoy and that is convenient for you to bring. And after the party, when people are cleaning up and sorting out the leftover food, you look for a job where you will be useful. If someone else brings the same food as you do or if you end up washing dishes, it is not a big deal. Do it well for a while and then do something else.

There will be another party and another opportunity. So too with life. I don't think, after 53 years of living—many of them spent agonizing over what I wanted to be—that what you do really matters for who you are any more than what you bring to the potluck.

What matters is that you show up, bring some food to the potluck and some skill to life. The interactions with other people are the main benefit.

The working counts more than the type of work.

I'm not saying the type of work doesn't matter. There are a lot of people stuck in shitty jobs. It matters to them and it will matter to you if that's the only job you can get. Refocusing on the practical, what you're good at or what you enjoy doing or what will help you get out of the shitty job and into a better one, these are efforts that can have satisfying and partially predictable outcomes.

But if you are at the point of contemplating what you would like to do and struggling with what it means about you, then you are engaged in a hypothetical exercise for which you cannot guess the outcome, important as it might be. So give up on it and do something you think is useful.

Giving up control over what you become makes you vulnerable to the serendipitous and the tragic. There is no escaping chance, but you are more favored by serendipity and overlooked by tragedy, I think, when you focus on how you can be useful rather than what you want to be.

On Being Expert at Nothing

I know a little about a lot, and that is satisfying in its own way, but I have never become expert at anything.

When I was younger, I found the archaic Jeffersonian ideal of independent farmer citizens compelling, but in the real world this notion had long since been replaced by the pervasive influence of that difficult genius Henry Ford and the assembly line mentality with its specialized and efficient tasks. One can't help but notice that Jefferson's model, at least in his case and his state, not so much here in Vermont, was dependent on slavery, whereas the Motor City gave rise to generalized economic opportunity and a large African American middle class, and this is reason enough to consider it an improvement.

As I get older, I increasingly feel envy for people who have expertise in some area.

For instance, a few years ago Bill and I helped a surveyor when he surveyed some land Bill had just purchased. Surveying has gotten enormously simplified by technology—from walkie-talkies, which have replaced the need for hand signals, to GPS and laser-guided transits—but this particular surveyor had worked out West in the old days of cumbersome equipment and limited technology. He had adapted, of course, to the modern equipment and so he had a range of knowledge and stories and the sort of command of his profession that a person gets when they have done it long enough to understand it from the inside. He was, in short, an expert. I do not want to be a surveyor, but I long for the sort of depth and range of knowledge he had in his field.

To become an expert, you need to work at

something for a long time—years, really, like the surveyor—until you have gotten the perspective that can only come by doing work over time through a changing knowledge base. And this is time that a person doesn't put in unless they have an innate love for the subject or a career pushing them along. I never had either the commitment or a career to push me along far enough to become an expert.

Once, when I was in my 20s, I set three tomatoes on the scale at the local market. The cashier said, in a conversational tone that I took to be not flirtatious, "I can tell by your hands that you are a woodworker. Or maybe a stonemason." She was remarkably accurate. I was a woodworker who, at the time, happened to be helping a stonemason.

We are identified to other people by our work, and sometimes that work leaves its mark on your body and mind. I wanted to have an identity in society because it would have been much easier, but I couldn't wrap my head around identifying myself by my work. The idea of dedicating myself to one occupation long enough to make it a career and become expert felt utterly false for me.

Deciding to become a plumber or a doctor seemed like a betrayal of who I was. And so I spent years doing things, mostly woodworking, and trying to do a good job but never feeling committed, as though I'd found my thing, because I didn't want to be one thing.

It was a misplaced fear to think my work would define me. The work leaves its mark, but it isn't the whole story. You really don't know and can't know how your life will work out. Worrying about what the work says about you seems to be mostly futile, in my observation.

There is a bit of a schism between the blue-collar world and the professional world. A person might say, "I'm a plumber," but in general no one who is a plumber defines their existence by being a plumber. Plumbing is a job. Plumbers do the job and usually take pride in doing good work. They understand that society categorizes them as a plumbers, but they realize there is more to them than plumbing.

For professional people, it is more difficult. The sacrifice necessary to become a doctor—or really any profession these days—makes necessary a conviction so strong that you are willing to go deeply into debt and forgo other interests. It's just not possible to believe in plumbing as some sort of higher calling, even though it is a fact that the greatest advances in human health and life expectancy are due to clean water and effective waste removal rather than to medicine, but doctors really do have to possess an almost single-minded devotion to their trade.

I think this is the reason that people in blue-collar jobs often have a much better and more multifaceted grip on who they are as a person. For the professional person, it is harder to separate self from profession.

At any rate, I didn't have enough conviction to become either a plumber or a doctor, so I worked with wood, which was rather natural for me and didn't require much commitment. I think now that I was both right and wrong. I was right not to cave in and force myself into some sort of career because that's what society expects and because having a public definition of myself would have made my life easier. A personal definition would have been a great relief too—or should I call it a personal concession. That's how I would have seen it at the time and that's why I avoided it.

And that gets to where I was wrong. A person is not one thing, even when they have to make sacrifices to become expert at that one thing. I didn't understand this when I was young. It seemed as though I had to choose what I wanted to be and, thinking this meant one thing, I refused.

I'm a generalist. There is nothing that says you can't have an area of expertise and also a general knowledge base, although I haven't succeeded at this. Something about our society, Henry Ford's influence, maybe, makes it seem as though a person can only excel at one thing. This makes choosing the right field seem unnecessarily important and implies that your other interests will be mere diversions, but this is not the case. A person can be really good at more than one thing.

The Project-Based Lifestyle

In the three-hour round trip between central Vermont and North Troy, Vermont, my friends and business partners Gordon and Hilton and I have discussed everything under the sun and listened to innumerable versions of the same tired stories. One new concept that emerged is the realization that we are all living project-based lifestyles.

I think all three of us were more or less resigned to our idiosyncratic lives by the time we started driving back and forth between our houses and our dilapidated hydro site. In my case, making peace with my place in society has not been an easy journey and I wish I had stumbled on this concept earlier.

A hundred and fifty years ago in this country, most people lived an agriculture-based lifestyle, with rhythms determined by animals and crops, weather, and seasons. Most people of my generation live a career-based lifestyle and they follow their career where it takes them, geographically and every other way.

Since I was unable to follow a career-based lifestyle, I had a hard time defining exactly what I was doing. It was completely apparent; I just didn't have words for it. Whether it was cutting firewood in the fall, building a furniture order, reroofing the house, or driving to the Canadian border to rebuild a hydro plant, I have always lived a project-based lifestyle. In other words, the structure of and schedule for my life is based on whatever project I'm engaged in at the moment.

It's not quite that simple. Usually there are multiple projects in various stages of activity, disrepair, outright neglect, or enthusiasm and they're all simultaneously being worked on or ignored to various degrees. But they are all projects, and working on them is the engine that drives my life forward.

I think lots of people aspire to the project-based lifestyle and for good reason, because it seems as though you would always be engaged in something you found interesting and have control over your life. The reality—for me, anyway—is that you are often discouraged about a project you formerly found interesting. Money comes in intermittently, which can tend to sour not only the project but other aspects of your life as well. And worst of all, you have the sinking feeling that you would be much more productive and possibly happier if someone else imposed a structure for you.

While our culture is dominated by the career lifestyle, there are other choices. I've named only three: career, project, and agricultural. But there are plenty of others: artist, student, traveler, just to name some more of the obvious. And, of course, a person doesn't have to be in one lifestyle for their whole life.

The point is not to critique the various lifestyles but to observe that by naming and defining the lifestyle you are choosing, it becomes easier and more comfortable to find your place in a society primarily promoting the career lifestyle.

It's a Feckless World

When Gordon and Hilton and I were running our small solar-electric installation business, we, like the owners of many other tiny businesses, often lamented our own shortcomings. There was the actual physical work of building a solar array, but there was also paperwork, ordering parts, keeping track of the various permitting requirements, making sure the money coming in from the customer got to us in time to pay the suppliers of panels, and, last but not least, remembering to reply in a timely way to potential future customers.

We inevitably dropped the ball on one or more of these tasks at some point during a project. When this happened, we joked, with bitter self-recrimination, that we ought to rename our business Feckless Solar. However, after several years of business, during which time we had to interact with various government agencies and also other businesses big and small, both as customers and suppliers, not to mention a variety of individuals, we came to the conclusion that our fecklessness, while regrettable, was the norm and, in fact, we were certainly no worse than average. The truth of the matter is, it's a feckless world.

Glory Days

Every once in a while when I'm driving, a song comes on the radio—"Glory Days" by Bruce Springsteen is on topic, but the iconic anthem "Born in the U.S.A." is probably more to the point— and I imagine how nice it would be to have at least one outstanding moment or achievement, one song so good I could look back at it and say, "Damn, that's what I accomplished. I may or may not do other worthwhile things in my life, but that's so good, I don't mind if I'm only remembered only for that."

I don't have this.

Instead, I, like pretty much everybody else, have a ragged, disorganized life. But when I regret not having a monumental achievement, I try to remember that life is the achievement. Every choice, every decision, is a brushstroke, a note in this ongoing creation. It doesn't have huge peaks that are mesmerizing, but it does have some peaks, little achievements, a few of which I am describing here, and many long, pleasant valleys.

This is where we are all the same and all

different. Everyone alive has a life, a unique life. Your life is a work of art, and this ongoing performance is the work that matters.

38- On Knowing Who You Are

I had an epiphany at the Tunbridge World's Fair. Credit the 150 years of agricultural history or the trashy dressing, the bright lights, loud noises, or the fragrance of beer, vomit, fried food, exhaust, sawdust, and animal smells mixed with human despair and ambition—whatever it was, something threw me off balance and allowed me to see the obvious. I'm a builder, not a farmer.

Beth Ann started to drift toward the chicken barn, away from the shiny orange tractors, and even the pull of the green and yellow tractors wasn't enough to stop her. I trailed behind. I love the chicken barn—for about five minutes. Same way with the pig barn. Even though it doesn't smell good, the distinctive odor of swine takes my mind back to the 19th century, when rural America was still the heart of the country. Industrial America was well on its way to greatness, at least by the end of that century, but throughout the whole century, everyone kept or was still associated with animals in some way. One hundred fifty years ago, everyone knew the difference between the smell of a horse and that of a hog. The variety of breeds in the chicken cages and pig pens, the spots and stripes, ornamental feathers and regional names, are an echo, a reminder that farming was everywhere in this country.

Leaning over the pen, looking at a Hampshire sow and her 10 piglets, I think it was a better time. Every small town in America was the center of its own little world, and out in the vast countryside millions of small farmers were building their places, raising their families, exercising local democracy and their independence. Then I remember that it was also a time of slavery and Jim Crow, horrifying rural poverty, and stupefying ignorance.

My parents were a little early of the back-to-the-land movement. Had they been consciously part of a movement, perhaps that would have prompted them to be more informed on the technicalities of farming. Instead, they plunged into animals, gardens, and children without much practical experience or knowledge. Among the many indelible marks this left on me were an excess of rustic skills and a conviction that raising animals and gardening were life's two most worthy endeavors equaled only, perhaps, by writing.

I've never been a farmer. My weed-filled attempts at gardening have yielded more guilt than vegetables. When it comes to tending animals, I'm more interested in the barns and hay feeders. A neighbor who was retired but had been a successful farmer told me once that he knew most of his cows by name but he could only say that his tractors were green and could hardly remember what brand they were. Now *that's* a farmer. I found this confession elucidating and also horrifying.

What is obvious, and has been since I was a child, is that my inclination is all toward the mechanical and structural. I'm not a farmer, I am a compulsive designer and builder. When I walk into a barn, old timber frame or modern metal frame, I notice how it was built. There is a language to structures, certain problems that must be managed one way or another, and these speak to me. My heart takes a little cheerful jump when I see that someone has solved a problem in a clever way. Just looking at a spruce log made into a floor joist and mortised into another log makes me happy.

When I was seven, my sister Molly, my mother, and I lived in Clarendon Springs, near Rutland, and my father was in Adamant, Vermont, starting his new job while we waited for our house to sell. We occasionally made the long hour and a half drive between the two places, and often we could persuade our parents to stop halfway at a diner near Bethel. It was there, in the bottomland below the diner, that I saw my first four-wheel-drive tractor with its unmistakable front tires. I knew by that point that there were two- and four-wheel-drive trucks but I had never seen a four-wheel-drive tractor, and this, apparently, caused me some perplexity because I still remember the sense of relief and satisfaction I got from seeing this tractor and validating what I suspected to be true—that if there were four-wheel-drive trucks, then there had to be four-wheel-drive tractors.

I would say that these are not typical concerns for a seven-year-old, but I don't think that is exactly the case. We all have natural inclinations and often they manifest themselves pretty early. It is hard to recognize them sometimes, especially when you are young, and so I spent my childhood thinking I wanted to be a farmer even though I was building things all the time.

By the time I was an adult and making a living by building furniture, the idea that I would someday be a farmer occupied that gauzy but rather capacious mental warehouse that we all possess and have labeled as Things I'd Do if I Won the Lottery.

Fifty-odd years into this experience of life, it seems, both personally and by observing other people, that most of us live our lives in reaction to our parents. The only possible alternative is being an orphan, and this, obviously, creates its own difficulties. Perhaps this reaction is to admire your parents' choices and emulate them. Perhaps it is in opposition to their actions. Perhaps it is a combination of rejection and appreciation. Perhaps you are trapped, measuring yourself against your perception of your parents' opinions and accomplishments. It doesn't matter. The point is that making an objective judgment about anything is very difficult because these decisions are made through a lens shaped by your childhood.

You can run but you can't hide. Running is a traditional American strategy for coping with difficulty of any kind—familial, economic, personal, or social. We go off and start somewhere else. That's what my parents did when they fled their small-town upbringing for rural Vermont. We are a country of immigrants and movers, eager for greener pastures and convinced we can leave behind our old selves and become something new and better in another place.

I had early and inept flirtations with the idea of starting a new life elsewhere, but these quickly ended with me returning home. My competence at doing things like splitting wood was matched by an equal incompetence in fitting myself into the rest of the world.

And I could recognize the obvious: Most of your problems are self-created, so you're going to be whoever you are no matter where you go. The clarity of this adolescent truth overwhelmed all the subtlety for me. I could see that by abandoning the lifestyles and values of their parents, my parents had not escaped their influences but had just reacted to them in a different environment. It stood to reason that I would not become different simply by leaving.

I see now, with the appreciation of nuance that 30 years of living can add to your understanding, that there are benefits to running. You don't escape yourself, but new territory and new problems stimulate your mind and open possibilities. Your own problems are going to follow you; that lens created by your childhood will still be there, refracting perception in its own particular way, and since perception is the greater part of reality, you will still be you. But the bumps of the new road dislodge things, and little pieces get through and alter your perspective. This doesn't change who you are, but if you want to change things, it gives you a little purchase, a little ledge to grip with the fingertips of your mind as you maneuver for a slightly different view, which makes for a slightly different reality.

It is always easier to see the advantage of whatever you are not doing. I can see the advantage of our restless society, of waves of people heading out into the unknown. Everyone is a little better in their own imagination than in reality. And maybe, on average, people succeeded a little bit, managed to get enough of a grip to pull themselves a little closer to the better person they imagined they could be. That's not nothing. Over time it adds up.

A human being is a kind of animal that is at its best when it confronts the unknown and is forced to use the special tool evolution gave it—an oversized brain—to understand something new and devise a solution. You're most likely to be yourself when your back is to the wall and you're facing something unexpected.

I took the other route. I stayed close, surrounded by the familiar. No illusion for me that I was going to be different because I was in a different place. There's a lot to be said for this choice. I've always lived near my family, so most of the people I love are nearby. I've seen saplings turn into trees. Hell, I've planted saplings that are now 30-foot-tall oaks. There are parts of the forest in where I've been hunting and watching the sun rise for over 40 years. But it's a long time to go to the fair feeling like you should be enjoying the animal barn when you really want to look at the tractors.

Would I have been different if I'd stayed in Montana or Santa Fe? Would I have been able to see my own abilities more clearly and been less constrained by the ridiculous idea that someday I wanted to try farming? Would chance have edged me more quickly toward the obvious? There's no way to tell.

The point is that one way or another you should try to understand who you are, and to do this you'll have to see through everything that made you who you are. I don't think there is any firm footing to make these judgments. However it happens, it is a back-and-forth game—observing yourself, observing how other people react to you, trying to triangulate an understanding of yourself.

Here's the thing: It is good to know yourself. What you do with that knowledge is a choice, but your choice is going to be only as informed as your understanding of who you are. Everything except reality has a loud voice in this contest. Society wants you to be something, your parents want you to be something, you want to be something. All these voices have their place, but they can crowd out the obvious, which is rather quiet but persistent and will always be there if you look.

39- What I've Learned about Writing

Creating and consuming writing is valued in our family—overvalued, some would say. Consequently, and unfortunately, I paid attention in high school when the teachers gave us writing instruction.

High school teachers are, in all my experience and observation, ill-equipped to teach writing. There are techniques and rules to the skill of writing, and as the teachers doled these out—topic sentences, punctuation, summaries, and introductions—I made notes and tried to follow their advice, assuming that this was the path to good writing. The results were mediocre, to say the least. I couldn't remember the specific rules of grammar and syntax and my attempts to follow the misremembered rules murdered any natural style I might have had.

Good writing is an art and like any art it requires skills, but in high school the emphasis gets placed almost entirely on the skills and rarely on the art, which is more difficult, or maybe impossible, to teach. I tried hard to write well because I had some good teachers who had mastered the art of teaching, but they were nonetheless unable to help me with the art of writing.

Although they couldn't help me become a better

writer—in fact, they set me back for years—they could still recognize good writing when they read it, just as a person who is not a good cook and can't teach cooking can still tell good meal from a bad one. And they knew they weren't getting good writing from me.

I knew I wasn't writing well because I could see the disappointment on my teachers' faces, as though they would have liked to have said to me, "You seem to be a smart enough kid with interesting things to say in class; what happens when you try to write it down?" But instead they just focused on trying to get me organized and pointed out run-on sentences and missing commas and suggested that maybe I should try writing notes on 3 x 5 cards.

When I was in high school, you were never supposed to try to write anything without outlining it first, so I tried harder and made more detailed outlines, planning my assignments sentence by sentence. This resulted in writing that was predictable, lifeless, and without any flow or power.

Neither my mother nor my father gave me much writing advice, which is odd given that my mother was working on a novel and my father was the managing editor of the local newspaper. They were encouraging and occasionally tried to help, but for the most part their attitude to this and most of life's challenges was, "Well, you'll figure it out."

There was one place, however, where my

mother gave me invaluable advice about reading, writing, and, by extension, life.

High school English teachers are fond of sending students searching for symbolism and hidden meanings in any work of fiction. At its worst, this approach reduces reading to a puzzle in which the reader guesses about a secret the writer understood but was supposedly too coy to say in plain English. The idea that the book might be about the world, a real and endlessly puzzling and intriguing place, is lost in this artificial cat-and-mouse game between the reader and writer.

I had one high school teacher who was particularly enthralled with this approach. He had studied journalism and maybe even done a short stint at some newspaper and so he pranced around the classroom telling us about "professional journalists" and saying "graphs" instead of paragraphs to show us how comfortable he was with the shop talk. I'd never heard my father, who was an actual journalist, abbreviate the word "paragraph," and so I suspected that the guy was a bit of a fraud. And when it came to fiction, this teacher was very insistent about the need to discover hidden and secret meanings intentionally concealed by authors.

My mother dismissed this idea. "Oh, that's just the sort of silly thing that teachers like to do because they don't know any better," she said. "Don't pay any attention." But what about the symbolism, hidden themes, and so forth? Well, she said, those things were in stories—sometimes, anyway—but the story wasn't constructed around the symbolism purely as camouflage to make a game for readers. You could find symbols in stories because good stories were like life, and in life lots of things were connected to other things.

I tried this idea out on my dandy English teacher, but he would have none of it. Conveying secret messages was the purpose of writing. The symbols were there, tucked away by the author with only their corners showing, and he was giving us good grades for uncovering them.

I found my mother's explanation much more compelling. The multiple layers and different meanings in a story came from its trueness, not from an intricate game of hide-and-seek. Focus on what is true and let the rest take care of itself. The game of understanding was life itself, not a ploy.

In college they didn't really teach us much about writing, but I could see the same vague disappointment on my professors' faces. My papers came back with comments like "Choppy" and "Disorganized" marked on them, especially when I organized the hell out of them.

Then I had to write a quick note as an explanation of a lab report. It was a short and relatively unimportant assignment and I was in a hurry, so I let the words out without benefit of notes or an outline or trying to make paragraphs that were approximately four or five sentences long with a topic sentence introducing the paragraph.

My professor (tutor, as we called them at St. John's College) liked this attempt better than any previous writing of mine, and this set me to thinking: less organizing seemed to be producing a better result. Although still young and naive, I was old enough to know you don't get something for nothing. That I got better marks for a quickly written but unimportant paper meant that something about the way I was laboring over my writing was making it worse, not better. My writing didn't improve much in college, but I did have a window to its problems.

Four or five years after I finished college, Louis and I decided to take a cross-country road trip. The trip was hard and disappointing, but I was determined to keep a journal every day and create a piece of writing about the trip.

A couple of weeks into the trip, the writing seemed like a complete failure to me. We had mediocre experiences, which I dutifully recorded in my journal. There was no real point to the trip other than wanting to take a road trip. Recording our mundane days seemed worse than pointless; it put the whole lack of direction in my life, day by eventless day, in front of my face every night when

I wrote in my journal. I kept trying to imagine a structure for my writing and daily came up with a new idea for what the writing was supposed to be, but every night it was the same old drivel.

Journal entry
Canaan Valley

Photo by
Louis Porter

We were at a campground in the Canaan (rhymes with inane) Valley in West Virginia. It was January 12 and cold. I knew I was on the verge of giving up because I couldn't force myself to write every night without knowing why or what I meant to be writing. So in a sense, I did give up. I held to the commitment to continue writing every day because this seemed like an act of defiance in the face of failure, but I decided I would simply record the day's events without knowing what or why or for what final purpose. I wouldn't worry about whether it was supposed to be a travelogue or a preamble to essays or just a throwaway, I'd just write it down. At the time, I felt strongly that this was a failure. I'd wanted to write something else, something that was complete and had a shape, and I was giving up on that.

Road Trip Journal, 1994
Jan. 12th

. . . I am beginning to see my life as a failure. I'm 28 years old and living in the back of a truck, driving around the country. I suppose, like everything else, it depends on how you look at it. Every man I've talked to envies us. Perhaps no one can be happy unless their expectations are in line with their lives, and yet, for how many is that true?

Jan. 13th

This morning I finish off yesterday's journal entry while lying in my sleeping bag. Louis, upon waking, says, "I could write a great Edgar Allan Poe story. It would start, 'As I lay there, dreading the first strike of the venomous keys.'"

I decided to let syntax, grammar, verb tenses, punctuation be damned. I would just write. Whatever came to my mind I pushed through the keys of my Olivetti portable typewriter. If I lost the thread mid-sentence, I just started a new sentence. The road trip was a failure in terms of what I'd wanted it to be. We were on the road for a couple more months. There were a few minor adventures and lots of unremarkable driving, but I kept the journal come hell or cold weather.

Then I came home, and when I reread those journal entries I saw a kind of vitality I'd never seen before in my writing. I read sentences and whole pages I didn't even remember writing. It was disorganized, as I suspected back in the Canaan Valley, but it was also alive. And the thoughts flowed better than I ever expected, despite the lack of an outline or organizing structure.

Here's how I've come to understand writing in the years since: No one is born knowing how to dance ballet or play a fiddle or write. These are unnatural actions that, when performed well, give so much the sense of effortlessness that the person watching or listening or reading is completely absorbed in the art and doesn't see the disjointed path that produced the smooth, finished creation. But this doesn't mean that the creation is accomplished in one try. Writing is a multistage process that requires the synthesis of contradictory actions.

The first stage of writing is like vomiting. You have to get it out, and depending on diet and individual constitution it comes out more easily for some people than others. Like vomiting, writing is best done alone. It hurts a bit, although the anticipation is usually worse than the actual event, and afterwards you are a little disgusted, but the repulsion is overwhelmed by a feeling of relief. After you have the regurgitated mess on paper, as with vomit the best thing you can do is walk away for a while. And as with the vomit, you (or somebody) eventually has to clean up the mess.

There are various aids for this first step: road trips, 3 x 5 cards, outlines, a vivid imagination, lots of research, alcohol, music—different things work for different people. What doesn't work is thinking that you know ahead of time how it will turn out. You may know how you want it to turn out or how you hope it will turn out, but mapping it out with a predetermined plan results in something that seems predictable.

Because writing is an art, it needs to have a life of its own, a vivacity. This comes in the beginning. When the sentences pour out, they are full of life, albeit a somewhat disorganized stream, and this flow pulls the reader along.

The persuasive or compelling power in writing does not come from logic. Logic is for math. Writing gets its power from a sleight of hand whereby the reader is convinced of the writer's story or argument not by a logical truth laid bare but by an art skillfully executed, like a dancer floating through the air, so the truth for the writer is transferred believably to the reader.

Writing is just an early version of the internet. All the internet does is allow one computer to access files on another computer. Writing does the same thing except between people; an idea in one person's head gets transferred to another person's head. Dance, music, speech—these are all ways of transferring ideas from one person to another, but until recently the only way that could happen over vast distances or over time was by writing it down.

The skills part of writing is what makes this stream of thought palatable to other people. I have never achieved more than a rudimentary mastery of syntax, grammar, and other basic writing skills, like spelling. Apparently, I will always be limited in this regard, but I do have some conceptual and practical observations on this second stage of writing. I think of these skills in metaphors—bridges, meat, mining, and sanding.

Writing is a bridge from one person's head to another. Since the ultimate objective is to get an idea across the gulf between two minds, the less bridge the better. Every time the reader makes a little cognitive leap and lands safely, knowing what the writer means, a little trust is created. The longer the jump, the greater the connection between the writer and reader. If the reader can pass easily over long gaps, then the reader and writer are almost bounding together.

Everyone likes meat. Even vegetarians who don't like to eat meat from animals still want to eat things that have meat-like qualities of high protein and a certain texture. So too with writing. Readers want meat. Not every sentence has to have meat but frequently you have to give the reader meat; otherwise, they get bored. Meat in writing is a sentence that means something. Elmore Leonard stated this more succinctly when he said, "Leave out the parts that the reader will skip anyway," and then he went on to follow his own advice a little too scrupulously until a steady diet of his writing could leave you starved for certain mental minerals and vitamins that are pleasant to have between bits of meats.

Every mine is surrounded by tailings, the offcast material that seems perfectly useable to the lay person and is recognized as a worthless obstruction by the miner. The first stage of writing creates a large pile of words, some that are meaty and many that are just tailings and need to be swept away. Tailings are an inevitable byproduct of writing and mining. Sometimes you hit a vein and sometimes you only produce waste. Sometimes you go back through your tailings and find nuggets.

When I made furniture, I used to notice that to other people it got about twice as nice when I sanded it. I would have a completed bed sitting on the floor of my shop, needing only sanding and finishing. When people looked at the bed in this state, they would nod and say that it looked nice but without too much conviction. Then I would sand

and oil it and the same people would have a different reaction; the wood was so beautiful, where did I get the idea, and so on. Although I was never very good at either sanding or finishing, I try to remember for writing that a little bit of polish and smoothing makes a huge difference to someone else.

Almost everyone who is creative, including me, wants to think their work is good and even hopes that it may be great. But what does an artist really do?

For me, the process of writing alternates between despair and euphoria. I travel back and forth, like a leopard in a cage at the zoo, between certainty that my observations are trivial, uninteresting, and worthless and the satisfying feeling that I've just written something great that is exactly what I meant to say. The obvious contradiction between feeling brilliant one minute and foolish the next gives me pause, like the leopard when he stops momentarily as though recognizing futility.

This is my answer, the best explanation my pacing against the cage has produced: All art is consumables, no more than a meal, a temporary diversion to be used up and replaced the next day or month or year by another similar offering.

The job is to produce another meal. It doesn't matter that two years ago there was a nearly identical book or song. The muse has to be released, the artist must create, and everyone has to eat. Art is one person's creative output, whose purpose is to feed whatever appetite and taste is lurking hungrily by the dumpster or impatiently fingering a salad fork.

The artist is no different than a cook or school bus driver. It's a job, it's work, creative work, and it fills a need for both the artist and the consumer of the art, just as the school bus driver and the cook fill a need. The artist has control over doing the job well, and that's usually a more complicated task than driving a school bus well. But beyond that, worrying about whether the art is great or not or whether it displays the artist's full range and potential, that's irrelevant and no one else cares. Time makes greatness, the rest of us make meals.

40- On Investing

Warren Buffett— "The first rule of an investment is: Don't lose. And the second rule of investment is: Don't forget the first rule. And that's all the rules there are."

Investing is the only subject I have studied in depth as an adult, and I didn't start until I was about 35. Here is what I think I've learned:

Over the 10 years I've been working on this book, I've modified and rewritten this chapter as my own understanding expanded. This is a conceptual explanation of investing, the sort of description I think I would have benefitted from when I started learning about this subject. The technical details—how to analyze a company or what "backwardation" means—you're better off getting from someone who has actual expertise.

Most of these ideas can be boiled down to two points: First, understand clearly the difference between investing and speculating. You must define these terms for yourself and be clear with yourself about which activity you are engaged in. Second, devise your own theory for everything you do. Continually modify this theory, improve it, write it down, whatever it takes to always operate from your own understanding.

When my father took early retirement from Green Mountain Power, he decided to take his retirement money in a lump sum and manage it himself instead of taking a pension. My parents are pioneers very much in the spirit of the people who headed out to the American frontier. Self-reliance and independence are necessary qualities for pioneers. When Bill and Ruth started raising children and animals on their small farm, and probably long before that, their underlying principle was "We can do this ourselves." This is a sort of faith in the innate ability of a human being to take care of itself and solve whatever problems come up.

On the other hand, exchange of labor is one of the cornerstones of civilization. It allows for specialization and increased efficiency. But it can also lead to narrow-mindedness and, worse, dependence and incompetence in all areas except your specialty. I think my parents, like countless pioneers before them, wanted to avoid dependence, and if this meant hardship or less efficiency, it was an exchange they were willing to make in order to feel in control of their lives.

Modern society has very little use for generalists, so as a generalist you have to pick your way along, carefully maintaining enough general skills to have an open mind while sharpening a specialty enough so that you can make a living. Every choice between doing it yourself and having someone else do it for you is a personal choice based on the difference between what you think your abilities are, what you think their abilities are, and how much or little you mind being dependent on someone else.

Choosing to manage his own money rather than taking a pension or giving his money to a professional money manager has proved to be a very good choice for Bill, although at the time people said, "That's crazy. You should trust your future financial security to a professional."

My father got the logical justification for his choice from the fact that 85 percent of professional money managers are beaten every year by the broad market. In other words, you have an 85 percent chance of being better off by investing broadly in the stock market, a low-cost index fund, for instance, than you do by paying for a money manager to pick stocks for you. But he got his motivation from the pioneer spirit that says, "I can do that myself." There is no more dangerous or powerful thing in the world generally, and in the world of investing specifically, than a person who is willing to think for himself.

A year or two after Bill started investing his retirement money, the tech bubble burst and the stock market crashed. He lost money, along with almost everyone else, but not quite as much, and then he made a little more than the market when it went up. He has now survived and prospered through two stock market crashes.

Gradually, prodded by Bill, I overcame the fear created by the crash of 2000 and started experimenting with investing myself. Bill gave me an article he had read in *Fortune* magazine written by Carol Loomis and based on a long interview with Warren Buffett. It was remarkably good luck on my part to have this article as an introduction to investing.

Warren Buffett is probably the world's greatest investor and is indisputably its best teacher. Buffett is like a martial arts master. Devotion to his discipline is his organizing and motivating force. People invest because they want to make money, and most people want money because they want to use it to buy things. Warren Buffett is not like this. He hasn't bought yachts or mansions to live in. The discipline of making money through investing is the end for him.

Take a moment to let this sink it. Monks take vows of celibacy and silence. A samurai warrior has an allegiance to his lord and he puts this loyalty before his own self-interest and life. Buffett is like this with making money; it comes before him. This makes him the perfect person to learn from because he is a master at the discipline. But there is a sort of monastic purity to his approach. If you're an average person, you want money because you can then buy things. This means you can't be Buffett. He wants money because more money allows him to make more money. Full stop. You can learn from him, but you can't really emulate him unless you want to make the commitment. Money is the purpose for him.

If you offered young investors the proposition "You can be rich, but you have to keep continually reinvesting the money instead of spending it, forever, until you die," how many would take that offer? That's the deal with the devil Buffett made.

Warren Buffett is an understated and tricky writer, and in addition to studying his investment theories it pays to stop and look closely whenever Buffett appears to be stating the obvious. When he says that the first rule of investing is not to lose money, this seems obvious and therefore easy to disregard. Examine it more closely and you see Buffett's style as a writer.

It is very difficult to paraphrase. One could try by saying that it means not to invest unless you are certain to get your money back. But certainty doesn't exist in investing or any other endeavor predicated on the future. Casting it as a rule avoids making this impossible request. Rules get broken.

Does it mean preserving capital is more important than making a return on the investment?

Yes, but the point of investing is to have a return. He doesn't say to ignore the return. So while the first rule is don't lose the money, it is in the context of investing, where loss is always a possibility and a satisfactory return always the goal. And remember that stuffing money in a safety deposit box means that it will lose to inflation, so this is not a way to follow the first rule because you would actually be losing money.

The first rule is the first rule for a reason: It is the most important. When you buy a stock or any asset because you're certain it will go up in price, you are completely ignoring the first rule. Your first thought should be whether the investment is worth more or less than you are paying for it. If it might be worth less than you are paying, then there is a good chance you won't get all of your money back. In fact, you want it to be worth a good deal more than you are paying.

After Bill gave me that article by Carol Loomis, I picked up a copy of the annual report for Warren Buffett's company, Berkshire Hathaway. On the opening pages of this report was a chart that showed the annual percentage gain or loss in value for the S&P 500 and the annual gain or loss for Berkshire Hathaway's book value. The book value was shown because that reflects the company's estimation of its value—at least, the value according to accounting rules. Were they to show gain or loss in the share price (as later versions of his annual letter do), that would reflect how the stock market sees their value and it would be much more subject to swings up and down, although it would almost always reflect a higher value.

From 1965 until 2017, the S&P gained an average of 9.9 percent annually. Berkshire Hathaway gained an average of 19.1 percent. So Buffett is a smart guy and he beat the stock market by an average of 9 percent; seems good but not that extraordinary.

And yet, under these numbers was the line that made no sense to me. The cumulative gains for the S&P were 15,508 percent, but for Berkshire Hathaway they were 1,088,029 percent. I looked twice to see if the numbers were right or if I'd missed a decimal point, since I was reading it in the low light of a movie theater while waiting for a movie to start. How was that possible?

One dollar invested in the S&P in 1965 would have grown to $156.08 by the end of 2017. But $1 invested in Berkshire Hathaway would have grown to $10,881.29 of book value and much more in share value. Every year Buffett got about twice the percentage return as the S&P, but after 52 years it added up to 70 times as much money.

This is the miracle of compounding. It is not really a miracle. It is just math, but it is so counterintuitive that it seems like it must be magic.

I was in my mid-30s when I learned about the miracle of compounding. This is a cornerstone of capitalism. Money is loaned at interest. Earnings are compounded. Small differences in the rate of compounding make a huge difference over time.

These are fundamental principles of nature, math, and the modern industrial economy. I owned a house, had kids, and had experienced a high-quality classics education, but somehow the miracle of compounding that underlies most of our economy had eluded my grasp. I had probably learned the math in one form or another, but no one had explained to me its real implications for life and making money.

These concepts and facts should be explained to kids in ninth grade and again before they graduate just to make sure they understand. The miracle of compounding can work against you or for you, but it is at work whenever a rate of growth is being compounded.

While the miracle of compounding is a bit of math that seems hard to believe, there's another side to the miracle of compounding and it has to do with the effect a slightly lower return has on your long-term gains. When you hire someone else to manage your money, they usually take a little money every year as payment. The fees and fee structures vary and are often artfully disguised.

Someone managing your money, whether it is a big mutual fund or a hedge fund, is doing the work because they get money in return. In other words, their motivation is self-interest, not your interest. Naturally, they try to sell themselves as your partners, and to some extent they structure their fees so they gain more if you gain more so as to make it seem as though you're in it together.

You're only in it together as far as it benefits them; after that, they're in it for themselves. You can't blame money managers. They manage money chiefly to make a living for themselves, not because they want to help you. But those supposedly modest fees they charge eat away at your long-term gains.

Now, if the money managers are making a greater return than you can get anywhere else and if the amount of this excess return surpasses the fees they are charging, then you're coming out ahead. But as Bill learned before he started investing, 85 percent of money managers are beaten by the S&P index. Since it is possible to invest in index funds that charge very low fees and simply mimic the movement of the S&P or some other index, paying some mutual fund a fee to manage your money is really, in the majority of cases, just paying them to underperform the market.

The theory of a public stock market is that it is the best way for a capitalistic economy to collect and allocate capital so that the capital can be efficiently deployed by businesses. In theory, this efficient use of capital benefits everyone in the country.

Here is an analogy for thinking about the broad stock market and the economy: Imagine a person walking down a street with a dog on a leash. The person represents the economy and progresses at a relatively steady and consistent rate, sometimes slower and sometimes faster but without a huge amount of variation. The dog is the stock market and it pulls ahead and then lags back to sniff a fire hydrant, then it runs off to the side, and sometimes it walks beside the person but never for very long. Over a long time period, the person and the dog progress down the street at the same rate, but when you look for a short time, it can seem as though the person and the dog are going in opposite directions. In fact, a sudden lunge by the dog can jerk the person forward or temporarily cause them to stop. And the opposite is also true; the person can stop for their own reasons and the dog may keep going for a while until it reaches the end of the leash, but ultimately the two are tied together.

Well, sort of. Any country's domestic stock market represents companies that do business all around the world. Plus, there are other factors, like the variability of corporate profits as a percentage of GDP, that affect how closely the domestic stock market must heel the national economy. But the point is to understand that there is an erratic correlation between the stock market and the economy. They are never completely disconnected even when they are going in opposite directions.

Obviously, the best time to invest in the stock market is when the person is walking briskly and the dog has stopped for its own reasons and is momentarily lagging behind. Then the dog—the stock market—looks for a while as though it has stalled when in fact that is just the moment it needs to spring forward to catch the person.

An investor like Buffett would be quick to point out that the stock market is not one dog or one company. It is a multitude of companies, each with a trajectory that will be affected by the general economy but not tethered to it on a leash. Betting on the movement of the broad market is speculating. Betting on the movement of individual companies is investing.

Warren Buffett began investing during a time in history when the U.S. economy was growing and the economy and stock market had been reformed after the excesses that helped cause the Great Depression. He is a practitioner of value investing, which is a type of investing ideally suited to freethinking individuals and an economic system that rewards innovation, efficiency, improvement, and growth—the traditional virtues of capitalism.

It is fair to ask whether his methods and insight are still relevant today. The concepts are enduring but the circumstances change, and the concepts may no longer apply in new circumstances. The basic premise of Buffett's investing is that a good business bought at a fair or cheap price will provide a cash flow that justifies the investment. This premise is based on the assumption that the business is operating in a competitive marketplace free enough from corruption so that the better businesses will eventually succeed.

I think it is reasonable to question this proposition in light of the fact that the government in 2009 rescued, rather than nationalizing and restructuring, many businesses in the financial sector, businesses that were, in some cases, engaged in illegal activities for which they have never been punished, businesses that would have gone bankrupt without government intervention. Not only did these actions reward the incompetent and dishonest businesses and their managers and shareholders, including Buffett, it penalized the competent who had to compete with them. For the system to work there needs to be a gradual churning where the competent and honest get rewarded with the assets of the incompetent. Only time will tell if our system, a system that has produced more wealth for more people than any other in history, has been permanently broken.

In my opinion, Buffett disgraced himself in the financial crisis of 2008. He vocally and materially supported investment banks that were actively thieving from the government and their own clients. The banks' actions and duplicity were so far beyond the pale ethically that anyone who helped them deserves to be painted with the same brush of derision and scorn.

Buffett is an example, I'm sorry to say, of the old adage that power corrupts. Much like his own quip about not losing money, the saying about power corrupting has no exceptions. Buffett, from his exalted and powerful position, is apparently unable to recognize the justifiable contempt that any even moderately ethical person must hold for the investment bankers, his friends, and allies. This is entirely consistent with his discipline. Just as a samurai warrior must follow the wishes of his lord even to death, there is a high and destructive price to be paid for making money your purpose in life, even when you do it motivated by the discipline of the art rather than by greed.

That said, Buffett was characteristically prescient about the changes taking place in the financial world and he positioned himself to make money from those changes, however odious and immoral his partners.

We now may have switched to a system where

privilege and connection are more important than competence. Buffett too has switched. When he started out, he was an investor, but as he and the country and his company prospered, he has become more of an insider. When the financial sector collapsed during the 2008 financial crisis, Buffett profited from his connections and from government intervention to save the companies in which he had huge investments.

Has the economy evolved—devolved, really— into a system where business and, by extension, investing success is dependent on your proximity to the throne? This is the case in many other countries; usually these are developing countries and often they stay in a state of permanent poverty, with a few incredibly wealthy families who are close to the government and reap basically all of the excess value created by the country as a whole. I think it is too early to say, but one can't help but observe that Buffett, the shrewdest of all investors, has allied himself not with the competent but instead with the corrupt and well connected.

The real genius of Buffett, more than his investing savvy, may have been in his quick recognition of how the system worked. He saw in the aftermath of the crash of '29, the Great Depression, and World War II a certain system taking shape, a meritocracy of sorts, where good, competent businesses would prosper. This doesn't mean there was an absence of corruption or influence, just that the tilt was slightly in favor of competence over political connection so that given enough time, competence would win out. Buffett's actions now would lead one to believe that political connection is more valuable than competence.

This brings up a comparison between investing and speculating and between two financial titans: Buffett and George Soros.

Soros is a speculator. He got his start and made some of his most famous investment moves in the currency markets. Trading currency is pretty close to pure speculation.

When you buy a stock as an investment, at least as a value investor like Buffett, you are betting that because of its probable future stream of cash flows, the business you are buying is worth more than you are paying for it.

When you exchange one currency for another, you are betting on the value of one thing relative to another. There is, theoretically, an underlying fundamental basis for the strength or weakness of a currency, and that is the relative strength of the economy behind the currency. But currency values are heavily manipulated by the central banks of the governments that issue the currency and by the motivations of the investors and speculators who buy the currency and by the industries that must use different currencies as they carry out global trade and hedge against currency movements. So betting on currency is entirely dependent on betting on the future moves of other investors and governments. It is almost pure speculation, and George Soros is the best ever at this game.

Separating investing from speculating is like separating lust from love; they are entwined and the persuasive powers of one tend to color your judgment of the other. Buffett, in his ideology if not his actions during the financial crisis, is a value investor. Value investing has to do with finding undervalued assets that provide a sufficient return and seem capable of sustaining that return. The underlying assumption is that you are starting from a safe position and things may get better, but if they don't, you'll be okay.

Speculating has to do with determining what you think will have a higher price at some point in the future for reasons that may be unrelated to the thing's intrinsic properties or use. As near as I can tell, all investing strategies other than value investing are actually forms of speculation and not true investing.

Investing is easier but more tedious. Speculating is harder but makes faster money. Investing assumes that things will stay more or less the same and that a good thing now will be a good thing in the future. The old saying "The more things change, the more they stay the same" works well for investors. Making money investing is an incremental process. Investing requires long periods of patient waiting punctuated by short bursts of activity when prices become favorable, often following a crash or market crisis of some sort. Investing is probably more suited to the reptilian than the mammalian parts of our minds.

So, at first, it seems that Soros, a speculator, is very different from Buffett. And yet these days, in light of Buffett's willingness to collaborate with the investment banks and the government—to bet, essentially, on the way things will work out rather than the quality of the underlying business—Buffett looks a lot more like Soros, a master at predicting the movements of the government and the other market players. Perhaps we now live in a system where value investing is simply not possible because the system is too corrupt. I don't know.

In his early days, so I've read, Buffett holed up in his home office poring over investment journals, looking for stocks that were unloved by the market and consequently undervalued. He bought these stocks, cream rises, and he became rich. Buying undervalued stocks required him to put his money into investments other people thought were no good. It also required hours of reading stock tables and the financial statements of obscure companies.

Times have changed. Technology has made it possible to replace Buffett's laborious reading with a computerized stock screener that can sift through every available publicly traded equity and sort them for whatever criteria of value you choose. At first this seems to be a wonderful advancement that allows someone to bypass all of Buffett's squinting at musty financial reports. But making something easier and more efficient also allows more people to do it.

In his early years, Buffett was doing something few people had the discipline or courage to do. Now everyone with a computer can drift around the internet looking for undervalued stocks and buying them online. It is harder for an undervalued stock to remain hidden these days, and Buffett's astounding success and high profile have spawned legions of computer jockeys who think they are value investors, including me.

The sustained period of low interest rates following the 2008-09 financial crisis has swept up all financial asset prices and made bad hunting for value investors, but there may still be a place for Buffett-style value investing: the real world. In Buffett's early days as an investor, the stock market was considered to be a scary place. Years of fraud and manipulation, followed by the infamous crash of '29, had made regular people suspicious of the stock market. Many companies provided actual pensions instead of 401(k)s, so investing in the stock market was considered more akin to gambling than planning for the future.

These days the same could be said, and with good reason, for owning or being an investor in an actual small business. For someone to take money they will need for retirement and invest it in a small business would be considered much riskier by any financial advisor than investing in a mutual fund complete with its fees and near certainty of underperforming the market. But finding the right opportunity to own or invest in a small business seems to me to be quite analogous to Buffett in his early years. It requires lonely searching for a company that fits your criteria and then putting your money on the line for an investment generally considered to be too risky for sober-minded people.

After the crash of 2008-09, when it became apparent that the Fed would do everything it could to prop up asset prices, I concluded that there wasn't much role for an independent investor. A market where the prices go up or down depending on the movements of the central bank or other government actions and almost without regard to the quality of the company is a market that even more strongly favors the inside players, who always have access to earlier and better information.

My disillusionment, which has run now for 10 years, is a good illustration of my foolishness and the wisdom of Buffett. The wealth created by investing comes from two places. First, if the investment was purchased with a substantial margin of safety—say, after a stock market crash—and therefore had greater value than the price you paid, then eventually this value will be recognized by other investors and this will push the share price up. The second and perhaps most important creation of wealth occurs through the growth of the company, which is partly due to its organic growth, innovation, and improved productivity and partly due to the growth of the economy of which it is a part.

Buffett's wisdom—to buy good companies at cheap prices and do very little else—takes advantage of the wealth-creating features of investing and provides an excuse for ignoring the wealth-destroying tendency of worrying about the day-to-day price. The gyrations of the stock market, the intentional manipulation of the stock market by the Fed and its prolonged low interest rate policy, this is just background noise.

Investing in the stock market and ignoring the obvious manipulation by the government and the Fed has been a winning strategy for the past ten years because the economy chugged along. If the system overall is tilted in favor of innovation and good products and services instead of toward connection and privilege—and I think this is an open question—then time and the rules of investing espoused by Buffett are on your side. If this is not the case, then it is all speculation; but even under this scenario, betting on the power of the government to manipulate assets' prices in the favor of the ruling class was an obvious and winning bet.

When the financial crisis happened in 2008–09, it felt for a few months as though the system might fall apart and the basic financial infrastructure might fail, as it did in 1929. What if, for instance, you went to the ATM but could not withdraw your money because the complicated and intricate financial web had broken? The financial authorities, the secretary of the Treasury, and the Fed chairman, among others, waded into this mess and started taking action.

Their actions seemed a bit tentative and uncoordinated. Several proposals in a row that were supposed to stabilize the markets fell flat. In retrospect, the authorities were eventually bold and creative enough to save the system. There is a lot of debate about whether their actions should have done more to reform the system or correct its excesses, but I want to focus on a different point.

At the time, I remember thinking that if huge financial corporations were failing, if the system was so broken that these aggressive companies, run by extremely intelligent and highly motivated people, were floundering and unable to save themselves, then a bunch of government bureaucrats probably wouldn't be able to do much.

I was wrong on several levels and I remember exactly when I got a clue about my mistake. Our crisis spread to Europe by 2009, and a year or two into that crisis I read an article by George Soros in the *Financial Times*. He said in effect that government authorities had intervened with decisive and aggressive actions and that this would end the crisis. (It wouldn't, he said, necessarily end the underlying structural problems.) This was counter to my assumption but consistent with what seemed to have happened in our country.

The government is bigger, way bigger, and way more powerful than any company. The markets, investing, and speculation all take place under the umbrella of the government and its competence or lack thereof. Managed competently by public servants, the power of the government dwarfs the titans of industry and the so-called masters of the universe. Perhaps this is why the aforementioned titans often can't seem to resist the seductive call of politics and government power. These powers include taxation, regulation, monetary and fiscal policy, the power to confiscate assets or save companies, to print money, and make war. When push comes to shove, the CEOs of huge corporations—men usually, who often make hundreds of times as much money as the president or the Fed chairman and who like to deride the government as incompetent and weak—come hat-in-hand begging for help from Uncle Sam.

This is a two-edged sword. Managed incompetently, as it was after the crash of 1929, the government creates a void that is filled by chaos and deprivation. Managed competently, as our government was in the period leading up to and for quite some time after World War II, it creates vast wealth.

Some final, random thoughts on investing:

When the stock market crashes, it doesn't really crash; it goes down fast but over a period of months. There is plenty of time to get out as long as you are willing to get out below the peak, which no one usually is, at least paradoxically, when they are still close to the peak.

Money changes the way you think. Notice how much easier it is to remember money owed to you than money you owe to someone else. There are built-in biases at work in our brains and these biases associate themselves with certain tendencies and feelings, so your thinking about money gets wrapped into all sorts of unexpected corners of your psyche. For this reason, playing with a mock investment portfolio is a fun exercise but is very different from actually investing.

The eccentric theory of market success. Warren Buffett is seemingly upfront about his investing principles, and they are a very simple, if difficult to follow, set of rules.

George Soros has his theory of reflexivity, which is very different from Buffett's approach.

Ray Dalio, who started and ran the world's biggest hedge fund, has his own somewhat peculiar mechanism for understanding the economy and markets.

Jeremy Grantham, who also started and ran a big and successful investment fund, also works within a framework, a description he has mostly created.

Charles Koch runs a huge and very successful company that is, of late, largely a financial and trading company, and he runs it according to his own peculiar philosophy.

What you can't help wondering, after reading descriptions of these different theories and observing their variance from each other, is whether developing a theory that makes sense to you is the most critical tool for investing success. Maybe there is no right theory. Perhaps the market is too complicated or too continually evolving to have any consistent explanation and the best anyone can hope for is a theory that makes sense to them.

All of these incredibly successful men have had their own theories, which they have modified and refined over the years. The only consistency between them and their theories is the existence of an idiosyncratic theory and the discipline to keep improving and testing it.

Thanks to the internet, it is possible to give yourself an excellent self-education about investing. Here is where I would start:

1- Carol Loomis's two articles interviewing Buffett for *Fortune* magazine, 11/22/1999 and 12/10/2001
2- Buffett's annual letter to shareholders in the Berkshire Hathaway annual report, especially the early years
3- Jeremy Grantham's quarterly letters at GMO
4- John Hussman also runs an investment fund and for years wrote weekly letters, which, being weekly, are somewhat repetitive and weaker than my other recommendations but still very worthwhile.

41- Regrets

The $15 come-along

In 1989, lying on a blanket at the Santa Fe Flea Market, I saw a come-along hand winch for sale for $15. It was superior to any other come-alongs I had ever seen, and I knew because in my adolescence I'd used and broken quite a few cheap come-alongs pulling rocks and logs and stuck tractors. This one had solid, cast-iron gears, a sturdy frame, a rugged ratchet mechanism, and a simple socket where you could insert a pipe for a handle.

I didn't buy it because $15, while a great price for such a well-made tool, was too much money to spend on something I didn't need right then. I regretted that choice almost immediately and the regret continued for a couple decades until I found another, identical come-along, only the second of that type I've ever seen, at a moving sale and purchased it—for $15.

That's the thing about regrets; we don't really know how time and life work. Is it like a circular bus route, and if you miss the bus then you hope to catch a later bus, like I did with the come-along? Or is it in one direction, so the little woodstove Beth Ann and I saw years ago at a yard sale for $25 and didn't buy because $25 was too much to spend on something we didn't need then will never come back around again?

If we'd bought the woodstove, which had a water jacket so you could use it both for heating your cabin and also heating your hot water, perhaps instead of converting a welding shop into a house, we might have built a little cabin in the woods, taken outdoor showers with the mosquitoes under the stars, and had entirely different lives. Or maybe it would have had no effect whatsoever and would simply be accumulating rust in the side yard.

I'm inclined to believe that the possibilities are so numerous, and therefore the decisions are so numerous, that eventually you would end up in more or less the same place even if you could go back and insert or remove a handful of decisions. But no one can tell.

To live a life without regrets means embracing the idea that most learning comes from mistakes. It is a comforting and sensible idea, which I entirely believe. But does this mean that if you have no regrets, you would make all the same decisions again, in which case you apparently didn't learn from your mistakes? I'm fairly certain there are some things I'd do differently if I had them to do over and that I'd be a damn fool not to feel this way.

So here are a couple things I would do differently given the chance to do it over:

Once, I said to a friend that I wished I'd taken bigger financial risks when I was younger. He said that he had taken big risks when he was young and he'd bankrupted a couple of businesses, which left him with debts he was still trying to repay. He wished he'd been more cautious.

When I was building furniture, I generally didn't invest in a new tool unless I needed it for a job and was pretty sure it would pay for itself over the course of the job. That's pretty typical behavior in the building trades, where people, whatever their political inclinations, tend to be conservative in their behavior.

But I regret that now. I think I was too cautious and I probably would have been more successful and had more fun with furniture if I'd taken bigger risks. I played it safe, got frustrated and sick of furniture, and eventually got into the hydroelectric business, where the nature of the business means bigger chunks of money and more risk.

I've thought about this over the years—wondered if I took the kind of financial chances with furniture that I've taken of necessity with the hydro business how it would have worked out. There is no way to know and I don't care, except I'd like to know what the lesson is.

For me, the lesson seems to be take bigger risks than you are comfortable with, but for my friend, it seems to be the opposite. I think the answer is that you need to play against type a little bit. He is probably a little too optimistic by nature and I am a little pessimistic. We all have certain predispositions. These are, by definition, comfort zones, but they are not necessarily a reflection of your abilities. I think now that it is probably a good idea observe your predispositions and experiment with acting against type.

In high school, my Modern European History teacher had us read *Thus Spoke Zarathustra.* We had one girl in our class who seemed to understand it. Nietzsche made absolutely no sense to me, and since our teacher had explained to us that it was an experiment to see how we would do reading something that difficult, I didn't try very hard.

In my senior year of college we read quite a bit of Nietzsche. By then I'd heard that Nietzsche's philosophy was used by the Nazis as justification for their persecution of the Jews, and so, while I did most of the readings, once again I had an excuse for not trying that hard to understand what I was reading.

I don't regret not understanding Kant and Hegel because I tried and they just didn't make much sense to me, but things happen in life and pieces of Nietzsche come back to me and I think to myself, "I wonder if that's what he was talking about." I wish I had paid more attention back when I was in a class full of other fresh young minds with a couple of professors leading a seminar. The bit about Nietzsche and the Nazis was mostly wrong and not his fault anyway. It is foolish to be prejudiced against ideas without understanding them.

And, yes, I really regret not buying the little woodstove with the water jacket, even though we still don't have a use for it.

42- The Underlying Algorithm

My friend Rob Squire told me that there were only two questions he wanted answered in his lifetime: *Is there a God?* and *Do we have free will?* I was already aware of these two questions, but in my mind they were piled together with lots of other problems I wanted answered, such as, *Why can't I stop the bandsaw mill from making a wavy cut?* and *In a fractional reserve banking system, do banks really create money out of thin air?*

Then I bumped into a research source, done years ago, that seemed to prove what we think of as making a decision is actually the conscious confirmation of a "choice" made a fraction of a second earlier and in a deeper part of our brain. And the experiment seemed to be supported by more recent experiments observing the electrical signals in a person's brain as they made a decision. This implied that instead of free will, we are just consciousness along for the ride on an animal, which, when you observe the world, does seem to be pretty much the case.

I found this depressing and confusing but pushed the question away and went on with my life. Instead of being able to forget about it, however, the idea that decisions are made on some level below our consciousness started to be the way I saw the world. The more I looked for ways to refute this possibility, the more validation I uncovered. In fact, this very realization seemed to be verification of exactly what I feared.

My conscious brain, either through lack of information or interest, or maybe because of fear, had dismissed this problem as not worth pursuing, and yet on some level it was occupying my thought process and reappearing in progressively more believable examples in my thoughts. Wasn't this proof that the choice of what to think about and which problems to contemplate was taking place outside of my conscious brain, which had decided to shelve this question? And moreover, wherever this hierarchy of choice existed, clearly my conscious choice wasn't winning.

I'm not trying to resolve the free-will question. My goal is simply to explain how I now see our decision-making process and to justify this explanation by showing how it explains things that formerly seemed contradictory or inexplicable.

We seem to be conscious creatures able to articulate our desires, and we attempt to achieve them with choices, some of which we perceive ourselves to have made based on conscious and logical reasoning. But the reality of human existence is that all of us repeatedly make the same mistakes, however illogical, especially in complicated areas like human interactions. We all also experience the logical function being subservient to some other motivation, a contest we resolve by a technique called rationalization, which means we create a fake logical explanation to justify an illogical action we "want" to take. And in many cases we admit that something is wrong, counterproductive, or unhealthy, yet we do it anyway. Hmmm. So how and where is the "choice" really being made?

Is the logical overlay there simply to provide a rubber stamp of approval to whatever algorithm exists deep in our brains and actually makes decisions? As though a Canada goose, when it feels the instinctive urge to fly south, would, if it had a human consciousness/logical overlay, say to itself, "It's time to go south because the weather is getting cold."

Whatever underlying decision process exists, in us or a Canada goose, millions of years of evolution have honed it to make choices that are in our best interests; otherwise, we would be extinct. But for humans living in the relatively recent complexity of modern civilization, often what works well and the underlying algorithm are not in accordance.

It is also confusing because the underlying algorithm is clearly not static, but even in geese it is a learning algorithm. These days, Canada geese have learned to overwinter in northern places they used to bypass because now there is ample food.

I present this idea not as a revelation or discovery but as a statement of the obvious. The idea that there is an underlying thought process is embedded in many figures of speech. "Follow your gut instinct" or "Sleep on it" or even the term "the subconscious"—all of these are references to what I now think of as the underlying algorithm.

When you start looking at yourself and the world this way, troubling patterns make more sense. We all know that certain patterns of negative behavior get replicated generation after generation; victim becoming victimizer in a cycle that is as nonsensical as it is hard to break. What is this but the underlying algorithm being encoded to produce behavior that the conscious mind logically and emotionally abhors but is unable to change?

Rote learning has never been my strength and so I welcome the current educational philosophies that encourage understanding rather than memorization and repetition. And yet, I have to admit that when I have had to do something repetitive, during the process of that monotony I have come to greater understanding. This perplexing reality makes more sense if I assume the real mechanism of understanding is not the conscious, logical brain open to clear explanation but rather some more concealed thought process whose doors to understanding do not open automatically just because a proposition makes logical sense but instead has other, less obvious requirements.

What is the statement "Power corrupts" but an epithet exposing the reality that the underlying algorithm learns and changes slowly over time, adapting to new circumstances, until the formerly incorruptible engage in actions that seem blatantly dishonest to the rest of us and would have seemed dishonest to their former selves.

Our conscious, logical brains interact with and in some ways affect this underlying algorithm, but the exact mechanism is not obvious; otherwise, it would be simple to say to yourself that you wanted to change your behavior and have it happen. And most of the time all aspects of our brain seem to work seamlessly together, like the Canada goose "deciding" to fly south. But the peculiarities, the contradictions, and inexplicable abilities, that's where this idea makes sense to me.

For instance, how is it possible that as you are running, you automatically start adjusting your steps to coordinate the right positioning for taking the stairs? Or take the ability to look at a pile of food remaining in a serving dish and pick the smallest container it will fit into. Or the ability to look at a piece of firewood that is slightly too long for the woodstove and instinctively understand that it will fit if it is twisted and angled just so. These are complicated mathematical, volumetric, and geometric calculations that take place almost instantaneously and without conscious or logical effort. Where are these calculations performed if not by some underlying algorithm? And if it is able to solve these problems with such ease, what other decisions is it making?

You always know when a gift has been successful rather than thoughtful or a tool is useful rather than pretty because the gift or tool shows up in regular circulation rather than being put away in a drawer. So it has been for me with the idea of an underlying algorithm. I find that without meaning for it to happen, this idea has gradually come to be the way I understand my mind to operate. Now I struggle less hard for a logical explanation and pay extra attention to the part of my brain that seems to produce answers and ideas on its own schedule and with its own somewhat mysterious mechanism. When confronted with any task involving some problem-solving, I tackle the problem for a while and then put it away. Giving yourself time to mull over a problem is hardly an innovation in thought. The difference is that now I welcome this step as part of the deeper thought process rather than seeing it as an irritating hinderance.

FOUR

43- The Inner African

One of these days I will get around to having a genetic profile and I will be pleasantly surprised if I have some African genes or maybe Native American or, who knows? some Asian blood, since the Mongols pillaged deeply into Europe. But in the end, we are all Africans.

In the summer, I have a tan line where the lighter skin of my palm meets the darker, tanned skin on the back of my hand. This distinction is more obvious in darker-skinned people, and after a long, sun-starved winter in Vermont it becomes almost invisible on my pale skin. But in the summer it reappears on my hand, and when I look at the curve between my thumb and forefinger, I think of it as the inner African, the reminder that we are all descended from Africa and possibly from the same woman.

The geneticists think that modern humans are about 200,000 years old. At 25 years to a generation, 200,000 years is 8,000 generations. Eight thousand is not an unconquerable number. Homer's *Iliad* is approximately 15,000 lines long, and before it was written down it was sustained orally. In other words, one person could theoretically have in their memory a one-line-per-generation history of modern humans all the way back to this one African woman, the so-called mitochondrial Eve, from whom we all may be descended.

The past often seems very distant, but while the past is irretrievable, it really isn't that long ago. The birth of Jesus was 2,000 years, or 80 generations, ago. Given a few days and some good stories to help keep everything straight, you could memorize your genealogy back to the time of Jesus's birth. For whatever reason and for good or ill, we don't keep much memory or family stories beyond a few generations. But that is not to say that the past is not with us. The familial habits, the cultural habits, are inculcated even if the specific personal stories are not.

Eight thousand generations is not a hugely long period of time, genetically speaking. Those seemingly ancient but really not-too-distant cousins roaming around and eventually out of Africa were pretty similar to us. This means all, or at least most, of our emotional and intellectual complexity was there. We were sitting around the campfire in those prehistoric times. How many generations does a habit last? The soft murmur of a woman's laughter, the curiosity on a young boy's face, hurt feelings, love—this was all there tens of thousands of years ago. This creature, us, was there squatting on his haunches, staring into the flames, contemplating, struggling, watching the stars, already wondering how and why.

Update, October 2016:
Thank you, kids, for a fascinating birthday present.
British and Irish 54.8%
French and German 23.2%
Scandinavian 3.2%
Broadly Northwestern European 13.7%
Spanish and Portuguese 4.1%
Eastern European .5%
Neanderthal variants 312

That's a lot of Neanderthal (although Beth Ann said she'd known for years). It's more Neanderthal than 94 percent of the other people tested by 23andMe.

Every time I check in with 23andMe the percentages they are assigning to different groups have changed. For a while they thought I was .1% Siberian and before that .1% Yakut and now those numbers have disappeared.

I do wish I knew more about that possible Siberian relative. By family lore, from the brief family history Granny wrote for me:

Perhaps I've drifted away from good stories, but here's one about Mother's mother. She was a two-year-old child, staying with her parents in a hotel in Virginia, when her parents died suddenly from some illness. There were two old ladies, sisters, staying at the hotel, and they simply took the little girl. You couldn't do that nowadays. So, of course, no one knows who she was or even what nationality. Her parents spoke French and signed the name "Gaston" on the hotel register, but Mother, perhaps embellishing, as I do, said that she may have been Russian. Upper-class Russians at the time spoke French as much as Russian, and she had Oriental eyes; Jenny has those eyes. Mother said "Gaston" is like Smith; a French person puts that down if he doesn't want to give his real name. She grew up to be very beautiful, with a lovely singing voice, but my father said she was cold and spoilt.

44- Some Key Intellectual Achievements

I had the benefit of a classical education. Starting at age 20, and for four years, the best and most sophisticated thoughts Western human beings have ever created in primary texts (not a textbook but the original works, fresh from the butcher, so to speak) were thrown in front of my naive, vulnerable, and relatively uneducated mind. I did my best with it, especially in the first couple of years. Here, in the hope of encouraging you to investigate these books yourselves, I want to describe the ideas that were a revelation when I learned them and have stayed fresh and beautiful all these years since.

Euclidean Geometry

I can't remember at which grade level I first encountered algebra—eighth or ninth, probably. I do remember that the teacher was one of those uninspired souls who should have been fired as an act of public safety to protect the minds of hundreds of young people from being deadened and turned against math. I suspect she clung on for years, gradually working her way up the seniority and wage scale until her job security was unassailable and her irredeemable teaching style had been inflicted on multiple generations. After algebra, I signed off on math as being a boring subject that I wasn't any good at.

Unlike music, where I have no natural talent, I probably could have been a passable mathematician, with the right instruction. Math is an incremental subject where a little slippage early on makes understanding what comes later almost impossible. So, knowing that I was starting way behind where I should have been, I approached my freshman college math class with a bit of trepidation.

At St. John's College, freshman math starts with geometry in the form of Euclid's *Elements*, written roughly 2,400 years ago. Euclid starts by defining a point as that which has no part, then he gives more definitions and then geometric proofs, which follow first from the definitions and then build on each other.

Here's the thing: Euclid's geometry is beautiful. I say this as a person predisposed to dislike math. If you want to see the beauty of the human mind solving a problem, Euclid can show you like no one else. Abe Lincoln, when he was a lawyer, studied Euclid because he thought it would make him better at reasoning and logic.

Maybe other animals actually use language, create art, and have complicated emotions, who knows? But no other animal sits down with a slate, a piece of chalk, and a handful of definitions and 40 or 50 exercises later is proving that "[i]f a straight line be cut at random, the square on the whole is equal to the squares on the segments and twice the rectangle contained by the segments" (Book II, proof four).

You can't completely appreciate what we are as creatures until you work your way through a book or two of Euclid's *Elements*. (Lincoln supposedly memorized most of the first six books.) This is the beautiful intellectual side of the human mind, polished and shining and waiting for you in Euclid's *Elements*. All you need in order to open this window into your heritage is the ability to accept that a point is that which has no part, that a line is breadthless length, and so on. Euclid builds from there. History is full of examples of the bestial side of human nature, horrible errors in judgment, and serial tragedies we've perpetrated on each other, so it is nice to have things to make you feel proud to be human.

It turns out that Euclid was wrong about some things. Space is curved, parallel lines converge, but none of this affects in the least the beauty of Euclid's *Elements*. So, sometime, preferably with a good friend, set aside an hour a day for a few weeks and work through some of the first proofs.

The Iliad

I read the *Iliad* in high school and I didn't really get it. I read the *Odyssey* too, and since the *Odyssey* is a much better story, I liked it better. I read them both again in college and felt the same way. But now I'm a middle-aged man and I think of the *Iliad* more often.

The *Iliad* is about war. It's about a war men fought hand to hand with spears and occasionally rocks. A war where the victor of a battle often knew his adversary personally and was looking into the eyes of the vanquished as he killed him. A war where the courage of one man could turn a battle.

When a man is killed in the *Iliad*, you get graphic details—the spear pierces his liver and the green bile runs down the spear shaft. It is a war with all of the standard features of war—treachery, bravery, love and valor, misunderstandings, and all carried on at an individual level.

I've never been to war and so, like most people, I learn about it from the sidelines. Today, wars are waged from a distance with guns and planes, but underneath there are people killing other people. In one form or another, every time someone is killed, bile is running down the spear shaft. It is harder to see this these days because the technology of war has changed. But the people are still the same. So while the technology has separated us from action, the personal consequences are still there, and this is where the *Iliad* gives you a window no modern description can give.

The Bible

There are two important reasons to read the Bible. One is to gather whatever bits of interesting information and wisdom you can collect from this amazing book. A second and related reason is that the Bible has been, for people descended through Western civilization, the single most influential source for ideas about justice, the meaning of life, and suffering.

At St. John's, I encountered the Bible for the first time in any significant way and read it as literature. I also encountered love in the form of Aliza, who was Jewish. William Faulkner called the Bible a fairy tale with which the ancient Hebrews conquered the Western world, and you could say that this was true for me personally in the being of Aliza.

The Bible is a family history. Imagine, for a moment, that you have an extended family, a tribe, and you want them to remember their history—who married whom and what kids they had and so on. And because science and the scientific method are unknown concepts, you also want to record your best explanation of how things work—metaphysical things, spiritual things, and also practical things. And because this is a big project and it goes on for a while, different people get involved and different theories get recorded and historical events get recorded from different points of view. That's the Bible, and the authors did an amazingly good job.

The family history stories are more lurid than any soap opera. Most people try to sanitize their family history and present an artificial version of events diminishing the evils and highlighting the virtues. As a result, their stories are predictable, boring, and without lasting importance. Not the Bible. Beheadings, fratricide, betrayals, talking animals, plenty of old-fashioned lies, and homicides—and that's just the first couple of books. And while these stories were compelling for me, I could see that for my girlfriend Aliza, they were equally compelling but more personal. This was a chain of stories handed down over 3,000 years in a direct line from her relatives to her.

We humans love stories, and when they are good they also seem true. It is here on the rather broad knife-edge of truth that I think it is easy to get confused about the Bible.

God didn't create the world in six days. The creation story in the book of Genesis is full of incorrect facts, but it is even more full of good stories. And a good story is truthful, meaning that it accurately describes the way things work, even if it gets some of the facts incorrect.

Imagine a wise old person sitting in a cafe in some modern city and talking to a grandchild of 13 or 14 who is just beginning to realize how fucked up the world is and that many adults are talking about things they don't understand and posturing to cover their ignorance. The kid wants to know how things got this way.

This old person wants an explanation that contains the truth about the human condition. He or she can do no better than the Garden of Eden story. There was no serpent, no tree of knowledge, no Adam and Eve; the facts are not true, but the story is still as truthful an account of the probably unique human condition of self-awareness as one can conjure.

The Old Testament of the Bible, which comprises the bulk of the content we commonly refer to as the Bible, contains everything from historical narrative to skepticism and poetry and tedious dietary rules. It reads like what it is, an amalgamation of stories assembled over generations. Inasmuch as it defines a religion, it is a primitive, personal, tribal-based religion. God plays a role as the most powerful and mysterious actor on a human stage where willful people can conflict with Him.

Then you get to the New Testament. The Gospels of Matthew, Mark, Luke, and John are four of the many narratives about the life of Jesus. These four, for whatever reason, got combined into the modern Bible, while other, somewhat contradictory but nonetheless contemporaneous accounts were excluded. Even 2,000 years later, you can feel the vibrancy of Jesus's ideas expressed by the authors of these stories.

Jesus's interpretation of his religion, the Hebrew religion described in the Old Testament, broadened it into an inclusive and forgiving religion rather than a limited and exclusive religion. The power of seeing the world this way, as a place where imperfect people could still be close to God, is a much more optimistic view of the world than the religion of the Old Testament.

These two religions—the old Hebrew religion that has transformed into modern Judaism, and the teaching of the Hebrew religion by Jesus, which has become Christianity—are written deeply into the history of modern America.

The biblical Hebrew Old Testament religion (which has to be distinguished from modern Judaism) is a tribal religion. Loyalties are prized, betrayals are punished, justice is praised when it is swift and severe. These are frontier values, necessary maybe, for a small group of people living a relatively hostile existence with the other tribes in the wilderness. The Old Testament values seem, to my reading anyway, to have been more appealing than Christian values to American pioneers.

The Hebrew religion evolved into the Jewish religion, which has as its mainstay its relationship to the first five books of the Old Testament. The meaning of these books has been constantly debated and commented on for several millennia, shaping the religion and culture.

In a remarkable analog, our founding document, the Constitution, has been debated and commented on since the beginning of the country, and this debate, which is carried on primarily through the Supreme Court decisions, literally shapes our culture. Our founders had the wisdom to remove God and all decisions about God from this debate, but inasmuch as discussion in both the Talmud and the Supreme Court is about justice, the parallel is almost perfect.

If the European immigrants, transplanted to a wilderness already peopled by other tribes, found themselves attracted to the harsh, exclusive justice of the Old Testament, the Africans, transported and enslaved here against their will, seemed to grasp the power of Jesus's teaching. Forgiveness, redemption, humility, inclusion, acceptance of imperfection—these Christian qualities seem to have been better understood by the slaves and their descendants than by the European settlers.

Everything after the Gospels, as near as I could understand, was written by priests and hangers-on and reads this way, without the power of the Gospels. Thomas Jefferson created a personal account of Jesus's life in which he edited the

Gospels, removing, as I have read that he put it, "the diamonds from the dung," meaning that he extracted the supernatural and maintained the central tenets of Christianity as he saw them.

Jefferson's model is a good approach to the whole Bible. Find the pieces that make sense to you and ignore the crazy stuff.

Early Chemists

For me, physics is a somewhat intuitive science, at least on its more elementary levels. Biology is based on observing the living world and seems also very approachable. But chemistry never made much sense to me. At St. John's College, we read the works of many pioneering scientists, but the chemists—Lavoisier and particularly Mendeleev, who created the periodic table—astounded me with their brilliance. I didn't and don't understand their work. What they did, figuring out the elements and how they combined with each other, this to me was like magic.

If I had lived in the 18th or 19th century and someone gave me a physics or biology question, I almost certainly wouldn't have gotten the right answer, but at least I would have been able to come up with some ideas for how to start looking and experimenting. With chemistry, I wouldn't have even known where to begin, and so I stand in awe of their accomplishments. It is well worth your time to read a little about the early chemists and understand the monumental intellectual achievements they made.

Newton and Darwin and Einstein

At St. John's, we had to read parts of Newton's *Principia,* where he creates laws of motion and gravitation. It is extraordinary to be able to read the words written by a man who forever changed the world. Here is a person altering all of human thought. He puts words on a page knowing full well that he is more right in his description of the world than anyone who has come before him and the world of human thought can never be the same after what he has written.

The same is true of Darwin. He seemed to me a gentler man, less arrogant than Newton but equally cataclysmic in his thoughts. Pause and consider what it is like to have thoughts, put pen to paper, and know with reasonable certainty that you are invalidating 50 centuries of creation myths. This has happened only a handful of times in human history. Einstein's theory of relativity is another example.

So, sometime, it is worth reading a little of their work to get a sense of what it looks like when one person changes everything. It is also worth understanding, in at least a basic sort of way, their theories, but there are easier ways to understand the theory of relativity than by reading it from Einstein.

There was history before Darwin. History after Darwin was changed by him. There was history before and after Jesus as well, and we in the Western world use his supposed birth date as a historical marking point. It is a perfectly adequate point to choose. Jesus's thinking and speaking created a new religion, and human history has been altered by his thoughts. But there is no way Jesus could have known at the time whether his ideas would sweep over the world or flicker out. On the other hand, there is no way Darwin or Newton or Einstein could not have known that they were changing everything. The consequences of their thoughts were unpredictable, but they must have had near certainty that they were erasing all previous thinking with a better theory and, of course, in Einstein's case, mostly eclipsing Newton. So for the purpose of dividing human history into before and after, we could just as well have chosen Newton or Darwin or Einstein.

Shakespeare

Like most high school students, I was compelled to force my way through one or two of Shakespeare's plays. They made a little sense to me, but not much. Occasionally, a few lines would stand out because of an interesting twist of phrase, but I couldn't really understand it well enough to follow the plot. Even a play like *Romeo and Juliet*, where I knew the plot before I started reading, made little sense to me.

In college, most of the Shakespeare we read was assigned for seminars where we discussed the plays. But in language class, probably as a break from trying to learn ancient Greek, we also read a little Shakespeare and we had to read it out loud. I'm not shy about talking in public but I'm a poor reader so, to prepare, I read the assignment multiple times before class.

The more times I read a selection, the more sense it made. The more sense it made, the more beautiful it seemed, and the whole play gradually took shape and made sense one beautiful little piece at a time.

I'm a person who grasps concepts better than details, but rote learning, in math or Shakespeare, has some use. When you do something repeatedly, even if you feel you are no longer paying attention, your brain is still engaged and looking for way to make connections and create understanding. I thought I was just rehearsing the lines so I wouldn't flub them when I had to read out loud, but actually I was also learning what they meant.

This sounds like a trite insight, but it is amazing how often people read something once and either think they understand it all or, on the other hand, are incapable of understanding it, when all they need to do is read it again and again.

Adam Smith and Karl Marx

You could easily go through your whole life, and even through a four-year college education, without ever reading Adam Smith or Karl Marx. Maybe that wouldn't be an entirely bad thing. At St. John's College we had to push our way through a lot of Adam Smith's *The Wealth of Nations* and also a lot of Karl Marx's *Capital,* and as you might expect, this can be somniferous reading.

We live in a world where economic ideas have been simplified to a sort of religious purity. Free markets are good, and state-controlled economies are bad. History has validated this point in a simplified sort of way with the collapse of the Soviet Union and the conversion of the Chinese communists to some indescribable form of capitalism.

What's a shame to miss, I think, is the humanity and nuance Smith and Marx had. Free markets don't exist. They never have and never will. All markets are to some extent manipulated, regulated, and controlled. You wouldn't know this when you listen to modern discourse on the subject because a belief in free markets has become akin to a religious belief in the United States, and religious believers always try to outdo each other's piety by professing to be purer than their competitors. But even there, in the founding principles, Adam Smith made some provision for regulation.

Likewise, you would never know from anything you could hear in popular conversation that Karl Marx, despite being the father of communism, which was an unrealistic idea from the beginning, was a lifelong student of capitalism who understood capitalism better than anyone else in his time. He was a harsh critic of capitalism who wrongly (so far) predicted that it would self-destruct.

So we live in a world where the ridiculous principle of a perfectly free market is the ideal that most people think we should be striving for even though it cannot exist in reality and did not exist in a pure form, even for Adam Smith. And we heap disdain and scorn on Marx, whose chief contribution was a thoughtful understanding and criticism of capitalism.

45- Basketball and Prejudice

In my life, racism has been so absent as to make it seem almost ludicrous to comment on it. And yet, as an American, the legacy of institutionalized racism is so prevalent in every aspect of our lives, the ongoing examples of racism are so many, and the prejudice and discrimination against women, gays, transgenders, Muslims, Mexicans, anyone with dark skin are so universal in our culture that everyone needs to think about it pretty much all the time.

This is the way it seems to me. Everybody is a racist. Categorizing people into groups based on the most superficial observations seems to be an inevitable part of human thought. Judging and valuing these groups follows almost immediately. What matters is how you work to overcome this tendency, which is a hard task to have any success at, especially if you deny the tendency in the first place.

I expressed these ideas to my father and he informed me that I was making the fundamental error of confusing prejudice and racism.

My father, 25 years my senior and from Alabama, grew up in a society with many dark-skinned people but so racially segregated that a light-skinned, lower-middle-class boy like Bill almost never interacted with other races. The racism was so overt that in the neighboring—and, apparently, all white—Franklin County, he remembers billboards that read "Nigger, don't let the sun set on your head in Franklin County."

When he started living in Vermont, because he had (in addition to his mumble) a strong Southern accent he seemed to bring out racial slurs from a surprising number of people who assumed wrongly that they had found a sympathetic ear.

Because I grew up in Vermont, one of the most ethnically and racially homogenous states in the country, the racism I experienced in my childhood was casual rather than institutional.

Several times in conversation, old-timers used the phrase "Jew me down" to explain how someone had tried hard to get a better price from them. I got the meaning but misunderstood the phrase and thought they were saying, "Chew me down." Usually this comment came out in the course of a long story about horses and different deals the men had done in the past, and since these old guys mumbled and often chewed tobacco and were missing teeth, it was difficult to understand their words and easy to imagine chewing as part of the story. It wasn't until I had heard the same phrase a number of times that I realized what they were actually saying. There it was—not the organized racism my father grew up in, just the general tendency to demean and degrade the "other" group.

Sometime in the late '80s, on a road trip returning home to New England after spring semester of college in Santa Fe, my girlfriend Aliza and I aimed for the northern route up through Colorado. We were on back roads to the west of the Front Range when we passed a pickup truck parked on the shoulder and a man trying to change a flat tire. We stopped to see if he needed help.

It has been many years and I don't remember whether he signaled us or whether something about his situation alerted us to the fact that it was slightly more than a simple tire change. What I do remember very clearly is a sense of apprehension. A guy and a girl stopping to help a stranded motorist has been the setup for more than one slasher movie. It was a lonely piece of road, which was both more reason to stop and more reason to keep going.

He turned out to be a cheerful, inventive sort who had a flat tire and no jack and so was doing his best to contrive a way to get the tire of the truck off the ground so he could change it. The recognition that he was just a guy with a flat tire and not an axe murderer/rapist came with a sense of relief.

Our jack was a little short for his truck axle, but we improvised by balancing the jack on stones and a couple pieces wood. With the truck up and the flat tire removed, we gingerly placed the spare tire on the hub and tightened a couple of lug nuts finger tight.

At this point it wouldn't have mattered much if the truck fell off the precarious jack, and we all straightened up with a sense of accomplishment and satisfaction. Aliza and I grinned at each other. Wasn't the world a great place, full of people helping each other, and weren't we swell for stopping to help this guy.

The guy looked at the jack and laughed, "Where I come from, we call that nigger riggin'," he said.

He didn't seem like a hate-filled guy. Was he a racist? Just some dude with bad taste? Was he feeling a little in our debt and so he reached out for that universal social salve, putting down someone outside the group? Does what he said represent prejudice or racism? Does it matter to draw that distinction?

Even on the telephone I try to figure out where a person is from based on their speech. Is this racism, nationalism, regionalism, prejudice, idle curiosity?

Human beings have discriminating minds. Synonyms for discriminating include discerning, insightful, keen, perspicacious—all characteristics generally considered to be admirable and that relate to our ability to divide and categorize things.

People like to say, to show their enlightenment, that they are color-blind. No one is color-blind to race in my experience. Our discriminating minds immediately notice racial features, gender, age, clothes, and stature.

Some of the most closed-minded people I have ever met professed to be color-blind. Sure, they had camouflaged, at least from acknowledging it to themselves, assumptions based on skin color and therefore they assumed they were pure and above fault. This left them blind to the most stunning sorts of prejudice in which they dismissed whole groups of people as being inferior based on where they lived or what type of music or food or politics they liked or how much education they had.

What I notice in myself is that I come at every new encounter with prejudice. It is not overt or intentional. I usually notice this in the small, undefined sense of discomfort that can only be resolved by examining your feelings and discovering you are slightly perturbed because something is not the way you expected it to be. When that something is a person, you have to ask yourself why you expected that person to be any particular way. The answer is because you assumed, based on something—skin color, clothes, height, gender, accent, whatever—that the person would be a certain way and then they proved to be different.

My conclusions from recognizing this thought pattern were two. First, we don't come at any situation completely color-blind. Instead, all of our past experiences combine as our minds try to organize and understand the information from the new experience. Second, if this equates to racism, then everyone is a racist without even knowing it, which means that the only defense against this kind of thinking is to commit to a continual effort of open-mindedness, just as you might commit to regular exercise or a healthy diet.

In other words, assuming, wanting, or declaring yourself to be, for instance, color-blind to race, while a presumably laudable intention, like saying that you are going to exercise, is actually valuable only if you do it. It is the effort that counts, and the effort is one of constantly overcoming your inevitable prejudices rather than a choice to declare that you want to be prejudice free.

Racism, according to my father, is the belief that another group is inferior, often considered to be not quite human, purely on the basis of a conviction about that group, usually designated by skin color and without any knowledge of individuals in the group.

Prejudice, to my father, is the set of preconceived biases that you bring to your interactions with other people. Those biases influence your thinking about them. He sees this as different than racism, and to me it looks like the foundation of racism.

Here's what I'm pretty certain of: The history of Europeans exploring the Americas begins with the genocide of the Native Americans, and this is followed quickly by the enslavement of Africans. The individuals in both of these groups continue to live, on average in this country, in states of economic deprivation and persecution relative to the rest of Americans.

The most recent example of mass persecution of the Jews, the Holocaust, is generally understood, for a person of Western tradition, as the greatest example of evil and moral failure in history.

If history doesn't repeat itself with respect to persecution of the Jews, then we will have entered a new and unprecedented period of human history.

When the most heinous of human actions look as though they are either continuing in some form or are likely to be repeated at some point, it is a good idea to at least have them and their causes on your mind and not hidden away from your thoughts by some delusion or wishful thinking.

Let me give an example of the subtle workings of our unexamined presumptions. No one would dispute that African American players are, proportional to the overall population (about 11 percent), heavily overrepresented on professional basketball teams. This observation itself is slightly taboo since it inevitably brings up all sorts of (racist) questions about whether or not African Americans are innately more athletic.

But in the beginning of the 20th century,

professional basketball was dominated by another ethnic group, Jews. At the time—a time when it was assumed by most people that different races had markedly different abilities—it was thought that Jewish players had certain inherited qualities that predisposed them to be good at basketball.

If the dominance in basketball by Jewish players seems startling and hard for you to believe, as it was at first for me, then you have exposed prejudice in yourself. After all, there is no scientific reason to think that any one group is by genetics and evolution more suited to basketball.

What you should really observe is that when a group excels at athletics, they are excelling in an area, maybe one of the few areas in the culture, where measurements are, relatively speaking, concrete. Intellectual prowess and moral strength are difficult to quantify and therefore very subject to prejudice on the part of the measurer, but the winner of a basketball game is hard to dispute.

Another example: A Jewish friend said to me once, "The Holocaust isn't the only genocide in history, just the best publicized." This is a cutting but true statement that reveals several aspects of the Holocaust.

The Holocaust has been well publicized, as it should be, but this creates a paradox. Because the Holocaust was an exceptionally horrible and well-organized persecution, it starts to seem unique and unusual rather than just the worst example of a horrible but not uncommon human story. This makes it seem as though there was something uniquely bad about the Germans, which is a convenient way for the rest of us to avoid contemplating the ugly but universal side of human nature the Germans exhibited when they tried to exterminate Jewish people.

Whether it is the doom of Auschwitz we felt looming over Anne Frank or Viktor Frankl's account of his time in that prison, when we read these magnificent books in high school, I assumed most of the Jews killed in the Holocaust were killed in concentration camps. This is, in fact, not the case. The majority of the Jewish people murdered in the Holocaust were murdered not in gas chambers but instead the old-fashioned way, by armed groups, not infrequently neighbors, who took them out of their houses and killed them.

My high school history teacher explained to us that the persecution of the Jews was a sideshow in World War II. This made absolutely no sense. Nazis were bad because they made gas chambers to kill people like Anne Frank. In much the same way, we perceived that the Civil War began in order to free the slaves held in the Southern states, who had been personalized to us in the character of Kunta Kinte from the TV series *Roots*. My history teacher tried to set the record straight about either war, but it didn't matter.

The larger causes of the Civil War, the fact that few people at the time thought that blacks were in any way equal to whites, or that during World War II few people really cared what happened to the Jews, none of this, to our young minds, had the same power as seeing slavery and the persecution of the Jews as an evil that had to be stopped.

The point is that with issues that are difficult or shameful or controversial, there is a narrative, a cultural narrative, that is easier to understand than messy reality—easier to understand, often, because it absolves people from seeing the same flaws in themselves. This narrative—idealistic Americans liberating the Jews or fighting a civil war to free African American slaves—is simple and comforting. It also takes certain difficult questions off the table.

For instance, it is my perception that although Jewish people are only about 2 percent of the total U.S. population, they make up a greater proportion of important and high-profile positions in American society. As near as I can tell from a few hours of casual and unscientific searching on the internet, Jewish students make up a disproportionately large segment of the students at elite colleges, maybe as much as 10 to 20 percent. Since elite colleges lead to elite jobs, my perception may be correct.

Different groups rise at different times as they

overcome discrimination and disadvantages. But it doesn't change the fact that when one small group rises to prominence, they are likely to be the object of envy and hatred, especially when they are Jewish. Even to make such observations is taboo.

The comfortable narrative is that the Nazis were uniquely evil, somehow different from the rest of humanity. To suggest that Jewish people, a small but prominent minority in the United States, could one day face some sort of persecution here—however logical that conclusion might be, based on history—is heresy to the comforting narrative.

Similarly, the overt slavery enforced by bondage and violence has been mostly (not entirely) eradicated in this country, but there are many people in this country—many of whom, not accidentally, are dark-skinned—who are still for the most part excluded from the rights and opportunities, intellectual and economic, that the rest of us enjoy. We don't think of this as slavery, but to think it is unrelated to the legacy of slavery is as delusional as thinking that persecution of Jews couldn't happen here.

46- American Culture

When I was young, I never thought much about culture and what it meant to be part of a culture. Now that I am older, I see examples of the influence of culture all the time. Culture, as I see it now, is the perspective you bring to everything. You experience the world intermediated, always, by your cultural assumptions. Culture is like a set of colored glasses that cover not only your eyes but all information coming to your brain. It is the operating system that governs how you process information. Your culture doesn't necessarily require that you look at the world one way, but it strongly encourages certain perspectives and discourages others. You can switch the lenses a bit and try on different cultures—traveling is one way to do this—but there is no such thing as an unfiltered perspective.

When you're young, it is impossible even to see the culture you live in because it is all you have known. But as you get older little fissures appear, like irritating cracks in a windshield, and as you crane your neck to look around these obstructions you start to realize that you have viewed the world mostly from one position and that there are other ways to see things. Getting slightly outside of your accustomed viewpoint allows you to see the details of your familiar culture and also the rough outline of other possibilities.

I have gone from criticism, deserved in many cases, that I felt toward my culture, to much greater admiration. This is not to excuse the ridiculous aspects of our culture or the sometimes terrible actions of the government. In my adult life, I watched in horrified amazement as President George W. Bush led the country down a trail of lies into war with Iraq. How many hundreds of thousands of lives were lost to satisfy this supposedly Christian president's desire for revenge?

Photo by Nick Marro

I shouldn't have been surprised since, when I was learning to crawl, I turned over the paint can while my mother painted "Peace in Viet Nam" on the wall of our old barn. Vietnam was another disastrous war begun with lies, prosecuted incompetently, and finished, if these things ever are, in shame. But government and culture are not, even in a democracy, exactly the same thing.

If you say to an American, "Your point of view doesn't matter and your individual life has little to no value," this is offensive on the deepest level, however logically and statistically true it may be. We are a culture based on individuality and the worth of the individual. In other cultures, the well-being of the whole group often is more important than any one individual, and individuals are seen to be contributing their small and, individually speaking, inconsequential efforts for the betterment of the whole.

This doesn't mean individuals in those cultures don't value themselves, a misconception most succinctly stated by General Jack D. Ripper in the movie *Dr. Strangelove* when he said, "Your commie has no regard for human life, not even his own." It just means that in those cultures, the perspective is more toward the value of the society as a whole rather than the individual.

For our culture, the individual is supreme, often to a ridiculous level where actions taken under the sanctity of individual rights threaten the well-being of everyone else. But the great strength of a culture based on the rights of individuals is that it encourages a melting-pot effect and helps dissolve sectarianism. Conflicts between sects—be they racial, religious, cultural, ethnic, or national—seem almost inevitable, given human nature, and likely to be worsened by technology.

As I've grown older, I've come to believe sectarianism is the chief scourge of modern humans. Disease, starvation, physical deprivations of all kinds—these are within our knowledge base to control. But solving these problems depends on our ability to overcome our innate tendency toward tribalism and its modern format, sectarianism.

The European financial crisis that began in 2009 is a good example of this problem. The Germans were unwilling to completely bail out the Greeks. The reason, in the final analysis, is that the Germans considered the Greeks lazy and wanted to teach them a lesson.

The inability of Europe to overcome its sectarianism, based mostly around nationality, may spell doom for the European Union. In the United States, however, we did much better. Rich and relatively conservative states, like New York, gave money to bail out profligate states, like Florida and Nevada. This happened not because New Yorkers are more enlightened than Germans but because of our system, a system based around the individual. The Europeans do not have a United States of Europe and so, despite the EU, their national identities are much stronger than our state identities. Because we are based on the value of the individual, we don't value a Floridian less than a New Yorker.

The Europeans also have a harder time because of their multiple languages. Here in America, our unifying language allows people to move around and mix with each other. So when New Yorkers were taxed by the federal government to send government support payments of various kinds to people in Florida, the system functioned smoothly, almost invisibly, treating people as individuals rather than groups.

It's not that we succeed so well as a culture based on individuality. Our history of genocide, slavery, and the perpetual oppression of women is positively horrible. But we have a chance, a fighting chance, to make a society based on equal individuals.

Hand in hand with the belief in the importance of the individual is the belief that all individuals are of equal value. Both of these are widely accepted points of view within our culture and we continue to successfully promulgate them around the world. Despite this, there is nothing logically obvious about either of these beliefs, and for most of history—and, indeed, probably in most of the world today—they would be taken as incorrect.

I saw an interview once with country music

singer George Strait. The interviewer asked him what he thought of the appellation King George, which people had taken to using as a nod to his long and prolific ability to produce popular country songs. Mr. Strait got an uncomfortable look on his face. "Well, I'm no better than anyone else," he said. George Strait is demonstrably better than pretty much anyone else at singing hit country songs, but his first thought upon hearing this praise is not what it means about his music but that he's not comfortable with the idea of being designated as somehow better than his fellow countrymen. This is American culture. On some level, illogical as it may appear, no one is any better than anyone else.

The intellectual roots of American culture are best summarized by two statements in our founding documents. The first, from the Declaration of Independence, is the unqualified and untrue statement that "all men are created equal." And the second is that amazing statement, the First Amendment, declaring that we will never afraid of ideas.

I'm not saying that these statements created the culture but that they represent its most succinct embodiment and have become the core concepts.

"All men are created equal" is contrary to what we can see and observe in nature, it is contrary to human experience, and it was clearly hypocritical for the slave owners who wrote it. Some people are born healthy, smart, and strong, others weak, stupid, and unfit. Even more unjustly, the strong and healthy are also likely to be rich and privileged while the weak are also often poor. And to make things even more unequal, the rich usually oppress and sometimes enslave the poor.

The scholars like to come in with their pedantic brooms and neaten this statement by saying that it means equal before the law. But it doesn't say equal before the law. It says that it is self-evident that all men are created equal. Reducing this statement to a more legally comprehensible concept deprives it of its greatest power.

When a group of people make a blatantly untrue but noble proposition, sign their names, and pledge their lives to it, other people should have enough good taste to recognize that they are striving to exceed the animal part of our nature and to reach for ideals that are beyond them. To limit our aspirations only to those we can say we have already accomplished would, by definition, be a low bar in a stagnant pool.

This is an ideal birthed in hypocrisy and existing in imperfection. But this is precisely because it is an ideal proposed for humans by humans. As humans, we can intuitively grasp the concept of no one being any better than anyone else. Equality *is* self-evident on some instinctive level, despite all logic and observation to the contrary. We can also understand that the implementation of this concept will always fall short. Most important, we understand that our culture is dedicated to the continual struggle for improvement. This makes us the shining city on the hill.

This genius sets an ideal—an unobtainable, unnatural ideal—as the basis for our collective existence. The signers pledged their lives and the future of the country to something that can never exist in reality but, contradictory as it is, nonetheless is instantly and intuitively understood by the human mind.

There is a quote attributed to Gandhi: when asked what he thought of American culture, he replied that it "is a very good idea," implying that we don't have a culture. It is a good line and a quick-witted commentary on our constantly changing society, and he manages also to contrast the newness of American culture with the ancientness of Indian culture. Fair enough.

Gandhi lived in and tried to improve an ages-old culture that addressed the difficult question of equality with a caste system whereby some human beings are designated "untouchable."

We are social animals, and social animals naturally have caste systems. Dogs, for instance, can be generous, even selfless, and unconditionally loving, but a dog doesn't understand the concept of all dogs created equal. One dog is better than another based on hierarchy. Maybe it is more pragmatic, more realistic, more honest in the sense of recognizing our limitations, to accept the baseness, the animal pragmatism of a caste system. But that is not our culture.

We are a culture based on ideals.

It is popular to note that Jefferson and many of the founders were slave owners and to use this as cause to assert that the whole basis of the country is flawed and hypocritical. To me this logic implies that only the perfect among us should be trusted or admired. I find this ludicrous. I'm in favor of making the best from what we've got. I accept that the best ideas we have will inevitably come from imperfect people.

The horror of institutionalized and culturally acceptable human slavery does not abrogate the genius of choosing equality as a first principle; rather, it shows in bold relief how an ideal can contain within itself implications that go far beyond the imagination of the conceivers.

Like many American six-year-olds, I learned about freedom of speech and its ambiguities on the playground. I responded to a taunt from a recess enemy by replying, "You can't say that about me because it isn't true," to which his buddy responded, "It's a free country, he can say what he wants." I sought recourse with a bigger kid who was a neighbor and friend. He confirmed that it was in fact a free country and the kid could say what he wanted but also that he could rub the kid's face in the snow for saying things that weren't true.

The idea of freedom of speech is one of the most courageous acts in human history.

The First Amendment defies fear and ignorance. "All men are created equal" is a noble and idealistic choice. The First Amendment is just pure bravery. For a social creature that depends not on strength but on knowledge for survival, to say it will not, as a society, be afraid of ideas is an enormously powerful position but also terribly risky.

What if it had turned out that the practitioners of witchcraft could indeed conjure evil forces into the world? You may laugh, but in a world where many natural phenomena were completely misunderstood, the courage to permit any sort of worship is extraordinary.

To put it in a scientific realm, what if it turns out that open inquiry into the nature of the universe gives us truths with which we destroy ourselves? Would we have been better to have stayed like the ants or ancient Egyptians, dutifully following the rote procedures laid down by our ancestors? Will Admiral Hyman Rickover, Father of the Nuclear Navy, be proved right in his comment to Congress that he thought we would destroy ourselves and leave the world to be populated by some other more intelligent species? There is a great risk to pursuing truth; you don't know where it will go or whether you can handle where it takes you.

According to the Declaration of Independence, governments derive "their just powers from the consent of the governed." In many cases, governments maintain their power, fair or unfair, by quashing dissent. Our government was formed on and embodied as a first principle the acceptance of dissent. The First Amendment says that the government will not be afraid of dissenting ideas.

We set as a first principle that the truths we personally hold most dear can be publicly disputed. You can't act any way you want, but you can say what you think and believe. We're equal to each other in our ignorance or our knowledge. On the one hand, we're not afraid to find out, and on the other, we admit we may not know. We are humble enough for the mightiest and richest to have no more claim on the truth than the meekest and poorest. The First Amendment extinguishes the ages-old power of priests and kings to pretend to possess secret knowledge that made them better than other people.

Making your first principle the freedom for people to speak their own minds is astoundingly brave. It says we are not afraid of what people may find. We're not afraid of what is new. Governments and religions are always afraid of what is new because the leaders get into power with old knowledge and so the new ideas are threatening to their power. But along come the founders of our government and they chose as the first right protected by the government the right to think and say what you want, even in matters of religion.

This is shoulder to shoulder with great advances, like learning to control fire or the theory of natural selection. Even more extraordinary, really, is that it didn't occur in one moment. Two hundred–odd years down the road and we've kept at it and are still working on defining what it means to make the ideas of equality and freedom of speech functional in a society.

All men created equal and freedom of speech fit together like a hand in a glove. When you pair this fearlessness about ideas, especially new ideas, with the statement that all men are created equal, then you've set the groundwork for unleashing human potential. The power of atomic energy was unimaginable before Einstein. I think a similar thing is true for human potential. Until the ideas of freedom of speech and equality were combined, the great bulk of humanity's extraordinary mental powers were wasted.

We are mostly hairless, weak creatures without claws. Then along comes this period in history when we surge forward. You can argue about what progress really means. Are things actually ever better or worse? But you can't dispute that there is something unprecedented about our time in history.

There is no such thing as achieving perfect equality or complete freedom of speech. Always there are ambiguities. Technology and times change, and human nature, the animal part of human nature, the part that instinctively seeks to oppress and dominate, the part that is terrified of new ideas, the part that holds fast to the innate security of tribal loyalties, the instinctively racist tendencies, these are constantly assailing the higher and fragile ideas of equality and freedom of speech.

It is simple to believe there is one right way, so easy, so true, to observe that people are not equal. Freedom of speech and equality are a leaky boat constantly taking water from an ocean of doubt and fear. The zealots who are certain they know the mind of God, the greedy with more than they could ever use who only want more, most of history has been written by them.

But the combination of equality and freedom of speech unleashed something new on the world, an advancement of ideas, freedom, and material wealth completely unprecedented in history. Yes, perhaps you can attribute some of that to fossil fuels and a continent with abundant natural resources, but not all, not even half.

At its heart, equality and freedom of speech are

incredibly optimistic points of view because they embrace a conviction that knowledge, inquiry, and understanding are the highest order of human pursuits.

47- American Inheritance

In our family, like a lot of other American families, we have some famous distant relatives who made contributions to the founding of the country and we also have slave-owning and slave-trading relatives.

When I look at you, Ford, my son, and picture the cheerful, goofy humor you have in common with many teenage boys, I think of a document that descended years ago in a box of other artifacts from some dead relative. It was a yellowed, time-brittled bill of sale, "Negro boy age 13." I think of the thin line between courage and terror, desperation and hope this barely teenaged boy faced. It was horrifying to look at that piece of paper, as though the past were alive and floating up off the page.

(I've looked for it in recent years and been unable to find it or the other document in that collection, the commutation of an execution sentence for some confederate relative signed by Abraham Lincoln. In a way, I was relieved not to find the bill of sale and disappointed to lose the execution sentence. A funny irony that these documents would get passed through the years together and lost together and entirely apropos to the point I am making in this essay.)

It is less than reassuring to acknowledge that your ancestors bought and sold other human

409

beings.

On the other side of the coin, however, it is nice to think that the admirable accomplishments of some dead relatives reflect well on you.

The problem is that if you take pride in your ancestors' good actions, then it seems inescapable that you should be embarrassed by their bad ones. Or, to be more direct about it, if you feel that your ancestors' good actions somehow make you better, then you must also accept that their bad actions make you worse.

There is a logical resolution to this personal problem entirely consistent with our national culture of individualism: The famous relatives are of no merit to me and the slave owners no shame. As a human being, I can take pride or shame in their various actions, but as an individual, they say very little about me.

This is simple logically but not so easy emotionally. In human relationships, perception and self-perception play the biggest role, so the person who is convinced that they are special often manages to persuade a lot of other people to their point of view. Woe to the person who thinks that maybe there is something wrong with them, some lingering not-quite-revealed defect or deficiency; this self-perception becomes a self-fulfilling prophecy as other people sense it and act accordingly.

Do I have a little bounce in my step when I ponder a famous dead relative? I'd like to say that logic and reason prevail over emotion. I'd like to think that when I see the sun come up in the morning, my first thought is that the earth is rotating, not that the sun is rising. And a human being, even a cynical one like myself, is more prone to remember a virtue, even a misperceived virtue, than a fault. It is quite natural to think that your ancestors' accomplishments somehow make you better without their faults detracting from you.

How would it be if I were dark-skinned and had to struggle against self-doubt in a society actively discriminating against me so that every failure caused by economic or legal injustice also chipped away at my confidence? Racial discrimination is a common topic, but we don't talk as much about how it works like lever and fulcrum, discrimination prying against the destructive legacy of slavery to triple or quadruple its power and keep people down.

So I believe that I am responsible for my actions but not those of my ancestors and, further, that you cannot have a peaceful modern society that is not based on individual responsibility, but I know that it is a muddy distinction.

I cannot in good conscience say that the deeds of my ancestors impart absolutely nothing about me, because just as a fast horse is more likely than a slow horse to sire another fast horse, so too it seems that whatever quality allowed one human being to own—presumably, without excessive pangs of conscience—another human being might also get passed on. But I'll add two notes. Observing that the quality of unrepentant slave owning is widespread in history, places, and races, it seems safe, if sad and scary, to assume that it is a universal rather than rare human characteristic and nothing particular to my ancestors. Second, that horse breeding is very tricky and a winning race horse does not always, or even often, produce winning descendants, but nurture also plays a strong role.

The current disfavor in some parts of the world with human slavery indicates the power of nurture over nature. I find in myself a deep abhorrence to the idea of owning other human beings—so deep that I would like to think that in any time or place I would not be a slave owner, but this flies in the face of logic. I am not markedly different from my ancestors or the rest of humanity. It is nurture, not nature, that guides this feeling. In ancient Rome, I probably would have been a Roman full of bloodlust at the Colosseum, and 200 years ago I, given the opportunity, might have been a slave owner as some of my ancestors were. And given a different role of the dice, I might have ended up with brown skin and living in slavery. Even if it is true that I share these traits with the rest of humanity, these are not comforting conclusions.

However, when Thomas Jefferson, slave owner, slave lover, penned the words "all men are created equal," he set our culture off in a direction. And we have progressed far enough in this quest, barring some sort of mass amnesia of history, to have disproved the racists who saw inferior and superior races (including Jefferson, sweet irony), the pragmatists who shrugged and said it had always been thus, and the avaricious who could not have enough unless they enslaved others.

In this country, every race has contributed music and science and literature, agriculture and invention and dance. And now a man from the race that was enslaved has been president, not once but twice, and discharged the duties—despite a perpetual and racist assault from the Republican party (irony again) —with the most evenhanded impartiality of any president in my lifetime.

We have made more wealth, more freedom, more power, more art, more of everything that has motivated people throughout history than any other society ever. Whatever intrinsic moral failure condoned slavery, whatever grasping reasons my ancestors may have told themselves, these are brought to a full stop by the historical facts. Individuals from every race, creed, color, and religion have made the country stronger by far than any other country that has ever existed.

I'd find more peace of mind thinking that some evolutionary advancement had dispensed forever with the inclination towards slavery, but I see no evidence for this. The mood of the moment in most of the world frowns on overt and obvious human bondage, but this emotion could be temporary.

Instead, I take some comfort in the knowledge that it has been proved forever and irrevocably that any society that subjugates a group based on race or gender or religion or sexual preference is willfully depriving itself of the talents and insights held by the individuals in that group and is therefore weaker as a society and culture.

As a case in point, in World War II, individuals from two groups persecuted by the Nazis—homosexuals and Jews—made such enormous contributions to the Allied war effort that it is reasonable to question whether we would have won without them. Nazi ideas were overcome and crushed by the ideas, imperfectly implemented but nonetheless, of equality and freedom. It has to be added that homosexuals and Jews were, at the time, strongly discriminated against in both the United States and the U.K. and also that they have come closer legally and culturally to equality since then.

I think the United States is the first time in history the evidence of the power of a culture based on freedom and equality has been so clearly and compellingly exhibited. Over time, weak cultures succumb to strong cultures, and there is a good chance, although not a certainty, that the social model of subjugation of one group by another will fade away, a relic of the past done away ultimately not by morality but by competition, the reliable propeller of evolution.

48- Salvation and Damnation through Commerce

The man's voice on the other end of the phone line had a thick Kentucky accent. We'd managed to fight and trick our way through eBay's best efforts to keep us from communicating directly with each other. He was selling, I was buying, two big pillow-block bearings sized to fit a 4 15/16" shaft. The price wasn't a problem. I was happy to pay $1,500 apiece and he was willing to sell at that price.

The question was whether the bearings would work in my application. I thought they would. The rolling elements were spherical rollers, which, because of their beer-barrel shape, have an inherent ability to accommodate some shaft misalignment. He feared that the type of locking collar on the bearing would get in the way. Eventually he convinced me. I thanked him and apologized for taking so much of his time. "That's all right, buddy. I just wanted to make sure it was going to work for you," he said.

I got off the phone, disappointed not to be buying the bearings but full of joy in every other way. This is what I think of as salvation through commerce. People interacting, each for their own individual purpose, but underlying is some unspoken yet shared belief in helping each other.

I'd made my best guess based on the picture and what I understood about the locking collar. No one could have faulted this guy for selling me the bearings. It's hard to see how he had any moral obligation because I'd told him I was sure they would work for me, but he still worried that they wouldn't work and lost the sale as a result. What was his motivation? Was it cultural? Personal?

There was a sense in our conversation that we are all in this together. If it didn't work for me, then it didn't work for him, even though, as a practical matter, I was very unlikely ever to be a customer of his again.

I don't know if humans have a predisposition, some sort of genetic programming, toward believing in mutually beneficial exchange. Maybe it is a learned behavior. It happens a lot. That's what I know.

I've been exposed to the average range of spontaneous feelings of genuine connection— hanging with old friends; sharing a laugh with someone in the checkout line; the woman, complete stranger in the seat next to me, who clutched my hand and started crying when our plane suddenly aborted its landing in Philadelphia and went around for another try—but it feels as though there is something special about salvation through commerce.

Usually it occurs in person, a one-to-one exchange, and usually the commercial transaction takes place instead of being cancelled. I'm standing in the mud that always surrounds sawmills, chatting with the sawyer and buying lumber for a shed I'm building for someone. He's happy to sell me the wood, I'm happy to buy, and the guy getting the shed is going to be happy when it is done. We're all in this together and everyone participating in the transaction is benefitting in some way. Money, the evil old pelf, isn't bringing us down; it is just the medium of exchange, another tool, like the sawmill or my hammer. Underneath the transaction there is an assumption that we are all doing what is in our self-interest, but talking to each other face-to-face, the sense of cooperative effort is much more present.

Perhaps that's why I found the bearings seller so inspiring. Our distance, me calling from Yankee Vermont, his accent south of the Mason Dixon; the natural tension between buyer and seller—he had plenty of reasons to put me in the "other" category. We were strangers who were never likely to meet or speak again. It is tougher to see someone as other when they are standing right in front of you, but here was a guy 800 miles away walking out on a $3,000 sale because he wasn't sure it would work for me.

The autonomy, or in some cases the anonymity, is, I think, what makes salvation through commerce more redemptive than, for instance, the good feeling of hanging out with your friends. With friends, by definition you have shared history and experiences, so it is natural for there to be a certain commonality of interests. The idea of two people, often strangers, perhaps even strangers with different ideologies, operating for their own autonomous motivations and yet doing so in a framework of mutual benefit, this experience embodies a world of peace and cooperation.

When I experience the salvation-through-commerce feeling, it makes me believe this whole thing can work out—the American experiment with democracy, evolution's experiment with self-aware creatures, the balance between self-interest and caring for each other. It can work; given the right structures, the right framework and assumptions, everybody can make life better for everybody else.

There are lots of shared experiences where strangers feel connected to each other. Some are spontaneous—like my experience on the plane—and some—a music concert, for instance—are planned, but the feelings are no less genuine. But the commerce is what makes the feeling of salvation through commerce special. You go to a concert to have a good time and feel connected with all of the other people having a good time. You engage in commerce to make money, and despite this you discover mutual benefit.

I'm not naive. I've been taken for a ride a time or two. There are plenty of people who will sell you some piece of shit knowing perfectly well what is wrong with it and that it will never work out for you. They see the world as being full of an endless stream of suckers they can take advantage of. For these people, it is not about mutually beneficial exchange but about one person getting ahead of another. That's what I think of as damnation through commerce, a world of perpetual strife.

Corporations often embody this attitude. They have calculated exactly how much they think they can charge. If I go bankrupt paying the phone company's confusing charges, it is immaterial to them; already factored into the program, so many customers are going to drop out every year. It is a purely commercial transaction.

Perhaps when I phone the call center I get a very helpful person who explains the bill to me and we share a moment where she is trying to help me get the right plan, but we both know this all takes place not between us as autonomous people but between us as actors on a stage with limits placed on us by the phone company, whose objective is to pilfer as much as possible from me.

The question of which structures encourage salvation through commerce and which structures lead to damnation through commerce is complicated. I don't have answers. Maybe somewhere there is an economist laboring to answer this question and produce a model that shows which regulations are most beneficial to human beings and not just the bottom line. Probably if this model is ever created and made public, it will be sneered at by the established economists working for universities with endowments funded by huge corporations that see the world composed of consumer units operating in a market of price takers and price makers.

I know nothing about the bearings seller from Kentucky except that I got off the phone feeling as though anything was possible. The point of this essay is to raise a flag so sometime in your life you'll be buying something or selling something and you'll have a feeling of connectedness and you'll know that's what I was talking about. It is one of the best things I've experienced.

49- Gates

When I was a kid, other than the incidental money from selling a few lambs or a half a pig, we never made any money from our farm. For this reason, to this day I feel slightly dishonest calling it a farm, even though we raised virtually all of our own food. Money isn't the definition of when a thing is or isn't, but the farm was not our income and so I never felt justified in saying that we were farmers. At school, around children whose parents really were farmers and actually owned the large and new tractors I longed for, I was especially careful not to say that we were farmers.

When I went to college and had to fill out financial aid forms, I put down my parents' occupations as journalist for my father and farmer for my mother. Back then, I felt the statement was justified more by defiance than truthfulness. Now I feel that the statement is justified by the countless hours of work, the sort of uncompensated, unacknowledged, at least by society at large, work my mother and millions of other women have done throughout history: tending a garden, preparing ingredients, cooking meals from scratch, preserving food, and tending to animals and fires and children.

When my parents started raising animals and children, they knew nothing more about farming and child raising than what they read in books, and those were novels. They became farmers by buying animals, bringing them home, and then dealing with the missing knowledge or fences. In this way, they established a menagerie of animals, machinery to cut hay for the animals, and children to tend the animals and fix the machines.

In the first years, the farm was a kind of adventure land. The leaning, decaying fences were helpfully inclined and easy to climb. If the sheep burst through the fence, scattering the chickens and pursued by the dogs, and this caused my dad to jump from the porch where he had been reading the newspaper and run shouting after the sheep, it was all to the good.

In the barn, I employed gates and doors as swings, hanging off them and pushing myself back and forth. "Goddamn it, son," my father said when he caught me, "I can't fix these gates fast enough for you to use them as swings."

Disaster and calamity seemed a continual and not distant threat on our farm. Everything was old or broken or insufficient, and there was no money. Escaped sheep, a broken car, or a puny woodpile were omnipresent. Our parents taught us to believe that this was the perpetual condition of farms and farmers, and since farming was the most natural and righteous occupation for human beings, it was also the perpetual condition for human life.

Nevertheless, the proper attitude was to try to overcome the difficulties and make the best of them. My siblings and I rose to the challenge with everything we had, maybe more. We attempted to fix, or at least hold at bay, all of the urgencies to which a farm gives rise. These were extensive: cutting hay, fencing and building, gardening, woodcutting, machinery repair, and animal care. It was a contradiction to try to hold things together in the face of a conviction that life is always in a state of disrepair, but our parents respected literature, if anything, above farming and saw contradiction and dramatic tension as a necessary and, at any rate, inevitable condition of life.

At night, before I went to sleep, I contemplated the farm I wanted to have someday. I ran through the list of trucks and tractors I would need and I planned to stable them in a proper machinery shed, unlike the open-air treatment our tractor got. When I was nine, we built an addition to the barn during my father's vacation from the newspaper. He and my mother moved the record player to the barn so we could have music, and we worked steadily for two weeks. From then on, I was always building. I spent hours designing carefully organized barns and I built wagon beds, chicken feeders, gates, stalls, ramps, and eventually, when I was 15, the horse barn, which by some physics-defying miracle is still standing 35 years later.

When it came to gates, I resented the extra time they took to make and was a little extra satisfied after I finished. A gate is a great convenience when it works. Most of my parents' gates were made by throwing whatever was handy, a door or a feeder, across the opening and tying it there with baling twine. My dad swore when he had to climb over a tied-shut gate and more  often than not he spilled water down his leg or caught his "britches" on a nail.

In a book, I saw a design for wooden-fence gate hinges and modified it to use on barn gates and doors. Wooden hinges had two advantages: They saved having to buy expensive metal hinges, and I felt they somehow ameliorated the damage I had done to gates by swinging on them.

The balance between parent and child, dependency and autonomy, love and vulnerability is a fragile thing. After I graduated from high school and before I left on my walking misadventure, my father wrote a letter for me to keep in my wallet. I don't remember any particular instructions as to what I was supposed to do with this letter or in what circumstances he imagined it might be useful. I do remember recognizing (in a way I would not be able to fully appreciate until I had my own children) his feeling of powerlessness. I found the letter five or six years ago and so I will reproduce it here:

The Times Argus

Vermont's Largest Afternoon Newspaper with Sunday Edition

October 25, 1983

To Whom It May Concern:

This will introduce my son, Bobby Porter, who has just turned 18, recently graduated from high school, has finished cutting our 12-cord winter wood supply and is setting out today to see the country.

Left to his own devices, I am confident he will get along fine; but if he gets into a jam along the way, I would appreciate any help you can give him. If need be, please call me collect.

Thanks,

William K. Porter
Managing Editor
802-479-0491
802-229-0691

When I returned home, sooner and less happily than I expected to, I found the broken gates and hastily repaired fences both reassuring and frustrating. In my footloose search for meaning, here was purpose and necessity. I could be useful but the problems didn't seem like mine anymore and, anyway, when I fixed them they came undone.

I left and returned again and again. When I eventually went to college, I settled into a routine. Haying in the summer and a little work on the barns before I left in the fall. At school I worried about my parents trying to tend to the self-imposed chaos of their lives.

One fall, I restored the sheep pen after it had been taken apart so the barn could be cleaned. I built a gate to make easier access to the chicken coop, which was on the other side of the sheep pen. The design was innovative: four boards built into a frame that slid down the sheep-pen fence. Multiple sliding rails often rack and bind, but I boxed these together so they would slide easily as one piece. It was a useful spot for a gate since the chickens needed water every day and climbing over the fence with a bucket was uncomfortable.

When I came home for Christmas, the gate latch was gone and the gate was tied shut with a frayed clot of baling twine to keep the sheep from scratching against it and working it open. My dad had tacked boards on the bottom to stop the new lambs from slipping under, but the boards kept the gate from being able to slide and open. It wasn't really a gate anymore, just another inconvenient piece of fencing.

I fixed the latch and corrected the bottom so the lambs couldn't get through and the gate could still open. That night during chores, my dad climbed over the gate. His boots left manure smeared on the top rail. On the way back across he looked sadly at the manure, avoided it, and shook his head. "Goddamn these gates." I showed him the latch and his face lit up in the way that always makes a child proud. "Ah, that's great, son." He scrutinized the latch for my benefit and worked it a few times. "Yeah. Nice, thanks." He slapped me affectionately on the back. "Nice to have you home."

When I came back in the spring, hay was piled against the gate and it was impossible to open. The top rail had broken from being climbed over and then had been lashed back together to prevent the lambs, who could jump now, from leaping out. I looked at it for a while and then tried to force it open, but the mound of discarded hay from the sheep feeder had been accumulating there all winter and it wouldn't budge. I knew they would never farm the way I thought they wanted to and the way I thought they should, but they would probably manage. Even if they didn't, there wasn't much I could do about it.

50- Conclusion

George Soros, who lived through the last global calamity, World War II, said that some of the best advice he ever got was from his father, who explained to him that in unusual times, unusual actions would be normal. Because this book started out as a father's advice to his children, perhaps it is not surprising that Soros's father's advice would come to my mind when I contemplated writing a conclusion. I hope it is the case that the current state of domestic and global affairs turns out to be an unsettled period akin to the McCarthy era or the unrest during the late 1960s and not the beginning of a global catastrophe, but the times do feel uniquely fraught. This feeling may be the inescapable result of living in the present; as time unfolds in front of our lives, it always seems as though we are living in unprecedented times because, of course, in some sense we always are. Only time will tell.

In the meantime, whether the future holds more of the same or some kind of upheaval, it seems fitting to close this book with some commentary on the current state of affairs. This is apt not only as a conclusion for the material in this book but also for you, Ceres and Ford, since you were small children when I began this book and now you are adults living in the current world, not the world of stories from my life.

People who know me do not generally consider me an optimist, although I beg to differ with that assessment. In the preceding pages you will find many examples of my optimism, which I feel is part of my heritage as an American. I think that things are good and they can be better. My nature, perhaps a little grim, does not expect the improvements to come without effort.

I bridle at the idea of original sin (even though I view acceptance of imperfection as one of the cornerstones of my personal beliefs), and I think our American history, despite its many horrible chapters, is one of human improvement and ennoblement, not as groveling supplicants before a wrathful god but as unique, self-aware creatures living in nature and doing their best. So it is with the assertion that I am an optimist and I think great things are possible in the future and that it is within our power to deliver them that I will make these observations about the present.

In this book I've tried not to comment except on things to which I had given some thought and come up with ideas I felt were at least a little original or constructive. You will have noticed, no doubt, that I don't offer much advice on child rearing, which is not from lack of effort or worry on my part but from lack of thinking that I could speak with any certainty on how it worked and should be done. Here I will stray from that path a little bit by offering speculations and criticisms with no solutions.

This, in short, is how I see the world now. I have mentioned earlier in this book that I view sectarianism as the greatest evil for modern humans. The founding fathers warned of the evils of political parties, although their advice was quickly ignored. The inherent tribal tendencies that human beings have exhibited through all of history have been exacerbated recently by technology and in particular by individuals and politicians, and especially the Fox News Corporation, who have seen an opportunity to profit by sowing the seeds of hatred and division between people.

I'm sorry to revert again to religious references but I can think of no better definition for the devil than hate mongering. This is, of course, hardly a new story and it is not yet even a particularly bad episode, historically speaking, but it seems to be rising and has been exploited brilliantly by Donald Trump and his allies. Truly, if Trump's opponents gave the devil his due and admired not his actions but the skill with which they were implemented, they would be better prepared to defend against them.

I hold out hope (the optimist in me) that the Trump era will prove, like so many episodes in our history, a lucky accident rather than a tragedy. It seems to me that in Trump we have an inoculation of sorts. He is not a true authoritarian or even an ideologue but instead that most American of creations, a brilliant salesman. In an attempt to wrap his hotel business with the grandeur of the presidency, he sold himself as presidential and, inadvertently I believe, became president. For him, that may be the crowning achievement or a terrible miscalculation. Once again, time will tell. But he is showing us how vulnerable our country is to an actual demagogue the same way a flu shot prepares your immune system to fend off an actual flu virus. Of course, the flu shot is never 100 percent effective and sometimes, even, the immunization makes you sick.

The real weakness, the one we should be concerned about, the infection inflaming our society and exploited so adroitly by Trump (and embodied perfectly by his values) is the financialization of everything. My uncle Jimmy told me that he thought his profession, the legal profession, went to hell when the lawyers started advertising their services, but everyone expects lawyers to end up in hell eventually anyway, so that was not a particularly surprising development. Somehow, the medical profession—arguably the profession with the most intelligent, disciplined, and, one would hope, most civic-minded individuals in the society—ceded control of its choices to accountants in the insurance industry. But my greatest contempt is for the academics who, seemingly without a whimper, have been complicit in turning higher education into a system for luring great numbers of children into permanent debt while simultaneously abandoning the cause of education as a value in itself in favor of college as glorified vocational training for the pursuit of dollars.

I said I was not going to offer solutions, and that's because I don't know what they are. Two forces that have shaped our country and the world for the past 100 years—fossil fuels and the relentless pursuit of money about all else—seem to be coming to some sort of crisis. These forces, harnessed haphazardly, wastefully, wantonly, have nonetheless, when combined with attempts at equality and freedom, delivered more wealth, more knowledge, more leisure, more life to more humans than in any other period in history. That is ultimately a testament to the underlying goodness of human nature.

It seems as though we have the technology to manage the climate crisis if only we could find the will and organization. The financial crisis might be trickier. Restructuring capitalism so we don't destroy each other and the planet is a tall order. And yet, the system itself seems to be begging for reform. A capitalistic system depends on a return on the capital. The trillions of dollars invested at negative rates are a huge warning light indicating that the system is failing. It's like going 70 miles an hour down the highway and having the oil light, the charge light, and the fuel light all come on simultaneously on the dashboard of your car, and when you look out the window you notice brushfires caused by climate change.

But I'm an optimist. These are solvable problems. The same American culture that eventually ended slavery and Hitler and put a man on the moon is already working away at solutions.

I said in the introduction, "There are things I want to tell you, but . . . I know before I open my mouth that I can't convey in that moment and with those overused words what I want you to understand. So I speak with a grimace, the kind of expression you might see on the face of a dog when it tries to beg a treat it knows you will not give."

Now, in this conclusion, these are just desperate cries yelled at departing children: "Have a good trip. Drive slowly. Watch out for potholes and keep an eye on those low interest rates. Don't forget to check the oil and try not to use too much of it." And remember the advice of George Soros's father. You have to figure out for yourself what applies to you and your situation.

I wrote the conclusion to this book on Friday night, February 21, 2020. I wrote it after prodding from Anita Warren, who had been working on editing the book and thought it needed a conclusion. I liked the way the book ended and in my heart of hearts I disagreed with her, but her suggestions had always been so thoughtful and measured that I suspended my own judgment for a while. I didn't expect to write anything, but I decided to leave the question open for a few days and by that evening an idea came to me. The words poured out rapidly and in a couple of hours I was pleased with what I had written.

It is a month later as I write these final paragraphs, and we live in a different world. In the opening paragraph of this conclusion I mentioned a global catastrophe; I was referring to the polarization, xenophobia, and hatred that seems prevalent now. As I wrote those words, another global catastrophe, the coronavirus, was already spreading across the world. I was aware of this pandemic and yet, even as I mused about the possibility of a global upheaval, I was oblivious to the obvious disruption already taking place.

Eventually this plague will lift, but not before it alters the world and our society. No one knows yet what these changes will be. It seems safe to say, however, that the cycles of nature—some of which are sweeping in scope, like this pandemic, and some of which are narrow and personal, like my inability to see the obvious—will continue. In this I find some hope, a little fear, and, best of all, some humor.

It is spring here now. My mother saw a red-winged blackbird this morning. After 54 years in this climate, the dripping water and receding ice still fill my heart with joy, ambition for the projects I have planned, and the sort of optimism that sprouts after surviving a long winter.

Made in the USA
Middletown, DE
18 June 2020